THE FLOCK

Joan Frances Casey

with Lynn Wilson

Afterword by Frances Howland, M.D.

Fawcett Columbine New York

A Fawcett Columbine Book
Published by Ballantine Books

This edition published by arrangement with Alfred A. Knopf, Inc.

Library of Congress Catalog Card Number: 92-90103

ISBN 0-449-90732-5

Cover design by Georgia Morrissey
Cover photo by Al Francekevich

Manufactured in the United States of America

First Ballantine Books Edition: July 1992

10 9 8 7 6 5

*Some names and places of persons and institutions have been changed to protect
the privacy of all involved. Joan Frances Casey and Lynn Wilson are pseudonyms.*

Prologue

This book is many things. It is the story of a child who was badly hurt, but survived. It is the story of a young woman who had many personalities and became one. It is also the story of how one therapist treated one patient. Most of all, however, it is the story of people who found each other at the right moment in their lives and performed magic. It's about two women who changed each other and about three people who became a family.

It is neither a manual nor a definitive statement of what ought to be done to treat Multiple Personality Disorder. It is an account of what Joan and I did and how it worked. A therapist more experienced with multiples might have treated Joan differently and much more efficiently. But, then, as I have learned to my sorrow, many clinicians might not have seen what was there to be treated, no matter how flamboyantly presented.

What happened between Joan and me was a product of the time, the place, and the people the two of us had become when we met. A year or two earlier or later, I might not have been able to respond to Joan's need. A year or two either way, Joan might have been dead or might have been strong enough to use me as she had used other therapists—to bury her problems further.

When I first met Joan, on a snowy March day in 1981, I was approaching a transition in my life. My daughter Lisa, youngest of five, was finishing her final year at home. For the first time in thirty years, I would have no children living with me. For the first time in our seventeen years of marriage, my second husband, Gordon, and I would be alone together.

I knew I would miss Lisa. By the time she was born, five years after her nearest sibling, Victor, I had relaxed enough about mothering to enjoy her completely without worrying much about how she would turn out.

Lisa had found it easy to confide in me, and we had spent joyful hours walking along the lake near our weekend cottage, talking about politics and about her hopes for the future. There were no younger children demanding my attention, so I had the time and energy to develop a personally gratifying relationship—not only with a daughter but with a delightful person. As much as I wanted Lisa to grow up and build her own life, I knew her departure would leave a gap.

Yet I felt a secret happiness at the prospect of *not* having her around. I was excited by the idea of being a spouse rather than a mother, of being able to make plans just for Gordon and me. Now we could spend hours, or even days, sailing. Gordon had a special love of the water and of his boats: a thirty-foot Catalina named *The Channel* and a fifteen-foot O-Day that he called *Mantra*. Some of the children grew to appreciate the beauty and solitude of being on the water, but I was often too distracted by some family or professional crisis to go out for a sail or to enjoy it when I did. Now I'd have the time.

The stack of books I had waiting to be read was two feet high. In anticipation of lazy hours on Lake Michigan, I had divided the stack in half: one for reading in bed, the other on the water.

I wanted also to do some work on the house that had been occupied by kids, cats, and dogs for so many years. I thought I might even get back to singing in a choir.

My career as a clinical social worker was gratifying too, and my job had changed recently in a way that promised growth. After sixteen years of doing both fieldwork and psychotherapy, I had become a member of a new "whole-patient" unit attached to the local university and teaching hospital. This outpatient unit was designed to serve as an interdisciplinary training ground for members of the medical and ancillary professions.

I enjoyed working with both students and community people, and I welcomed being able to teach as well. My colleagues were enthusiastic about the concept of treating a "whole" person and concentrating on wellness rather than disease. The mix of doctors, nurse clinicians, and social workers collaborating for the good of patients generated new and challenging ideas. But the program was slow in getting started. Not all the doctors were thrilled with interdisciplinary treatment, and some were resistant. Referrals were scarce and sometimes inappropriate.

Although I worked hard to show the doctors how useful a social worker could be in patient care, I was not as busy as I would have liked. The first time Joan called me, it was easy for me to respond to her apparent desperation with an immediate appointment, and equally easy to schedule additional sessions as the complexity of her problem became obvious. This is a rare situation for most clinicians.

In the years that have passed since I met Joan, many things have changed. I know that if Joan were approaching me for the first time now I would respond to her differently. The bureaucratic structure has changed, and I have more administrative duties. I am also treating other multiples and have begun supervising a colleague who is treating them. The two of us are conducting group-therapy sessions for adults who were molested as children. Most of these are people who suffer from Multiple Personality Disorder. Sheer numbers, if nothing else, have forced me to find other ways of treating MPD than those I used with Joan. And as my understanding of and competence in treating the disorder have grown, multiple personality has come to seem, though still horrendous, less unique and incomprehensible, and thus more manageable.

Six years ago, treating one multiple was unsettling enough to me. Now I can treat several at once, because of what I learned from Joan. I have also found that both therapist and patients benefit from cutting down on the mystique and the feelings of isolated strangeness that so often accompany the disorder.

I must emphasize that I am not apologizing for my approach to treating Joan. Despite the "reparenting" style of treatment described in this book, I was not "overinvolved," nor did I experience "messianic countertransference," as some of the clinical literature would suggest. I have often tried to imagine how I might have acted differently. Always I end up in the same place. For us, at that time, it was the only way. To treat my first multiple, as to raise my first child, I had to commit myself deeply to the experience in order to tolerate the uncertainty, fear, pain, and intensity. With Joan, I came close to burnout, over and over again, but was continually rescued by the depth of my caring.

Treating Joan changed me and my life. It confirmed deeply felt values, sharpened my awareness, honed my perceptions, and gave me a sense of confidence about my skills and abilities that is reflected both in my work and in my being. It remains a priceless gift.

As I write this, I think how remarkable it is that I now feel so clear about the connection Joan and I made, the relationship that weaves like a shining thread through all the pain and confusion that existed for so long. It is this honest connection between two human beings that, in the end, makes what we endured together understandable and meaningful.

To me, the essential task of any therapy is the same as that of life—to recognize, experience, and affirm our common humanity as we integrate within, with one another, and with the universe.

LYNN WILSON

June 1988

Author's Note

I had multiple personalities from infancy until I was almost thirty years old. My sense of identity changed drastically as I began to accept my diagnosis and progressed through successful treatment. Even my ability to say "I" in a self-referential way is a relatively new experience for me. I have been integrated—well—for six years.

Before my integration, "I" meant, at various times, any of twenty-four personalities. It's a confusing way to live and, with twenty-four points of view, a confusing tale to tell. My story is told here through the perspective of one major, growing, and changing personality—a personality who called herself Renee.

BOOK I

1

Anyone can walk a tightrope. All it takes is practice and luck.

I had the practice. For as long as I could remember, I had walked cautiously through life, careful to please whoever might be near. I was so expert that hardly anybody noticed I didn't have feelings or thoughts of my own.

Practice and luck. I used to be very lucky. School was easy; I never had a job that I couldn't handle. It used to be that everybody always liked me.

It was different now. Keith wanted us to separate. Maybe he didn't want to be married to anyone, certainly not to me.

I figured that he didn't really mean it. He must be warning me to shape up. Sometimes I forgot about trying to please him.

When he first told me that we should live apart for a while, I tried to do everything I thought he wanted. I let him stay in our house and found an apartment for myself to make it easier for him. That should have counted for something, but after three months, just as I was getting ready to ask him if I could come home, he said he wanted a divorce.

There had to be a solution. If I could just figure out the right button to push, he'd like me again. But when I tried to think about it, I got scared, so scared that the tightrope swayed and I began to fall.

I leaned back and jerked reflexively to regain my balance, startling myself awake. I was no longer sitting at my desk. The typewriter I had been working at continued to hum, but now I was ten feet away, sitting on the wide windowsill.

I had no memory of leaving my desk, of crossing the room, of climbing onto this perch. Nevertheless, I was now tucked against the old mullioned window, chilled by the March cold that seeped through the pane.

"Damn it," I muttered, "what's going on?" The blankness throbbed within, so I looked out at the gray urban sprawl. My life was centered here, at the University of Chicago.

I was working on a master's degree in political science. My lover was a biology professor; my job was secretary in his department. I could see my apartment, clearly visible in the afternoon sun. And if I faced north and squinted just right, I could pick out the United Way building, where Keith worked as a fund-raiser.

Then I looked down.

"Jump!" I heard the voice, felt the nudge. "Jump!"

As if I had been mentally rehearsing a part in a play, I envisioned myself pushing the large window open, hopping to my feet, pausing briefly in exhilaration, and then diving strong and hard at the parked cars five stories below.

I shook my head to flick away the mental scene and hopped back down quickly from the window, as though the ledge itself might compel me to leap.

I returned to the typewriter, breathed deeply for a moment to relax, and set trembling fingers on the keys.

"Jump!"

Where had that come from? I didn't want to die. I wanted to be married.

It didn't matter where it had come from. I knew this kind of thing was dangerous.

It had happened before. I didn't want to kill myself, but suicide was on my mind.

"I've got enough to deal with without this," I said, giving up on the typing and resting my head in my hand.

It had to be the drugs. High school had been a series of psychedelic experiments, a little LSD, a little mescaline, more than a little marijuana and hash, enough of something so that I had virtually no memories prior to the summer I was fifteen.

My memory was spotty even now, ten years later. Mostly I didn't worry about it. Proper payment, I figured, for having had so much fun. It was only a problem when someone guessed that I didn't know something I should have known. But that didn't happen often. When I walked my tightrope with care, no one seemed to know that I sometimes lost it.

But suicide was different. I had been frightened like this before: once

I'd discovered pills hidden in my dresser; then a collection of razor blades; this was the second time I had found myself looking longingly from a window ledge and fighting the urge to jump.

In college, after I uncovered the cache of pills, I happened on a way to relieve the pressure at the campus counseling center.

I didn't tell the counselor about the pills or feeling out of control. I just played a game that proved to make me feel better.

I relaxed and let my inside come out.

Sometimes I could sit on my shoulder and watch. Sometimes I watched with interest, sometimes with apathy, while a detached part of me talked to the therapist. And sometimes I forgot to watch altogether.

It was a lot like what happened to me when I got high on drugs. Whatever it was, it worked, and the out-of-control feeling subsided. After three visits, I couldn't do that "inside-out" thing in the counselor's office. I stopped seeing him, but everything was OK for a while.

This quick-fix therapy worked so well that I had subsequently seen eight counselors or therapists or psychologists. I always went somewhere different and stayed for no more than three or four visits. Sometimes I felt a little guilty about wasting their time, but I figured that's what they were paid for.

One therapist told me that I was passive-aggressive. I growled at her when I left.

The last guy I saw just after I moved out of the house I shared with Keith and into my apartment. I thought he could help me figure out a way to get Keith back. He didn't and he scared me away when he started asking questions that made me uncomfortable. I had been woolgathering in my "inside-out" position when I suddenly woke up and realized that he was looking at me curiously. "I asked you if you ever forgot things," he said.

That jarred me.

"Yeah, sometimes," I said teasingly and ran my tongue over my lip. "What about you?"

"I'm asking the questions," he said lightly, "like when do you forget? At work, in bed, here?"

"Oh, sometimes I get distracted and find that I got someplace without planning to." I grinned, letting my eyes convey that I thought he was sexy.

"Like where?"

"Like the shopping mall or work."

"You mean that you drive yourself places and don't really think about it?"

"Something like that," I said.

This seemed to satisfy him, and he explained that a lot of people get distracted when they're under stress.

I didn't tell him that sometimes I found myself in distant cities when I had gotten *really* distracted. I didn't want to get into discussing the drug use with him. And he didn't ask me out, even though I made it clear that I was interested, so I never went back.

Now I turned off the typewriter and went into Steve's office. "I'm going to knock off a little early," I said.

He looked up from his book and smiled at me. "Has anyone told you today that you're lovely?" he asked. "How about if I take you out to dinner?"

"Not tonight—I'm tired and need to get home." But I kissed him goodbye so that he wouldn't feel rejected.

I drove home, changed into sweat pants and running shoes, and raced outside with my two springer spaniels. They bounced along, black and white, then brindle and white. It was easy to slip into fantasy while my body stretched and moved, the dogs yelping at my bursts of energy: After my run, I'd find myself back at the house I shared with Keith, back where I belonged. I'd make something interesting for dinner. Thai. With lots of lemon grass. Keith liked that.

The fantasy dissolved, and I was at the door of my temporary home. I showered, lit a cigarette, and called the nurse practitioner whom I had seen a couple of months ago when I had a virus. "I'm feeling kind of stressed out right now," I said. "Do you know someone I could talk to?"

Lynn Wilson was the name, and she was a social worker. I hadn't liked that woman therapist who called me passive-aggressive, and generally preferred to be around men, but I decided that the gender of the therapist didn't matter. I only needed to see her a few times. Within a month, everything would be fine: no scary suicide thoughts, and I'd probably be home with Keith.

2

Early Friday morning, I left my desk and let myself into an empty faculty office. Fridays were quiet in the Biology Department; no one would notice the secretary's brief absence. I needed to make this call in private.

"Lynn Wilson, Mental Health Clinic." I couldn't conjure up a face to go with the name but had no trouble visualizing the mental-health clinic. Lots of little offices and a waiting room filled with tense-looking students who pretended to concentrate on their textbooks until the invariably late therapist condescended to see them. When called, a student would hop up nervously and follow a cool professional into an office from which, exactly fifty minutes later, she would emerge, sobbing over some overwhelming personal trauma. Late in the day, after all the students had gone, the therapists would get together and laugh about the ridiculous tales they had been told.

I shook the scene from my mind and dialed the number. I'd never be like those other students. I would walk in bouncy and smiling and leave the same way. I had no real problem, no *feeling* that required going to a mental-health clinic. I was only going so that I could be more in balance and stop the threat of suicide.

While I waited for Lynn Wilson to answer her phone, I rehearsed my speech. I knew what therapists wanted to hear.

"My name is Joan Frances Casey, and I'm going through a stressful period right now," I began. "I'm in the process of a divorce that I don't want. I'm a secretary in the Biology Department, and I'm having an affair with a professor there. I'm also a graduate student in political science, and I'm feeling a little overwhelmed by it all."

I took a deep breath. "Just right," I thought, "I sound serious, but not panicky."

The therapist paused. "Let's see, can you come in Wednesday afternoon?" she asked. My hands felt clammy as I searched for a response. Five more days until Wednesday. I couldn't make it that long. The tightrope swayed.

"Umm, OK," I answered uncertainly, "but could you tell me how to get through the weekend?"

I waited while she weighed the new urgency in my voice. "I can make some time today," she said.

The waiting room was just as I had imagined. A half-dozen young women, some with small children, flipped through books or stared out the window at the falling snow. I smiled and made eye contact where possible. You don't have to let your problems get you down.

"Ms. Casey?" I stood casually and smiled at the tall dark-haired woman, then followed her down the hall. I liked that she called me Casey. I liked that name, liked it so much that I had kept it even after I got married. "Casey" seemed more descriptive to me than a mere family label. I definitely liked "Ms. Casey" more than "Jo" or "Joan Frances" or "Josie" or "Missy" or any of the other names that people called me.

Privately, I called myself Renee. Like one of T. S. Eliot's cats, I assumed everyone had a private name. "Renee" felt comfortable on my tongue, on my being, even if I rarely said it out loud.

We sat. The therapist pulled out a notebook and pencil from her desk. I smiled at my own understanding of the process, seeing that she knew her role as well as I knew mine. She waited expectantly.

I felt relaxed and a little drowsy. It was a calm that I recognized. I knew what was going on, and my words flowed with little effort or input. I let my inside out.

"My name is Joan Frances Casey," I heard myself say, "but I prefer to be called Jo." It was odd, I thought, hearing myself say that. It was not what I really felt. *I* certainly didn't like to be called Jo.

I listened while I answered the therapist's questions. Most of it I could have predicted. I had heard the spiel before.

I heard myself say that I was the younger of two children and that I had never been close to my mother or to my sister, Carol. I didn't feel energetic enough to clarify that I didn't see how I was part of any of this.

But I did feel a twinge about Carol's child John. Three years old and already so furtive in his movements, so unsure of himself. The phrase he knew best was "I'm sorry." John had heard often enough that "Mommy won't love you if you do that" so that he sensed Mommy's love was dependent on his intuiting her wants.

The pain gave way to sharper hurt when Father was discussed. "I was always close to my father," I heard myself say. "Literally all my childhood memories are of time with him."

The therapist listened intently to the description of a special father-daughter closeness, a closeness that had ended in death. "In the spring of 1977, my father knew his cancer was terminal and he told me that he wanted me with him when he died. I think I hated him for saying that. I knew I wasn't strong enough to watch him die. A few weeks later, my mother called and said to come home. I was living in Chicago, and they were in Richmond. I made plane reservations to go to Richmond, but I hoped that he would die before I arrived. He didn't.

"I walked into his hospital room, and he glared at me through glittering yellow eyes. The tumor in his belly had grown so large that he looked pregnant. 'Giving birth to death,' I thought."

The therapist put her pencil down and laid her notebook aside. I stopped the monologue, suspicious that she had stepped outside her role. She smiled at my nonverbal question and nodded for me to continue. I relaxed and allowed the unrehearsed monologue to continue. I hadn't heard this before.

"I was afraid of his dying, afraid of the finality and ugliness of death. I clung to the door frame, wanting to race from the room. Then my father talked to me. He needed me. He was scared. I had never heard him say those words before.

"My father took ten days to die. He did most things in his own time. For the first time in my life, I gave to him, offering him sips of water, rubbing lotion on his body. When he died, his hand was in mine.

"I understood then that my father was even wiser than I had thought. He knew that I needed to watch him die. I had always worshipped my father as though he were a god. At the moment of his death, I finally loved him as a person."

I shook myself from the telling. I felt wrung out. There was a strength, an intensity that I had not before experienced when I let my inside out.

Lynn Wilson looked touched, her eyes misty. "Well," she said, "that's quite a story."

The word "story" was jarring. "Does she think I'm making this up?

Am I?" I hadn't known what I was going to say until I heard it. Was my description of his death accurate? I realized suddenly that I didn't feel too much about him alive or dead.

I pushed my confusion aside, too threatened to relax again yet not knowing what I'd say if the therapist asked a direct question. My session time was almost up anyway.

"See you later," I said as I stood; stretching and smiling, I tried to be nonchalant as I made for the door.

"Wait, what about getting through the weekend?" the therapist asked.

"Oh, that's right," I said, but made no move to return to the chair.

"It sounds as though you need to do something for yourself, something that would make you feel good," she said.

I smiled, nodded, and said, "What a great idea. Why didn't I think of that?"

I was no longer worried; the pressure was already subsiding. I knew that I'd be safe this weekend. There'd be no suicidal thoughts or gestures now. That was all the help I really needed.

CASE NOTE *March 6, 1981*

Ms. Casey called me for an appointment at the suggestion of the nurse practitioner on our team. She was seen the same day because of her apparent high degree of anxiety.

Ms. Casey is a small-boned, thin, tall, fragile-looking young woman with large eyes, wearing glasses and no makeup. She has long brown curly hair, is well groomed, neatly and unobtrusively dressed.

On first entering the room, she shook hands firmly, looked me directly in the eye, and spoke clearly and rationally. However, from the start of the interview, she appeared limp, her shoulders drooped, and she looked away or down at her clasped hands.

Ms. Casey engaged very quickly.

However, at the end of the interview, she seemed uneasy about her disclosures—limited and offered with little affect—and I told her she had done "just fine." I said that she has a right to take time for herself on the weekends and gave her permission to do so.

Ms. Casey is a bright, articulate young woman, introspective and in-

sightful to a degree. She has a number of ego strengths and coping skills but is currently overwhelmed by an extremely stressful life situation in which she does not have any unconflicted supportive relationships. She has difficulty expressing and owning her anger and tends to turn it inward, accepting blame and behaving self-destructively—tends to separate intellect and feeling. Could profit from long-term treatment.

PLAN: *1. Appointment at least weekly to provide support. 2. Attempt to foster corrective emotional relationship. 3. Insight development.*

3

I had a second appointment the following week. All I wanted was the "fix" I needed to feel a better balance, but I realized too that an electric anticipation flowed through me at the prospect of seeing Lynn again. The feeling was mine, but not mine.

"That's not so strange," I thought. It was like keeping my mind on some office activity while looking forward to going out to dinner. It was OK to feel two things at once. And I had to admit that there was something intriguing about Lynn Wilson.

I knew Lynn was a "professional." Like all of the therapists I had seen before her, she was talking to me because she was getting paid to do so. But she was better at pretending that she cared. Her body language and sympathetic "umm" suggested that she really listened. I decided that this visit I'd talk with Lynn directly instead of letting the drowsiness take over so that I didn't care what was said.

"I really want to find a way to get my husband back," I said at the beginning of the hour. She nodded and asked me why and how I planned to do so.

Lynn was easy to talk to, so easy that I found myself telling her about the internal urge to jump. "I don't want to die," I assured her, "but I guess I wouldn't mind if I got hurt a little. So Keith would understand how much I need him."

"That won't work!" Lynn said sharply. Then her voice softened. "I don't want you hurt for any reason," she said.

I felt humiliated and tricked into admitting my real feelings, and stepped back into the drowsiness, not wanting to invest myself again.

I heard myself stumble and stammer in confusion and left the office in that state. "So what," I thought.

CASE NOTE *March 9, 1981*

Ms. Casey came in saying that things had gone well over the weekend.
She discussed her marriage and feelings concerning her husband, Keith.
She admitted thinking that if she hurts herself Keith will know how much
the divorce pains her. She became very withdrawn when I told her this
would not work. She closed her eyes. Became silent. Seemed dazed when
she left and did not make new appointment.

Because of Ms. Casey's apparent confusion, I will ask the clerk to call
and confirm next appointment. It seems obvious to me that this patient is
in a great deal of pain (e.g., allusions to self-destructive behavior and
sudden periods of confusion). I will suggest twice-weekly appointments.

. . .

Later that afternoon, the clinic clerk called to say that the therapist
wanted an additional appointment later in the week. I was too surprised
to do anything but comply. This wasn't the way professionals were supposed to act. Lynn wasn't supposed to care if I came back.

Anyway, the extra appointment seemed like a gift. You're supposed
to accept gifts graciously. I wouldn't hurt her feelings by refusing.

CASE NOTE *March 12, 1981*

Looked very well—less frightened, less suspicious. Still subject to
strong mood shifts during sessions and presented many contradictions
concerning present and past relationships. For example, she said, "My
mother says that my sister is just like my father"—negative connotation.
Yet she told me with pride that she is like her father. She reported feeling
manipulated by her mother yet also occasionally mentioned their "close
supportive relationship. . . . We're like friends."

She boasted that she's "good with people—I know how to please
them," but also said, "People always stop liking me; they stop loving
me"—referring to Keith, Mother, high-school and college friends. Ms.
Casey did not seem aware of these contradictions.

PLAN: *Encourage her to identify and explore feelings of ambivalence as a lead to helping her deal with these contradictory feelings.*

. . .

I was embarrassed when I thought about how obvious the contradictions must have been. Before the drowsiness took over, I told Lynn how wonderful Keith was and how important it was to me to fight the divorce, and then later in the session I heard myself saying that the marriage had never been quite right. Keith wanted a fun-loving wife and ridiculed me when I said that there was more meaning to life and that other people's feelings really mattered.

I heard myself tell Lynn about my current relationship with Steve, and about how inadequate I felt when I compared myself with his beautiful, brilliant wife, who had recently died of a chronic heart disease. I couldn't overcome my trancelike apathy to keep from saying this. But early in another session I told Lynn the truth: Steve was an old drag. He never wanted to go to bars or dances. I couldn't be what he wanted, and, as far as I was concerned, Steve was just someone to fill the time until Keith realized that he wanted me back.

Lynn didn't mention the contradictions—she must not be paying close enough attention. No matter, in a few weeks I'd stop seeing her.

The thought of not seeing Lynn brought a flash of pain and then the familiar panic of swaying, being off balance. "Damn it. That's always my problem," I thought. "I get attached to people, but they have their own lives, their own problems, and really don't give a shit about anyone else." I knew that was true, and it didn't bother me most of the time. I had learned to be a friend without expecting anything in return. I had learned not to be surprised when people decided that I no longer fit into their lives.

I was furious with myself for letting this Lynn Wilson get to me. "She's not even pretending to be your friend," I reminded myself. "She's just a professional, just listening because that's her job."

4

I continued to go twice weekly to see Lynn. The suicidal urges had ended, but the more I listened as the inside part of me talked, the more intrigued I became. The part of me who spoke without my input felt special, validated by Lynn's attention. Lynn's questions often made that inside part uncomfortable, because there seemed to be so much that that part didn't really remember. But for the first time I heard that part of me sound safe in saying, "I don't know." Lynn didn't call me a liar, as so many other people had, and she didn't laugh when that part of me who liked being called Jo admitted not knowing what clothes I was wearing without looking down to see.

I listened attentively but apathetically—interested but with no desire to act—and thought that Lynn must be incredibly naïve. She acted as though she believed me. And her belief in me made me feel confused. After I left Lynn's office, I felt guilty about not doing a better job to control what I was saying.

Surely I was playing an elaborate game of make-believe with Lynn. Surely I could stop anytime I wanted to, but in Lynn's office I often felt too drowsy to stop anything.

Effortlessly I was presenting Lynn with characterizations unlike the real me, characterizations that I thought of as "them," not me. With other therapists I had quickly begun to feel so foolish that I couldn't let my inside out. I realized, only after the sessions, that Lynn touched different nerves at different times, called forth varied responses, even as I watched, uncaring, from my internal perch.

Sometimes I saw myself react as a little girl who peered out at this lady through half-closed eyes. Curling up in the big chair was the only way to respond when Lynn reached out and said, "It hurts so bad, doesn't it?"

Sometimes I heard myself defending the mother who never felt like mine.

"Your mother doesn't sound like a very supportive person to me," Lynn observed one day.

I heard myself saying unequivocally, "My mother knows that there isn't anything wrong with me. There never is. I'm a very, very lucky girl, and I can't let myself get caught up in self-pity. My mother is a lab technician. She spends her time helping sick people who really need her. She knows what's best for me."

But, whatever turmoil might trap me mid-session, I usually managed to shake it free and feel fully in control at the end. I'd smile and stretch, telling Lynn through my cat-cozy manner that I attached no significance to the bullshit she had observed in the last hour. None of it had anything to do with me.

Lynn always smiled back and asked, "Feeling better?"

"Much," I answered cheerfully and went on my way.

CASE NOTE *March 30, 1981*

Ms. Casey clearly has periods of dissociation. She described two such incidents within the past six months. One evening, her mother-in-law, who reportedly never cared for her, called to tell Ms. Casey that she was happy Keith was getting a divorce. After her mother-in-law said, "You ruined my son's life," Ms. Casey "woke up" at a shopping mall with no idea of how she had gotten there or what had happened in the intervening time.

Another episode occurred after her own mother called to cancel a trip to Chicago. Ms. Casey's mother had not visited her for two years, and she was counting on her mother's support in helping her deal with the divorce. Ms. Casey reported "waking up" in the car, parked in front of a friend's house, uncertain as to whether she was on her way to see her friend or on her way home.

Since I suspect that Ms. Casey has also been dissociating during her sessions with me, I will continue encouraging her to talk about these incidents. The patient who bounces in and out of my office with a "what-the-hell" attitude is very different from the aspect I'm talking with during the majority of the treatment session. And that aspect is different, again, from the "scared child" and the "mother advocate." I'm beginning to think that Ms. Casey may suffer from Multiple Personality Disorder. But this is unsettling for me. I've never seen a case, nor have my colleagues.

PLAN: *1. Reread* Three Faces of Eve *and* Sybil *and see if I'm on the right track. 2. Search for a knowledgeable consult. 3. Explore the possibility with Ms. Casey and continue supporting all parts of this very complex patient.*

. . .

Early in my first appointment in April, Lynn told me that she suspected that I suffered from Multiple Personality Disorder. "Oh, brother," I thought, "what's this lady's problem?" She might as well have told me that I was possessed by demons. I was more worried about *her* mental state than my own when she said that, but I refrained from expressing my derision. Professionals don't like their diagnoses questioned.

I spent the evening ticking off why I wasn't a multiple. Sure, I forgot things sometimes and failed to pay attention to everything I was doing. So did everybody else. Occasionally I heard myself saying something I didn't believe, something that seemed to pop out of nowhere. Eric Berne's Transactional Analysis explained it perfectly: we all have various parts— parent, adult, child—within us.

People said I had a flair for the dramatic, but what Lynn suggested was just plain weird. Multiple personality was some sort of mental illness. I certainly didn't need psychiatric care.

I was fine unless the pressure of doing so much or being rejected put me off balance. And I *had* done a lot. I had completed my B.A. at the University of Virginia in three and a half years—longer than I expected because Keith and I didn't have the money for me to take as many courses as I wanted each semester—*and* I worked full-time. I had interned with a state legislator, completed my teaching certification here in Chicago, was doing graduate study, again working full-time—and still pursuing my hobby of breeding, training, and showing springer spaniels. Now I was applying for high-school teaching jobs.

People called me compulsive, a workaholic, overenergized, an overachiever, too intense, but no one would call me crazy.

5

Ms. Casey is terrified at the thought that she might be a multiple. I decided not to force a discussion of the diagnosis until I am more certain myself of how to deal with this—my patient requires unquestioned support far more now than she needs debate over a particular psychiatric label—but as soon as I made that decision, Ms. Casey presented her multiplicity in a more florid way.

Ms. Casey was working on an annual fund-raiser with United Way, where her husband is employed. During our sessions, she talked of her fear of this intense involvement with Keith and the people who used to be their mutual friends. But still she felt compelled to meet her responsibilities.

However, in direct contrast with this "fearful" presentation at the beginning of our last session, she proceeded to talk animatedly about the event—about how much fun she would have there. Since I knew I would be out of town during the weekend of the fund-raiser, I encouraged Ms. Casey to use the on-call number, advising her that she would find somebody to talk to, and stressed that I would see her for our Monday appointment after the weekend. She said that she would be very busy with United Way and felt she probably wouldn't need any support.

Because of poor flying conditions and airline cancellations, I was unable to get back in time on Monday and had to have the receptionist reschedule the appointment.

When I finally saw Ms. Casey today, she seemed different. Bright, gay, bouncy, and happy, she told me that she hadn't minded missing our appointment. She inquired whether I had had a good time and said she had had a ball at the fund-raiser. She had explained to her friends there that she and Keith were having a little trouble now but that she was sure it would all work out.

I remarked on the change, and Ms. Casey insisted that Keith was just angry and that he had a right to be—"she really fucked it up." When I asked who "she" was, Ms. Casey replied, "Jo, of course." When I asked her name, she told me "Renee."

. . .

I was stronger, more in control, than I had been before meeting Lynn, and the suicidal impulses were gone. But that inside-out part of me was stronger as well. This was not the way the game was supposed to work—before it had just gotten quiet inside.

Now I noticed at least one voice engaged in active thinking—the voice that most often talked when I turned inside out in Lynn's office. The voice muttering "It's better without Keith. I really need a lot of private time right now" concerned me when I thought about ways to remind Keith that he loved me. The voice mumbling "I'm bad. Nobody could really like me" when Lynn rescheduled the appointment made me certain that it was time to get out of therapy.

But I was sad at the prospect of not seeing Lynn anymore. She seemed more like a real person than had any of the previous therapists, and I felt guilty about turning inside out in her office. I had just been playing that game to release pressure and had deceived her into thinking I had multiple personalities.

This would be my last visit. If I explained to Lynn what was going on, she'd understand that I really didn't need to see a social worker. She could give the time to somebody who needed it.

I told Lynn my real name so that I could help her understand the game.

"Today's the last day," I said, "and I'm just going to talk to you as the person I really am." I tried to be earnest enough so that she'd know I was serious, but light enough so that she'd feel free to tell me to stop that nonsense.

"You ought to feel really special," I said extravagantly. "I hardly ever tell anyone that my name is Renee. But if you're going to understand the game I play, you've got to separate me from the voice I made up that said to call her Jo."

Lynn nodded, but seemed more cautious than she had the other times I had seen her. "I do feel flattered that you've told me your name, Renee," she said, without even smiling. "Could you talk in the Jo voice for me, just so that I'll know the difference?"

I sighed. This was going to be complicated to explain. "I heard that voice say that nobody would ever like her," I said. "It's as though she felt bad that you canceled the appointment and then she got mad because she felt bad and so I just can't make it happen now. But it's just a game anyway."

"Renee," Lynn said gently, "this is a little confusing, but I think that you're describing a lot more than a voice there."

I groaned. I was trying to own up to the game I had been playing, and Lynn was taking this as more evidence for her diagnosis.

"How could a voice feel bad or get mad?" Lynn asked.

"It was just me pretending to feel that way," I said, feeling flustered. I couldn't believe that Lynn was even bothering to argue. What did she care? "I know everything that's happened in here, but sometimes I just feel too lazy to stop it." The more I tried to explain, the more confused and humiliated I felt. "It's kind of a habit," I finished, feeling as lame as I sounded. That wasn't what I meant but I didn't know what to say. "I screwed up!" I said. "I'm sorry."

"It's OK, Renee, you haven't done anything wrong," Lynn said. "Whatever it is, we can handle it together, but I think that's going to take longer than this session. So, for right now, why don't you not worry about quitting therapy and tell me more about the voices. It really is OK to tell me about it."

"It's just a game," I said again, but I felt less frightened. Lynn really wanted to help me, and she wasn't upset with me for having wasted her time. "I sort of relax and let my inside out."

"And when your inside comes out, it speaks in a different voice that you made up."

I nodded a couple of times and gritted my teeth, grateful that Lynn was beginning to understand. I was still a little afraid that she might get angry and throw me out of her office.

"The voices must go with characters," Lynn said. "Don't worry about how it sounds. Just tell me about the characters that you've been presenting to me."

"Well, there's the one who introduced herself the first day and told you about her father's death. That's Jo. That part is always so serious! She really likes Steve and is glad that Keith wants a divorce.

"And there's a little girl whose name is Missy. She knows that it's bad to come outside, but somehow in here it occasionally happens. She likes it when you touch her, but she's afraid to talk.

"And there's one more. You've talked to one other voice: Joan Frances. She thinks that her mother is great. When Jo says that her father was great, Joan Frances thinks she has to stick up for her mom.

"I don't know why I say those things, but when I do, I feel really bad and then tell you the truth. I love Keith, not Steve. Nancy and Ray never really felt like parents to me."

Lynn smiled at me. "That's why so much of what I said in here seemed contradictory," I said, smiling a little. "I really didn't mean to lie."

"I know, sweetie," Lynn said. "I don't think that what you were doing counts as lying." Her eyes were kind and soft, but her body rocked in concentration.

"Help me understand how the game is played," Lynn said. "Where does Renee go when Missy comes out?"

"I go inside, but I'm nearby," I said. "It's like I'm at the back of a theatre, watching a play. But if I get bored watching, without really meaning to, I leave the theatre and go inside another room in my head. Sometimes a question or some sort of warning bell calls me out. When I come back, I know what happened, but I don't feel like I really did anything."

Lynn listened thoughtfully. She acted as though she believed me. "That voice you call Jo, why can't she remember like you? Why does she seem so confused and uncertain?"

I felt triumphant and finally able to make my point. "It's because she's just a voice, or like a character in a play. I'm the real person."

"In your game," Lynn said, "do the voices look like anything?"

"Missy is an ugly little girl, about five. She has fuzzy brown hair and skinny arms and legs. Jo is an ugly twenty-five-year-old. Jo has brown, stringy hair and a long face, like this," I said, mimicking Jo's expression, "and she'd spend her life in shirts and jeans unless I came out to get dressed in the morning. Joan Frances wants to look like her pretty mother and sister, so she likes to put on makeup and always sits up straight.

"And, of course, you can see me. I'm pretty and younger than Jo and

Joan Frances—I'm only nineteen—and my hair is soft and wavy. Surely you can see the difference."

"OK, Renee, let me tell you what I think," Lynn said. "I know that you want to believe that you have control over all of this, but I really don't think you do. You get scared about what the others do because sometimes you've been forced to realize that you don't have control.

"I do feel really special that you're letting me close enough to help you with all of this. And I'm going to have to ask you to trust me even a little more. What you want is to never again worry about losing control to one of those voices, right?"

"Right," I said, but felt trembly, scared of what Lynn might do now that she knew the truth.

"You've told me about the game," she said. "Now let me play. Our time is up for today, but next time, just relax and let the 'inside out' if you can. And try to stay close enough to watch without interfering with anything. I think you might be surprised at what you learn."

"I need to think about it," I said as I got up to leave.

"But you'll come back?" Lynn asked.

"Sure, I guess so," I said.

"I think you are a very remarkable woman," she said.

I left Lynn's office that day unable to sort it all out. I knew that Lynn was likely to be furious when she fully comprehended the game, but I felt intrigued too. I had never had the chance before to understand why the pressure built up inside or why I got suicidal without wanting to die. Lynn seemed confident. I guess I did trust her a little.

At the start of the next session, Lynn met me in the waiting room and put her arm around my shoulders as we walked back to her office. Once inside, she said, "I'm tremendously proud of you for giving this a try. Do you think you can relax and let Jo out?"

"I guess so," I said, took a deep breath, and slipped in.

Jo found herself face to face with a sympathetic but determined therapist. "I'm sorry that we missed an appointment, Jo," Lynn said, "but I'm glad to see you."

Jo said nothing, uncomfortable with Lynn's new directness.

"Did anyone ever call you Missy?" Lynn asked.

"My father," Jo said with surprise.

"How about Joan Frances?"

"That's what my mother calls me," Jo answered and wondered if Lynn had had a conversation with her mother.

"Does the name Renee mean anything to you?" Lynn asked.

Jo blushed and wondered where Lynn had heard that name. She had never told her mother about Renee Montecalm. "That's a name I made up myself," Jo said.

When Jo was nine years old, she decided that she wanted to spend her life hiding away and writing books. "I knew that my books would have a limited audience and wouldn't earn enough to support me, so I decided that I'd write for money as well, but I didn't want to publish that under my own name. Renee Montecalm is my pseudonym, but I actually imagined her as more.

"Now it seems childish," Jo explained to Lynn, "but at the time I thought commercial writing would damage my credibility as a scholar. The 'Renee' that I dreamed of was bright, witty, social. It was kind of a flashy veneer to protect the real me from dealing with the public."

"It's not at all childish," Lynn said. "What you've described is exactly what's happened."

Jo looked at her, silent but afraid.

"You've got Renee and Missy and Joan Frances too, who all help protect you," Lynn said reassuringly. "You're so unsure of things because these personalities handle a lot of your life when you're not looking."

Jo looked squarely back at Lynn. "That's crazy," she said.

"No, not at all," Lynn responded, "it's very creative. I'll prove it to you. Tell me what was going on during the hour before you came in here."

Jo felt the blankness stab at her, the familiar lack of answer and accompanying panic. The room swam before her and she closed her eyes.

Joan Frances, who lacked Jo's amnesia, twisted the panic into cool anger. She glared briefly at Lynn before she responded with a slight smile of derision.

"I spent the last hour before my appointment ordering supplies for the Biology Department. It was requisition number four-oh-oh-seven. The order included a dozen dissection kits, some tubing, and more animals than I care to list. I left the office, got my car out of the parking lot, and drove here. I parked at a meter in front of the building. And if I don't leave on time, I'll get a ticket."

"I am impressed," Lynn said. "You have good recall, Joan Frances."

She smiled thinly in return. I gave Joan Frances's anger a wide berth as I struggled back out. I needed to talk to Lynn for a minute before I left.

"Wow," I said, grinning sheepishly at her.

"Renee," Lynn said, "so what do you think now?"

"I guess maybe you're right," I said. "Maybe they do think independently of me, but I think it's happening because you let it. If you just said stop, it would."

"No, sweetie, it's not like that," Lynn said. "You don't have that control and neither do I, but together you and I will find a way to figure it out."

"I'm not so sure about that," I said with a flash of insight. "Joan Frances doesn't even have as much control as I have, but she's pretty sure that her mother will make this stop."

Joan Frances got to the car before she got a ticket and hurried back to the apartment. She was filled with a sense of dread. Her mother would be furious if she knew about this. But if Joan Frances tried to conceal it, her mother would find it out. She always did. And, either way, her mother might disown her.

That evening, Joan Frances called her mother. She mentioned offhandedly that she was seeing a therapist, and her mother reacted as she had feared.

"That's a waste of time," Nancy said. Her anger was clear even through the phone lines. "Look at me. You don't see me running to a therapist with every little crisis. My stepfather abused me—you've seen the scars on my back from the beatings—and I came through it without a therapist.

"Your father treated me like dirt, but I still took care of him when he was dying. I see really sick people every day, and I've learned from them that I can't go around feeling sorry for myself. You're a very lucky girl, and it's time you realized that. It's time you stood on your own two feet."

Joan Frances told her mother that she was right and shakily called the clinic's after-hours number. She left a message for Lynn to call. "I can't see you anymore," Joan Frances said when Lynn returned the call. "There's nothing wrong with me. I have to stop feeling sorry for myself."

Lynn said, "I'm here. I want to see you. I can help you. I think that you should come in for your appointment."

CASE NOTE *May 1, 1981*

Ms. Casey has become quite dependent on evening phone calls. "Missy," who is afraid to speak when she's in my office, is the most frequent caller, although I usually end the conversation by finding "Jo" on the line, and sometimes I talk to these two along with "Renee" and "Joan Frances" during a single phone call. I am continually surprised that I have no difficulty in distinguishing which one I am talking to.

There is a problem, however, in getting to me through the hospital on-call service. I am particularly concerned because of my upcoming trip to New Orleans. I have made arrangements to let the hospital know of my whereabouts each night so that I can be notified of any calls, even though I am told that when Ms. Casey reaches the on-call number, she says that I am not to be bothered. It's as though she expects to find me at the other end of the line and feels confused that I'm not there.

I feel strongly that it is important to remain accessible even during my trip. I am not sure that she really understands when I am away and when I am in town.

"Missy" is not in touch with outside reality. She doesn't seem to have the resources to tell the on-call operator anything more than her first name. I find the next day only that "Missy" called for me, that this "very confused person" hung up when asked for further information, such as her last name or whether this was an emergency. The problem with the on-call operator is compounded by the fact that Missy refers to herself not in the first person but, rather, as "you," as though she has no sense of identity aside from the references provided by other people. For example, she tells the on-call operator "You want to talk to your friend Lynn."

When she does get through (with, I suspect, the helpful intervention of another personality), and I call her back, Missy tells me secrets that she won't yet talk about in the office. She has told me that she did not want to grow up to be a woman like her mother, so she "prayed to God every night to make you a boy. Until God makes you a boy, you're not going to get any bigger."

Missy is giving me information that is vital in my understanding of this patient; e.g., she was supposed to have been a boy, and is told by her mommy and daddy that she remembers things all wrong. She tells me that she's not allowed (by the other personalities?) to talk to people face to face. She also hints that there are many things she knows that the "other girls inside" consider dangerous to tell. If she is unable to reach me, she may withdraw completely.

. . .

I couldn't understand why Lynn would ruin her vacation by staying in touch, but she did, three times via telephone from New Orleans. At our first session after she returned, I told her that she was making a mistake. She was only encouraging Jo and Missy to think that they had someone to depend on. I knew it was good for them to learn that people couldn't always be available—other people had their own lives and their own problems. If Jo and Missy didn't understand that by now, it was time they figured it out.

Even Jo told Lynn that she didn't have to be so nice. "People can't be there just because I need them," Jo said. "My father taught me that! My parents were separated when I was in high school. My father insisted that I live with my mother, and then he refused to give me his phone number or tell me where he lived. No one has ever been there constantly for me. I don't know why you're doing this."

6

I will keep case notes concerning Ms. Casey's progress as required by the unit, but feel more free to explore my personal and clinical reactions in writings that are less subject to the scrutiny of others. I don't think I'm being paranoid. I feel like a pioneer, but I also am beginning to feel misunderstood.

Some of my colleagues and even my supervisor seem concerned about the amount of attention I'm giving Jo. Yesterday, during the staff's case-reporting session, Harry suggested that Jo might be manipulating me by telling me secrets over the telephone. I think he was surprised that I bristled in response. I told him that I knew she was becoming dependent on me. And I explained (rather testily, I admit) that Jo came into my office with her pathological dependency; I didn't create it. I said that it was only natural that the dependency would be expressed if I was providing adequate treatment.

Later, in private, I apologized to him; I had reacted defensively at the meeting because I had been informed that some of the staff "didn't believe in MPD." I told Harry that I wanted his approval for any unorthodox treatment techniques and that I wanted to talk with him about the case, but didn't want it open for peer review right now. I need to be able to explore treatment ideas without defending the diagnosis at every turn.

I am well aware that Jo, in all of her various parts, is testing me to see if I'll come through with what I promise. Despite Harry's concern, I am being very careful not to promise more than I can give.

I can tell that rejection would actually be easier for some of the person-alities to handle than my sincerely and willingly responding to their needs. When I cuddle or comfort little Missy, she cringes as though expecting punishment for her expression of need. Both Renee and Joan Frances have given me obviously parent-inspired warnings that "you don't know what you're getting yourself into" by responding to the personalities' needs. The Jo personality refuses to acknowledge openly that she has any needs whatsoever.

I find that the pathology, dependency, need, and fear of rejection all make far more sense than talk of malingering or manipulation if one accepts the diagnosis of Multiple Personality Disorder. That is a very large "if" for my colleagues! Their uncertainty is making me take stock of my own psyche and of my professional intuitions as well.

I'm so sure of the diagnosis during the sessions. The transformations are undeniable. I usually see at least Renee and Jo during each appointment, and I can tell when a personality switch is occurring. There's always a pause, a lowering of eyelids. Then Renee comes in a flash—bright, gay, and immediately oriented. Jo comes slowly, seeming dazed, fuzzy, almost drugged—not sure of where she is or how much time she has lost. Sometimes the transformation period, which lasts no more than half a minute, brings yet someone else. Those same eyes, so pleading and full of pain in Jo, so twinkling and merry in Renee, grow cold and full of contempt. This is Joan Frances, who despises herself for her "playacting" and who hates me for "allowing it to continue." Renee has at least tacitly given up her description of this all as "a game," but Joan Frances seems wedded to the idea.

I even see physical differences among them. Renee's hands seem delicate and long-fingered, and then turn rough and spatulate when Jo has control. The whole body seems to shrink when Missy is out. I can't deny that I'm both intrigued and overwhelmed by this patient. Treating Jo is a challenge that I haven't known in twenty years of clinical work. Despite the skepticism around the office, I'm pleased to have the chance to work with a disorder that is apparently so rare.

Treating a multiple raises so many new questions for me. The legal and ethical tenets of confidentiality, for example, usually so straightforward, now have me stumped. I'd never repeat what a patient told me to some other patient, but I am not sure how this applies to information that is offered by one personality.

Should I keep Missy's secrets as though she were alone in her body? I would certainly keep my promise to a personality if I had verbally assured her that I would not tell something to another personality, but otherwise I think that it is up to me to decide what to share. Missy's secrets are important for Jo, Joan Frances, and Renee to hear. I am sharing them with Jo because I think that Jo needs to confront the fact that she was most probably a victim of child abuse. So far, Missy seems unaware of or unconcerned about my talks with Jo. If Missy reacts in a negative way to my sharing her secrets, I will re-evaluate the situation.

The lack of support I feel among my colleagues makes me unwilling to talk with them about this case. In what is probably a far greater breach of confidentiality, I have been taking my own uncertainty and excitement home.

Since we've been married, Gordon and I have shared many clinical experiences. At his inner-city high school, Gordon has worked with his share of abused and dysfunctional children, and he has been the object of misplaced hostility. He says that Jo (in all of her various personalities) acts and reacts much like his abused students. Gordon has answered the phone when the personalities call and has learned to distinguish the different voices and vocal mannerisms. His willingness to accept the reality of the disorder—even hearing most of it second-hand—and his insight from twenty years of teaching make him a very valuable colleague and confidant. Unlike my discussions at the office, I can talk out my dilemmas with him without his stopping to ask me if I am sure she is multiple.

I honestly care about Ms. Casey and want her to be well. I know that she will take more time, energy, and commitment than my other patients, but I'm willing to do what is needed. It feels very good to know that I'll have Gordon's caring for me and his empathy for Jo to support me through the process.

. . .

Who is this Lynn Wilson and what is she trying to prove?

Two months into treatment. I thought that by now Lynn would be sick of me, but instead she seemed more and more accommodating. Lynn gave each personality her home phone number and bought an answering machine so she'd know if anyone tried to reach her.

I figured that one of the reasons she was so willing to schedule extra time was that money was not an issue. Lynn worked for the university-hospital outpatient clinic on salary. She didn't depend on her patients' fees, as did therapists in private practice. My student health-insurance plan paid for psychotherapy as long as I used the university clinic.

I liked that Lynn liked me, and she had convinced me that the "voices" had minds and experiences of their own.

"Jo," for example, told Lynn that she had always felt out of place but had never suspected that she might have a problem that could be fixed. Now that she had the diagnosis to explain her sense of reality, she sorted some of the chaotic jumble of thoughts and memories.

"I'd feel funny having 'daydreamed' my way through whole seasons," Jo said, "but then I'd hear someone say, 'Time flies,' or 'How did it get to be three o'clock already?' and I'd think that everyone was like me.

"But I guess I never quite convinced myself, because I'm so afraid of people. It's like I'm carrying around this huge secret that I'm never supposed to tell. But since I don't remember just what I'm supposed to keep secret, I'm afraid I'll tell it by mistake."

"Oh, sweetie, you've got a potful of secrets," Lynn said. "Missy's just now beginning to tell me some of them."

"Don't say that name," Jo said. "It makes me feel stupid for you to talk about 'Missy' as though it were some other person. I don't want to hear what I say in my sleep."

During the sessions, Lynn recognized when Missy appeared and told her that it was safe to talk to her there. Missy refused to speak. But when Lynn got out of her chair and sat down on the rug and said, "Come on, sweetie, you can sit with me," she eagerly scrambled from her chair into Lynn's arms. She felt lulled by Lynn's warmth, her rocking, and her gentle voice.

"It's your hand," she whispered one night to Lynn on the phone.

"What about your hand, sweetie?" Lynn asked.

"It's bad. Bad hand."

"No, Missy, your hands are good hands," Lynn said, "I like to hold your hands when you sit with me in my office."

"Bad hand," Missy insisted. "Sister Mary said so. 'Right hand right, left hand bad.' "

Missy had not been allowed to use her naturally dominant left hand. The nuns who taught her slapped her hand with a ruler or made her sit on it when they found her holding a crayon or pencil with her left hand.

"Mommy says you're bad. Daddy says you're bad. Daddy says you're stupid. Mommy says you're lazy."

"You're a very good girl," Lynn reassured Missy. "I want you to come see me at my office, and you can color with whatever hand you like."

At peace after such conversations, Missy slipped back inside, and Jo often "woke up" clutching the telephone, hearing Lynn's comforting voice through the receiver.

"I'm sorry that I bothered you," Jo said, "but I didn't know that I called you tonight. I'm sorry."

"Don't worry about it, Jo," Lynn said. "You didn't call me. Missy did. Everything's OK. We'll talk about it next time we're together."

Back in the office, Lynn said, "Missy acts like an abused child."

"But that's not true," Jo said, "I couldn't have been abused."

"Just how do you know, Jo, that your parents never abused you?" Lynn asked.

"That's simple," Jo said. "I don't remember my mother or father ever being mean to me."

Jo stopped, struck by a new understanding. "You know, I don't have any preschool memories of being alone with my mother." Now that she thought about it, that was strange. Although both her parents had worked full-time since she was three, she had very early memories of being with her father, and no memories of being alone with her mother. She remembered babysitters, but not her mother.

Jo dismissed her new insight. Her father wouldn't let her be hurt. Jo did recall that one time when she was three or four her father had asked how she had gotten a new bruise on her leg. Mother's explanation seemed reasonable even now: "Joan Frances is a very clumsy child."

Jo knew she had to be utterly truthful, even when her version of the truth conflicted with what Lynn wanted to hear. Truth was vital to Jo, because she had a hard enough time keeping track of the spotty reality she experienced. Jo realized that she wasn't clear enough about what really happened ever to be a convincing liar.

Jo tried to think about her suspicion that Lynn liked her. She figured that Lynn was nice to her because she was a patient. Jo's mother had shown her what it meant to have a professional mask. The times Jo saw her mother at work in the lab, busy and efficient as she drew blood and marked vials, Nancy smiled warmly at the patients, ready with a sympathetic comment. If a patient or a doctor called Nancy at home, she immediately became the caring professional, no matter what had been happening before the phone rang. When Lynn hung up after an evening phone call from Missy, Jo suspected that Lynn resumed screaming at her husband or kids.

Lynn told Jo that she honestly cared about her, but Jo couldn't trust that. Her parents had said that they cared, but they didn't seem to like her much. She figured that they *had* to care for her. They didn't have a choice.

Other people seemed to care about her for short periods—some teachers in high school, Keith—but they had all gone away, no matter how much Jo had come to depend on them.

Jo supposed she was lonely, but her aloneness was an integral part of her life. She sometimes wondered what it would be like to have a friend, to feel intimate connection with another person.

Jo understood that Lynn's concern, genuine or not, was a precious but temporary gift. She continually apologized for all the phone calls she didn't remember making. Lynn said that she wouldn't let Jo interfere in a way that would lead to rejection. "It would be bad for both of us, Jo, if I let you take more than I have to give. Don't worry. I can take care of myself."

Jo reacted to Lynn's assurances with humiliation. "Of course you take care of yourself," Jo said. "You protect yourself so that I don't intrude. I know that you need to protect yourself from me. But I feel so bad, so guilty, when you remind me of that—as though I could presume to be important enough to intrude."

While Jo worried that her dependency on the therapist would lead to Lynn's rejection, the Joan Frances personality worried that that same dependency would lead to her mother's abandonment.

Joan Frances knew that her mother would not approve of her seeing Lynn, but, no matter how strongly she made the resolution to stop therapy, she found herself sitting in Lynn's office or leaving the building after a vaguely remembered appointment session. Joan Frances pleaded with Lynn to help her. "Please make me better before my mother tells me that I must stop seeing you. Please make me a better person so that she will love me."

DIARY *May 8, 1981*

It is clear that the various personalities I am seeing are quite different from one another.

The physical changes are startling. I have come to know Missy, Jo,

Renee, and Joan Frances well and am no longer surprised by the move from one personality to another. In fact, I experience each of them as different from the others in the same way as my other patients are different from one another. Although they share the same body, they are not the same and do not wear the body in the same way. It may be more accurate to say that the various personalities share the same physical space in a serial manner.

Their descriptions of their parents have virtually nothing in common. Renee even denies that they are her parents. She doesn't claim different parents. She doesn't claim any at all, saying that she is "a creation of this entity alone."

Jo worshipped her father and describes him as wise, gentle, and loving. His only flaw she claims as her own biological problem—she was resigned to never completely pleasing him because she turned out to be his daughter instead of his son.

Jo pities her mother for not being as "rational" as she describes herself and her father but denies that Nancy could have abused her.

Joan Frances says her mother is perfect, someone she models herself after. She is tortured because she is disobeying her mother by seeing me. Nancy reportedly told her daughter the other day, "For Mother's Day, I want a happy girl who realizes how lucky she is." Since Mother's Day is a couple days away, it would take a miracle to deliver that present. And so the pressure and guilt continue to grow. But Joan Frances's regular calls home make me sure that Nancy offers limited support and acceptance, as well as her dose of unrealistic expectations.

Her father, Joan Frances said, was "a cold, insensitive bastard who made life hell for my mother."

Missy sees Daddy as a refuge from her terrifying mother. She remembers long hours sitting in a place she calls "The Dark" until it was time for Daddy to come home. I'm not yet sure if Missy purposely hid there or if she was placed there.

My guess right now is that both parents offered a mixture of good parenting and abuse. I think that Nancy and Ray Casey were both very troubled themselves.

. . .

7

I don't expect to have a fully verified story of how Jo's disorder developed, but I don't think that historical accuracy is as important as what I call "emotional truth." People attach different levels of significance to the same events. No two participants in any event remember it in exactly the same way. A single broken promise, for example, among thousands of promises kept, might not be remembered by a parent, but may never be forgotten by the child who was disappointed.

So, when the Jo or Joan Frances personality says that an event remembered by another personality could not possibly have happened, I temper that need to deny by saying that what is recalled has significant "emotional truth" for the one who remembers. What's important is not the verifiability of the memory, but the significance of the memory to the teller.

But even with the amnesia and denial that accompany Multiple Personality Disorder, I'm amazed by the completeness of some memories of early childhood. I think now that the multiple mind must be a receptacle lacking the normal filters that allow for true repression. What one personality represses, another personality stores completely. The memories have sight, sound, texture. They are vivid in the retelling.

So, verifiable or not, I've been able to piece together a family history. Bits of family lore were duly recorded by Renee and by the Reagan and Robin personalities (two personalities who seem to exist solely to provide a storehouse for relevant information that was overheard in early childhood).

Reagan introduced herself one day with a calm "Perhaps I can be of assistance" when I was pushing Jo for some childhood memory. She said that she and Robin have always been around to "listen but not get in anyone's way."

Through these personalities, and through Missy's sharing of "secrets," I've come to make sense of the family background. There has been no reactive behavior, no abreaction of trauma, accompanying the retelling of this information. I suppose that's because Renee, Reagan, and Robin do not consider themselves members of the biological family. They have resisted all my attempts to make them see that they might have had some involvement in the early-childhood experiences.

Missy doesn't seem particularly troubled by the memories she shares with me either. I think she has been waiting for a long time to tell someone her secrets. And the other personalities are now allowing her to talk with me freely in the office. Missy has shared some memories from infancy and has even reported remembering the first split in personality—when, as she says, "the other girls came." She reports that this split occurred before she was a year old.

Missy apparently sensed (or someone else in the group told her) that I was incredulous that she could remember back so far. She explained these prelanguage memories to me by making an analogy with voice recordings on tape or phonograph records. "Things that happen and what people say make scratches on your mind," Missy said. "You don't know yet what the marks mean, but they're there anyway. And then, one day, you know what sounds and things mean. You can talk and know what words are. Then you can play back what happened before, and now you know what happened." Her aplomb makes it clear that she's satisfied with her explanation.

I'm not really concerned about whether or not Missy's explanation fits with theories of child language development or of memory. I suspect that few if any accepted theories of human potential adequately describe multiple personalities. I'm sure that her memories hold a great deal of "emotional truth." I am convinced that the seeds of this disorder were there long before my patient's birth.

If I write the narrative as it has been presented to me, it might help me understand what I think I know about Jo's beginnings. It's important that I keep in mind, both for me and for Jo, that what's important is that this is the scenario believed by my patient. Exact truth—who felt what, who did what to whom—matters less than how the personalities react to these beliefs.

Raymond Casey was born at home in a small manufacturing town outside of Syracuse, New York, in January 1925. A sickly baby, the last of twelve children, he spent the first months of his life coddled by his older sisters.

The family was not poor by the town's standards. As Ray later told his children, there was always "food on the table and love in the house." The strict Irish-Catholic traditions were ingrained by Ray's immigrant parents and by the shadow of the church, towering next door to the Casey home. Ray's father worked in the town's garment factory, as did Ray's older brothers.

By the time Ray had completed high school, the family depended on the income of the children to survive. Ray's father was killed in a factory accident, and two of Ray's older brothers died fighting in World War II. One brother left the family for the priesthood; a sister become a nun. Two other brothers moved to Richmond, Virginia. Ray was the only man in the house.

Ray's sisters Christine, Cathy, and Marie, who were also still living at home, worked as store clerks while they waited to get married. Ray worked in his uncle's hardware store and brought most of his salary home to Mother.

He lived another life as well. "Me and Tom Clancy," he later boasted, "broke into them places that I worked once fixing pinball machines. I knew them machines real good. We just jiggled the slots and took out all the money."

Ray told stories of how he and Tom set up bar bets that provoked brawls. When the others fought, Ray and Tom made for the door with the money. There were stories of wild car chases and equally wild women.

Ray made it clear that the women in his life were objects. His friendships were with men, Tom in particular. In his early twenties, Ray felt restless and bored; he wanted to get out of town for a while but couldn't just walk away. Ray decided that he would get married and join the Navy.

Ray chose Nancy Fitzgerald, the sister of his friend John. Nancy was a farm girl from the other side of the tracks. She was young, pretty, and shy.

Nancy's parents were also immigrants, and she had been raised by strict Catholic rules. There, however, the similarity with Ray's large, protective family ended. Nancy had spent most of her childhood watching her mother go through a succession of stepfathers. Nancy never knew her biological father. The men who shared her mother's bed—each of them for no more than a few years—either abused Nancy or ignored her.

Nancy found solace at the local convent, where she felt love and security that seemed absent at home. On her thirteenth birthday, Nancy asked to join the order. Although some girls were admitted at that age, Nancy was denied and counseled to ask again in five years. She decided that she was wanted at the convent no more than at home.

She turned her attention toward school, and there her brilliance was rewarded. She finished high school early and began to study blood chemistry at the local college. While in school, she worked as a lab technician at a nearby hospital.

On her eighteenth birthday, a year of college-level biology courses behind her, she married Ray, with little thought as to other options. Nancy felt trapped by her family's poverty. She was grateful to this man who, in his own words, "picked her up out of the gutter."

"She was some baby doll," Ray said of Nancy. Pregnant with their first child, Nancy stayed in Syracuse while Ray left for his adventures at sea. She didn't mind: being Mrs. Ray Casey gave her a ticket to the right side of town. She moved in with her mother-in-law, worked at the lab, and gratefully brought her salary home to her new family. She grew close to Ray's sister Marie, who also had a husband in the service.

Ray loved his three years in the Navy. "Stole an A-rab's horses once," he later confided; "turned out they was owned by some damn sheik or something, and me and my buddy got sentenced to twenty years of hard labor. We was sure lucky the U.S. government got us out."

"Seen every country in this world except Russia," he later reminisced. Ray claimed to have gotten drunk in a bar in every port. He said Argentina was the most beautiful country, Australia the friendliest. He loved those years so much that, whenever he felt particularly trapped, he'd pull out his wrinkled maritime certifications and sigh: "Maybe I'll just go back to sea."

It was to meet his "family responsibilities" that Ray left the Navy. He returned to Syracuse, packed up Nancy and his three-year-old daughter, Carol, and headed for Richmond, where his older brother had gotten him a job in a garment factory. Ray bought a small house outside of the city and settled into "doing right by his family." Nancy felt terribly homesick for the life she had known in Syracuse, but eventually loneliness overcame shyness, and she made friends with the other young mothers in the neighborhood.

Soon Nancy recognized that her new life had its advantages. Here no one knew about her past. Her wise, well-traveled husband taught her city manners. Since Ray said he could support his family, Nancy stayed home to raise Carol, and to wait for the baby boy who would complete her family.

In 1955, Nancy was pregnant again. This was the third time since she and Ray had moved to Richmond; she had miscarried twice before. Nancy felt a bond with this pregnancy, different from what she had felt at the same point with the last two. This time she knew she would carry the baby full-term. Nancy would give Ray his son.

In July, Ray drove Nancy and Carol back to Syracuse, where Nancy would be cared for by family before and after the baby's birth. When she was strong enough, she would return to Virginia with her daughter and longed-for son.

Nancy felt indulged by being back in New York. Despite an uncomfortable pregnancy—"I threw up for nine months," she said—her big belly gave her status, which she shared with her sister-in-law. Christine and Nancy, whose babies were due the same day, stayed with Ray's mother; they went to the hospital hours apart on the morning of August 22, 1955. Later that evening, Christine gave birth to a son; and Nancy returned home, for her labor pains had subsided. When Nancy visited newborn Matthew a few days later, she smiled at Christine over her rippling stomach. "It will be such fun for our boys to grow up together," she said.

Nancy never wavered in her belief that she was carrying Ray's son. She fancied that her miscarriages had been girl babies, and that her womb would reject all except the baby fit to carry the name she had picked out years ago—Joseph Raymond Casey.

Nancy awoke in agony on August 31, the day before her twenty-eighth birthday. The intermittent contractions she had experienced for ten days were nothing like this. Brother-in-law Jack took her back to the hospital and called Ray, who was still in Richmond. "You better come up," Jack said; "the doctors say it's the real thing."

The doctor and nurses kept close to Nancy's side, listening to the baby's heartbeat and trying to calm her. Although she had given birth before, she was more anxious than most first-time mothers, and her anxiety was working against her body. After she had been in labor a full twenty-four hours, and the fetal heart rate had become noticeably weaker, the doctor performed an emergency cesarean. He carefully uncoiled the umbilical cord, which was wrapped around the baby's neck, and got the slightly blue infant into oxygen.

"You have a beautiful baby girl," the doctor told Ray. "She's in some distress, but I think she's going to make it." The doctor gave Nancy the news in the recovery room. Nancy began to protest, then realized that she didn't have the strength. A girl. That wasn't possible. "Somebody made a mistake," Nancy said, and drifted back to sleep.

The next day, Nancy had to accept the truth. No other babies had been born September 1. No mistake, no chance for a mix-up. She had given birth to a girl. It was hard for Nancy to believe, harder still since she hadn't seen the baby yet. The baby was small, only five pounds, and not breathing well. Nancy hoped it would die. She had no need for another girl.

Nancy hurt from surgery, from the ordeal of labor, and from the knowledge that she had failed Ray. Even though Ray acted happy with the baby, she knew her husband well enough to recognize the undertone of bitter disappointment.

Nancy had no interest in naming the child, so Ray did it on his own. He named her Joan—because that was close to the "Joseph" Nancy had selected—and Frances because Saint Francis was a particular favorite of his. Joan Frances Casey. Even as he watched the baby struggle to breathe, Ray saw, through the glass wall of the newborn nursery, a resemblance to him that was less evident in Carol.

Ray willed his strength into the incubator. "Come on, peanut, get strong," he muttered, and watched through the night to make sure she did just that. This kid, Ray decided, was his special kid. Maybe a girl of his own would be OK.

Within a few days, the baby was out of danger, but Nancy's recovery was slow.

Three weeks after the baby's birth, Nancy took her new daughter home to Richmond.

She had to admit that the hospital nurses were right to say this was an easy baby. It slept through the night, ate on schedule, and rarely cried. Sometimes when she fed the baby, she pretended that it was a boy; she felt some love for the child then. "Joey, my little Joey," she crooned while the infant's hand played in her long brown hair, "are you my big boy?"

Other times Nancy felt nothing toward it. She would stare at the baby as it lay still, not crying, not moving, not sleeping. The infant seemed content to study objects or the movement of light on the wall for hours at a time. Nancy felt unnerved by this abnormal behavior.

The baby perked up when Ray was around. Ray headed straight for the crib the minute he walked in the door from work. He lifted the baby high in the air and told her in animated ways what had happened to him that day. She listened intently to her father's voice and made noises right back. The baby's first smiles were for Daddy.

The more the baby responded to her father, the more distant Nancy became. "It's not fair. I'm her mother. She should like me best." Nancy didn't see that the infant was sensing her mother's disappointment as surely as she felt her father's acceptance.

Nancy picked the baby up only when Joan Frances needed to be fed or changed. And she told Carol to keep away from the crib. "You leave that baby alone. You'll make her cry," she told the eight-year-old.

Nancy had to admit that Ray loved the baby, even if it wasn't a boy. He referred to the baby as Jo or Joan Frances as she did, but also called her Missy or Pixie or other crazy baby names. Nancy thought Ray looked very unmanly playing with the baby. It irked her to see him babbling baby talk or rocking the baby to sleep. She wished he would pay some attention to her and to Carol. "You've got two daughters, you know," she snapped.

Nancy saw innumerable differences between Joan Frances and the infant Carol had been. Carol was a screaming, colicky baby. This one was quiet, too quiet. Carol's constant crying had driven Nancy crazy, but at least she had known there was a baby in the house. This one didn't seem to care about anything except her father. She even refused to crawl.

One morning, in the baby's sixth month, while Ray was at work and Carol at school, Nancy placed the baby in the middle of a yellow blanket on the kitchen floor. She set an assortment of toys on the blanket, just out of the infant's reach, then picked up the jack-in-the-box and turned the crank. The baby responded to the sound by looking up at Mommy, who was crouched down, long hair hanging over her shoulder.

"That's right, Joan Frances," Nancy said, "come get your toy. Come to Mommy." The baby gurgled and reached. She could see the soft cloud of Mommy's hair; her fingers remembered its softness. She reached and felt only air. Mommy and the toy were too far away. She made no move to crawl.

Mommy picked up the child's favorite stuffed monkey and shook it so the monkey's head waved from side to side. The baby liked her monkey. The monkey's fur tickled her skin, and the hard plastic hat and monkey face felt good in her mouth. She stretched her arm out, but couldn't reach the monkey. She began to cry. But still she wouldn't crawl.

"Come on, you can do it." Hands picked her up. When the baby opened her eyes, she was on her hands and knees.

She froze. Whenever she got on her hands and knees in the crib and rocked so that the crib hit the wall, Mommy or Daddy came in to put her on her back. Now she didn't move, waiting for Mommy to act. When nothing happened, she pushed with her hands and tucked her legs until she was sitting again.

"Look, I'll move the jack-in-the-box closer." Mommy's voice dripped sweetness from an angry edge. The box played its tune and the baby reached out. This time she reached too far and threw herself off balance. Her hands hit the floor at the edge of the blanket. Now she was on her hands and knees.

The sticky, cold linoleum caught her interest, and she slapped a hand on the floor. It made a nice noise. She did it again, chortling at her new discovery. A brown shoe with a skinny sharp heel flattened her hand to the floor, and pain shattered the baby's being.

Her first internal struggle took place. The part that was becoming the Jo personality wanted to think about this turn of events and determine what had happened to cause the pain. Was it the floor? Was it the shoe? The jack-in-the-box? She had better avoid all three until she could figure it out. . . .

The part that was becoming the Joan Frances personality howled in anger and pain. She hurt. She wanted Mommy to fix it. . . .

The part that was becoming the Missy personality longed for the safety of her crib, lined with pastel beads that she could differentiate but not yet name. She could look at the beads and feel safe. . . .

The three desires, the three forming personalities, raged against one another, evenly matched. Then, abruptly, Missy won. She pushed the two new personalities into safe mental pockets and proceeded to follow the memory of her crib deep into her mind.

Nancy put the limp child back in the crib and wondered why God had punished her with this.

. . .

8

I helped Lynn and the other parts by showing up for the sessions. In return, Lynn inadvertently helped me by letting me see my life from a new perspective. I had some irrational fears. Now those phobias were shown to have causes, causes that made Lynn's diagnosis of Multiple Personality Disorder more plausible to me.

For example, if Nancy had really stepped on her infant daughter's hand, it was not surprising that I would feel an irrational fear and disgust whenever I looked at high-heeled shoes. I told people that I didn't wear high heels because at five ten I didn't need to be any taller. But, truthfully, I loathed them.

If Missy had felt confined to small dark places by fear or by physical incarceration, my terror of elevators made sense. No matter how long I scolded myself and paced in front of an elevator, I simply could not force myself to enter the small boxlike enclosure unless another passenger got on. I was late for many appointments because I had to wait in the lobby for someone to come along and ride with me. I never spoke to these stranger-guardians on elevators; their presence alone made me feel safe. But I broke out in a clammy sweat if my unknowing escort punched the button for a floor before my destination.

In the past, I hadn't thought much about my phobias. Now I was like a scientist attempting to find causes for newly recognized effects. Linking the early-childhood memories to the phobias didn't stop the irrational fears, but it did give me new respect for Lynn. No therapist had even understood the voices, and Lynn was showing me how important they were. Their effect was more pervasive than occasional suicidal episodes. I recognized that they controlled my life even on good days. I was ready to exorcise these ghosts from my past, once and for all. It upset me that Lynn continued to tell the Jo part that she, Jo, would someday be less confused.

Lynn often pointed out to me the contradictory feelings expressed by the different personalities. I couldn't help noticing that Lynn was being inconsistent. How did she think that she was going to help me feel more comfortable—as she promised—and also help the Jo part feel more comfortable? Maybe it was just her inexperience in treating multiples.

When professionals say that they don't know what they're going to do, it usually means they are not going to do anything. Nancy often said, "You help the patients you can and don't worry about those you can't." But Lynn made a mistake in encouraging me to think that she really cared about me and about the other parts as well. She couldn't suddenly become formal and cold, or pretend I was cured. Lynn's only way out was by talking to someone who could say with certainty that I was not a multiple personality. If someone with authority told Lynn that she had been wrong, she could conveniently forget or reinterpret all she had seen. Then she could terminate treatment with a clear conscience.

9

I've now been treating Ms. Casey for three months and have told her that I would be professionally irresponsible if I didn't seek a consultation.

Jo, who seems to be what the clinical literature refers to as the "core" or "host" personality, exploits my admitted ignorance about treating multiples when I try to tell her she was abused.

Renee wavers but usually sides with her partner, Steve, in saying that the disorder doesn't exist. She agrees that she's not playing "a game" but doesn't like hearing her condition labeled MPD.

Joan Frances would betray her mother in accepting the diagnosis. That personality won't even listen to me talk about it.

Missy doesn't care what I call it as long as she feels safe and loved.

The Robin and Reagan personalities are probably the only ones who would have no trouble admitting the diagnosis, and I haven't seen them in weeks!

I have no doubt that the personalities are real; each behaves consistently, no matter how many days elapse between visits with them. I cannot question Jo's claims that she often experiences no intervening time between sessions with me. For example, she has "come to" in my office, picking up the conversation that she left last time without realizing that days have passed. More than once, I've listened to Jo resume, in mid-thought, a week-old conversation. I've become scrambled and given up, unable to find my own thread of memory to lead me back to the previous discussion. When Jo realizes that time has passed, she's humiliated by her faux pas but able and willing to provide enough details so that I too can pick up where that last conversation left off.

Whether or not expert consultation helps my patient, I could certainly use the reassurance. I am the first in the office to work with a multiple. I'm sure of the diagnosis but uncertain about how to treat it. Though Gordon is supportive, he knows no more than I about the disorder. The problem lies in finding someone to consult on the case.

The theoretical literature is not of much help. I've read the relatively few clinical articles on MPD, and I've been surprised to find that Sybil, the book by Flora Schreiber, seems continually to be my best source of information. I read Sybil when it was first published, but dismissed it as overdramatized and fictionalized. Now it has become my bible. Sybil's story mirrors much of the reality I am seeing, but there are some disturbing differences between Jo and Sybil. For instance, Sybil's Vicky personality was described as a memory trace who said that she knew "everything about everybody," whereas Renee (who seems to serve the same sort of "managerial" function within Jo's group as Vicky did in Sybil's) is honestly surprised by the tales the other personalities have told about their childhood.

. . .

"Lynn, look," I said, "My boyfriend said last night that if there were other personalities he'd know about them. Steve and I are practically living together, for heaven's sake!" Lynn and I were again arguing about the diagnosis.

"Renee, you've already told me that you hide your problems from Steve, just as you did with Keith," Lynn countered with some exasperation, shaking her head. She was clearly getting tired of these debates. Suddenly Lynn looked up at me, eyes sparkling with determination. "You know I can't find any other therapists around here who have treated multiples. I'm going to call Cornelia Wilbur about you."

"Sybil's doctor?" I asked with astonishment and dread. I knew how taken Lynn was with that book. She sometimes started discussions with me by telling me something that Sybil or one of her personalities had thought. When I tried to tell Lynn that she was probably mistaken and that I was NOT a multiple, she often said, "You know, Sybil felt the same way."

I was frightened by the thought of Lynn's consulting a nationally known expert because of me. Why would Dr. Wilbur talk to some social worker from Chicago? And if she did, what would happen when Dr. Wilbur laughed at Lynn's naïveté and her misdiagnosis? I really felt that

Lynn liked me. I didn't care if her liking me was based on her obsession with multiple personality, but I felt uncomfortable about the reaction she would have when she found out that I wasn't.

I tried not to worry about it, yet still to be prepared for my time with Lynn to end. I had received a scholarship to attend a two-week workshop designed to prepare teachers to help precollege students understand political systems. While I was in the Smoky Mountains, where the seminar would be held, Lynn would be taking a month's vacation. She hoped to consult with Dr. Wilbur at that time.

Lynn and I parted as friends. I hugged her and told her I'd see her in a month. But I knew that that was not likely. A month away from Lynn would be time enough for me to get over any need to see her. I felt even more certain that, after a consultation with this "multiple expert," Lynn would never want to see me again.

DIARY *July 13, 1981*

Now, after a two-hour consultation with Dr. Wilbur, I see what a mistake both Renee and I made in imagining Connie Wilbur "larger than life." When she answered her own office phone, I should have known that she was more like my colleagues than like a celebrity. But, despite her easy telephone manner and her complete lack of amazement that I might have found another "Sybil," I still felt nervous about seeing her. I wondered how my style of therapy might appear to someone who didn't know me and who didn't know my patient. I thought Dr. Wilbur might disregard what I had to say when she understood that, in a single session, I joined in with Renee's laughter, held the trembling Missy, and allowed Jo to maintain her intellectual distance.

In the two weeks before the appointment, I condensed our three-months' work into a twenty-five-page summary. Ultimately, I didn't send Dr. Wilbur the material (fearing that she'd meet me at the door with "I've read your material and you're wasting my time"), but just writing a letter helped me focus my own concerns about the consultation.

Dear Dr. Wilbur,
Somehow I feel I'm coming for this consultation too soon, with both too much material and too little. I want to be able to give you

a clear idea of the experience Jo (Joan, Frances, Renee, Missy, Robin, and Reagan) and I have had and of the unique and lovely person they are.

I feel protective of them, of myself, and of our relationship. As Jo, Renee, and Missy are fearful that you will change things in some way, so am I. Jo is afraid you will say she is a fraud. Renee is sure you'll say she is not a multiple and I've been "too nice" to them. Missy thinks you'll make me see that she is bad and make me stop liking her.

I'm afraid that you'll say that I don't know enough, that I'm overinvolved, that I will hurt rather than help, that I'm being too optimistic, and that I don't understand what I'm dealing with. At the same time, I tell myself that surely you will see that I am the one who has to do the treatment, that if I don't know enough I'll have to learn—and not turn her over to someone else. Surely you will say that treatment requires a high level of involvement, and that it is more important for Jo that I care deeply about her and delight in her and in her growth than it is that I know and understand everything.

I have tried to organize this case summary so that you can read as little or as much as you need or want for clarification. Of course, I have found every scrap and morsel to be of consuming interest. I realize this may not be true for you—at least I can admit that intellectually. Emotionally, I am bringing this to you because I think that you, of all people, are likely to be as delighted with and as sad for Jo as I am, and therefore may really want and be able to help me help her.

My anxiety was unfounded. Dr. Wilbur saw the consultation as a way of helping me understand how best to treat the disorder. She reassured me that my commitment to seeing Jo through the treatment was indeed the most important thing.

Dr. Wilbur made some predictions about the case based on her experience with Sybil and with other multiples. She said that treatment would be long and difficult for both Jo and me, probably lasting three to five years. She said that there was no doubt that many more personalities existed than those I had met. All of those that Renee said were "in the past" and "now dead" were still around, said Wilbur, just not yet ready to present them-

selves. She also said that Missy's refusal to grow up to be a woman suggested that this patient had been sexually abused. I'm not sure how much of this I'll share with Jo, or how quickly I will share it. But I promised Jo that I would call after I had talked to Dr. Wilbur.

.   .   .

While Lynn was consulting Dr. Wilbur, I was at the Smoky Mountains seminar, working at impressing the coordinators with my energy and talent. They had paid for me to be here, and I was determined that they get their money's worth.

I settled into quick friendships with the other participants. The isolated mountain setting, the intensity of our ten-hour-a-day work sessions and equally energized nightly gatherings encouraged easy camaraderie. I was an expert at quickly formed friendships, at my best in strange settings. I knew that my new friends would leave this retreat marveling at my empathy and willingness to join in (and often instigate) anything from midnight pot-smoking and kitchen raids to theoretical discussions. They wouldn't know me long enough to see the other parts' interference with my ability to be friendly and empathic.

I used my acceptance in the group to reassure myself that I didn't need Lynn. I had managed quite well before meeting her. The four months of treatment was the longest chunk of therapy I had ever allowed. I had learned a tremendous amount about myself. Even though I didn't have the complete control I would have liked, life was certainly better now. I was grateful for Lynn's help and also grateful that I didn't need her anymore. It didn't matter what horrible things Dr. Wilbur said about me. I was through with therapy.

The Missy part comforted herself that, even if she never saw Lynn again, she had all the memories of their time together.

Jo walked the mountain trails in the early mornings wondering how she'd ever again cope with the confusion alone.

Joan Frances was glad she could stop lying to her mother.

Lynn called me after her visit with Dr. Wilbur. Lynn's simple statement resonated through me to all of the personalities. The message was clear: "Diagnosis confirmed."

10

Today was the first appointment after vacation. I felt sure that the personalities would have many contradictory feelings concerning Dr. Wilbur's confirmation of the diagnosis. I knew they would all be anxious about the continuation of our work. As a result, I expected to see only the Renee personality. I thought that she would come in and check things out for the group by using this session to chat about our separate vacations, and actually looked forward to a fairly nonintense re-establishment of our relationship. I felt new confidence after my consultation, and I had really missed Jo and her various manifestations. Consequently, I was already at my door when she glided gracefully into the waiting room and smiled distantly at the receptionist.

I rushed to greet her and then slowed with uncertainty as I looked more closely at this svelte, remote woman. She looked different—tan and elegant in her tank top and wraparound skirt, her hair tucked into a knot at the nape of her neck. But I realized that the greatest difference was not in her appearance but in her expression. She seemed distant and ever so slightly amused. I omitted using a name as I gestured toward my office and said, "Won't you come in?" I pointed to a chair, closed the door, then turned to hear her say in a polished tone, "Hello. I know you are Lynn, but we haven't formally met. I am Isis."

I remembered that Renee had mentioned this Isis personality as one who kept a great deal of distance from any trauma.

I felt all the strange and conflicting sensations that I've come to associate with seeing how profoundly Jo could change. Facial expression, muscle tension, voice, and vocabulary all indicated that this was someone I hadn't met. Isis's mannerisms were so distinct from the other personalities that I knew I would recognize her instantly when I saw her again.

"Why don't you tell me something about yourself?" I offered, and restrained my impulse to take off my shoes and curl up in the chair, as I would have if Renee or Missy had been present. Such a casual approach would have been out of place.

"There really isn't much to tell. I'm only here talking with you today because the others were too frightened to come," she said. As I watched Isis clench her jaw and raise her chin before speaking, I was reminded of all the pseudo-sophisticated and very scared teenagers I had treated over the years. I leaned forward to hear more.

. . .

I watched with interest from my internal seat as Isis chose her words. I may have been the personality who did the best job of running things, but I honestly didn't know Isis well. In fact, I had told Lynn that this was one of the personalities who had disappeared long ago. An hour before the appointment, as I felt defeated by my inability to decide what to wear to the session, I realized that I was as frightened as Jo about seeing Lynn after our long absence. Isis spoke to me then, for the first time in many years. Softly and confidently, she said, "Renee, I will go. I would like to meet this woman face to face." She chose the clothes.

Now Isis spoke to Lynn, doling out her words as though each was precious and intended to be noticed. "I am committed to beauty, but beauty isn't always easy to find. Among this personality group, I seldom take center stage. More often I cast shadows of myself on the overt actions of the others. When there is something that interests me, I take control, but that is rare.

"The others are so frightened. Their fear detracts from the joy that I might feel at sharing in their life. But otherwise they are irrelevant. I'll always be, no matter what happens to them or to this body. I'm a roving spirit of the universe. I will continue long after the end of the others."

"Always young and beautiful," Lynn murmured.

"Or old and beautiful," Isis rejoined. "Age and physical being mean little to me."

I remembered from years past that Isis believed she transcended mere mortality and had fascinated a group of high-school friends with her stories of cosmic being. I wondered if Lynn would encourage a monologue on existence beyond life.

Lynn, however, seemed more confident and determined than I had seen her before. She was staying on track today. "If you were always there," Lynn said, "you must know many things about the other personalities. What can you tell me?"

Isis hesitated. "I've existed in a spiritual sense forever, but I didn't join this particular body until Jo was thirteen years old. I have always felt free to leave it when it wasn't to my liking."

"Isis, why did you join the body when you did?" Lynn prodded.

Isis paused and groped for memory; I could feel her momentary irritation with the question. "It was the summer," Isis said. "I found myself by a large glass door, looking out at beautiful flowers and feeling calmed by the splendor of the season. I was glad to find that my temporary physical home was long and lean. I taught the body to move gracefully and to dance."

Lynn nodded. "Renee says that she doesn't remember anything before the summer she turned fifteen. How interesting that you two came to be when Jo was an adolescent. Do you know what was happening right before you found yourself in the body?"

"Well done!" I silently complimented Lynn on her determination. I paid close attention, since I didn't know the answer, and I suspected that Isis had run out of easy answers as well. Her uncertainty was a rare, humiliating experience for her. Isis pounced on a thread of memory. Following it silently, she frowned. She did not like where this was going to lead.

"It was him, Rusty," Isis said flatly. "You haven't met the boy."

"The boy?" Lynn asked.

"Rusty," Isis said again.

"Missy said that 'Rusty' was her friend," Lynn responded, "but I didn't know he was one of the personalities."

"Doesn't it seem logical that Missy's friend would be another of the personalities?" Isis asked with a touch of ridicule.

"You won't have to worry about dealing with Rusty," she added reassuringly. "He's not about to come out here. His father taught him to hate women."

Without giving Lynn a chance to reply, Isis continued: "Rusty left and I came. It's as simple as that."

"What did Rusty have to do with your joining the body?" Lynn pressed.

Isis shuddered, then pulled away from the emotion attached to the memory blossoming in her mind. "It was the father. The father created Rusty and couldn't decide if he wanted the daughter or the son. He praised the son, but desired the daughter." She paused, her voice drifting.

"How did he desire her, sweetie?" Lynn coaxed softly.

Isis's voice drained of all emotion; her eyes and speech became flat. "He wanted her sexually. The father got an erection while holding Rusty. Rusty felt confused and scared. I was there." Her voice hardened. "I pushed the father away from me and never let him touch me again. I hate men!"

She returned to her remoteness. "Of course, this really isn't my concern. I only happened into this body at that time. I'll leave it for good soon."

"Poor little girl," Lynn said, and reached to pat Isis's hand as she might have Missy's. "How upset you must have been."

Isis smiled in surprise and deftly moved her hand out of Lynn's reach. "Upset?" she asked incredulously. "No, not at all. Violent emotions are majestic. There is beauty in hatred—vivid reds and purples. But since that time I have left the body whenever a man moves to touch it. I do my hating from a distance.

"There are far too many men around this body," Isis added parenthetically. "Renee likes that."

Lynn nodded. "Renee has told me about a period of promiscuity."

"I'm different," Isis said with quiet pride. "I love women. I enjoy the grace of female bodies, at rest and in motion. I've written about my lovers; I've sketched them; I've danced with them." Her sexual preference thus adamantly expressed, Isis seemed to fade.

"Isis," Lynn said quickly, "I think you are very important, and I hope you'll come out and talk with me often." But even as she completed her sentence, Isis was gone.

Muscles tensed and hands clenched as Jo regained awareness. Lynn recognized the change. "Hi, Jo," she said cheerfully as she watched the personality fight through amnestic fog. "I'm glad you're back."

Lynn recounted her visit to Dr. Wilbur, and Jo listened carefully for anything that might threaten her relationship with Lynn. Hearing nothing frightening, and sensing from Lynn's reaction to her that their relationship was still intact, Jo focused on her most important concern. "Did Dr. Wilbur say when I will be well?" Wellness to Jo meant no more amnesia. She had no awareness of Isis's thirty-minute conversation with Lynn.

How long would it be before her life was normal? Lynn said that Dr. Wilbur had no definite answer for that.

Jo told Lynn that during her walks in the mountains she had realized how large a piece of her past she was missing. She had begun to work at reconstructing all of her twenty-five years on those walks and found that there were holes in her memory as large as several months. Jo said she wouldn't be surprised to find that she had missed entire years. She now understood why she couldn't do even basic math computations—Jo couldn't remember a single math lesson after the fourth grade.

Now she tried again to get an answer from Lynn. "So, how do we do it?" she asked. "Did Dr. Wilbur tell you how to make me well?"

"No," Lynn replied, "Dr. Wilbur said we were doing everything right. We have to work our way through this together, a little at a time."

Jo felt deceived. She thought she was being the "good patient," and accepting the confirming second opinion without question. She expected honesty in return. But Lynn seemed to be holding out on her, manipulating her. She knew she needed Lynn and wouldn't get angry. Jo's parents had taught her long ago that it was not safe to get angry at someone she depended on.

11

By the middle of August, Lynn was seeing us every weekday afternoon. Our sessions settled into a pattern. I went in, chatted for a few minutes about what had happened during the day, and then sped inside so that Lynn could work with the personalities who really needed her help. I usually reappeared at the end of the session to take the body on its way.

I found that I didn't mind giving up time for the other personalities to spend in therapy. In fact, I had an easier job maintaining control throughout the day when the others had an opportunity to interact with Lynn. I thought I was performing an important service by structuring my schedule so that I could get them to Lynn every day, but she wouldn't let me stay uninvolved.

"Renee," she asked, "just how many of you are there inside?"

I really wasn't sure, and didn't like my uncertainty. I thought that the only way I could survive was if Lynn understood that I was the most important personality in the group. Otherwise she'd support Jo or the others to the extent that I'd lose control over my life.

However, as the months went by and I monitored what the others said during sessions, I was continually surprised at the new information I gained. I was honestly interested in what I was learning about the group, but concerned that Lynn would begin to discount me. So I spoke with more confidence than I felt.

"I know there used to be a lot more personalities," I said, "but they served their purpose and then disappeared, like Robin and Reagan. A lot of them are just leftovers from the past. I'm sure they're gone for good now. You've already met the five who are around now—Jo, Missy, Joan Frances, Isis, and me. I think that's probably it."

Lynn wasn't satisfied. She wanted to know the names and functions of all the personalities who used to come out. As I tried to answer her questions, listened carefully to the bits of information that the other personalities could supply, and became more willing to share with her the gaps in my knowledge, I realized that the group of personalities was not as chaotic as I had first thought. The group seemed to have a structure all its own. I saw that there were different kinds of personalities in the group, and that each personality had its own sense of self.

Joan Frances, Isis, Jo, and Missy all thought they had as much potential as I had for living life as independent beings. They were foiled in their separate existences, as was I, by the interference of the others. Yet it became easier for me to see how each personality would live her life if she were alone in the body.

The Joan Frances personality would be neurotic, clinging to her need for Mother's approval, but that need for approval would spur her on to success. Joan Frances would be as productive and unhappy as any other person who has an overwhelming drive to succeed but finds no joy in her success.

Isis would be a dancer. Although dance instruction hadn't begun until Isis's creation at age thirteen, she had been teaching at the dance school and performing in community shows within a year after starting ballet lessons. Without the rest of the personalities to get in her way, she would be accomplished and bohemian, unapproachable, but respected by her peers.

If Jo were alone in the body, she'd be a recluse. Content with her books, her ideas, and her daydreams, uncomfortable in social situations, she'd live a quiet but productive life in some academic greenhouse. She'd be one of the many intellectuals who are inept with people despite their brilliance as scholars.

Even Missy, if she decided to grow up, could function autonomously. She had a range of moods and expressions that made her a full person in her own right.

If I were alone in the body, I'd have lots of friends and be satisfied with my life as long as I felt people needed me. If I were alone in the body, I'd be happy.

I entered therapy with Lynn because I wanted total control over my being. Now, almost six months into treatment, I felt less sure about being able to achieve this goal. The other personalities were getting stronger; I was seeing more of my own weaknesses. And I was becoming unsure that they would ever disappear entirely from my life. But I continued to cooperate with Lynn. I wanted her to like me. And although doing the things Lynn asked made me uncomfortable about my own future, I squelched my fears, as I had done in other relationships.

Lynn wanted to know increasingly more about childhood, but the information any personality could provide was sketchy.

Missy told her story from a perpetual five-year-old's point of view.

Jo had more experience of blank periods than of memories.

Joan Frances admitted no blankness, no multiplicity, but provided only vague statements about the ideal childhood her mother claimed she had had.

Robin and Reagan had disappeared months ago, after telling Lynn kindly but firmly that they had no further information to give her.

Isis simply didn't care.

And I couldn't remember anything before I turned fifteen. Lynn and I both suspected that my lack of childhood memories had more to do with my belated birth as a personality than with the aftereffects of drug use.

But I had an idea. "Lynn, do you think the group's medical history would help?" Medical records could fix with certainty what schools were attended and where the family had lived at various periods of childhood. The records of emergency-room treatments and hospital admissions might even corroborate the stories of abuse.

There was one obstacle to getting the records. Nancy worked in the small group practice where Jo had received most of her medical treatment. I could not request the records without Nancy's knowledge. So I decided to enlist her help.

I called Nancy that evening and told her that my internist in Chicago had asked me to have my medical records sent. Nancy said she didn't see why that was necessary. Having guessed that this might be her reaction, I told her the signed release was already in the mail. Nancy promised then to take care of it.

A month later, when the records had not arrived, I called Nancy to inquire about them. "Oh, your doctor didn't get them?" she asked, sounding surprised. "They must have gotten lost in the mail."

I suggested that she send copies. "We didn't make any copies."

Frustration flared in the sharpness of my voice. "Don't you usually make copies of records you send from your office?" Well, yes, they usually did, but Nancy had told the office staff not to bother this time.

Lost or destroyed, the records were gone. The sudden lack of history frightened me and the other personalities as well. Even the maternally dependent Joan Frances had a difficult time accepting what she called her mother's negligence. The rest of us suspected that Nancy had destroyed the records. Lynn seemed to have no doubt about what had happened. She had never questioned the stories of abuse, and she said that this incident suggested that Nancy herself was afraid that something from the past might come out.

Now my own lack of memory bothered me as it never had before. I accepted that the other personalities had lived fifteen years without my involvement, but I didn't trust their memories. I wanted to verify the truthfulness of their accounts. Had Nancy and Ray really been abusive, as the other personalities said, or had innocent parental actions been misinterpreted through the eyes of a child? Something in the records might have helped me answer this.

The Jo personality was also troubled by the records' disappearance. She refused to believe that her father had hurt her; she refused to believe that her father would have allowed her mother to hurt her. She had no choice but to think that Missy and the other personalities were lying about the childhood abuse. Jo had counted on the medical records to back up her contention that nothing bad had happened to her.

Lynn seemed convinced that Jo had been abused, and now Jo had no way of proving otherwise. More than ever, Jo just wanted those other personalities to go away and leave her alone.

DIARY *August 16, 1981*

I have been attempting to increase communication among the personalities. I am concerned that they now seem to be growing further apart rather than closer together and I fear that my efforts have only increased resistance. In addition, I am unable to find the "memory-trace" or "internal-self-helper" personality that Dr. Wilbur said would be there. Renee seems threatened by the holes in her knowledge and worries that I will think less of her and her importance to the group if I know how large these gaps sometimes are. Jo apparently feels completely helpless to deal with any of it.

It seems clear to me that, since my consultation with Dr. Wilbur, my patient interprets any change or new direction in treatment as a threat.

Somehow, mistakes I might make based on my own ineptness are less frightening for her than mistakes I might make based on the advice of an expert! There seem to be a number of factors contributing to her fear.

Jo is isolated because of the rarity of her disorder. Not many people know anything about multiple personality. She cannot discuss her problems or treatment with colleagues or friends without encountering disbelief or lack of comprehension. This leaves her extremely and painfully dependent on me and on my view of her. Being forced to take so much on faith puts her in a vulnerable position, without any kind of a support group.

The fact that Jo's mother is a medical professional makes trust, always an issue in treatment, inordinately difficult. The consultation with Dr. Wilbur only added to the difficulty, because any communication between Jo's mother and the doctors Jo saw during her childhood meant big trouble. No confidence the little girl offered was respected.

Jo is also aware that I have never treated a multiple and is continually dealing with her fears that, on the one hand, I don't know what I'm doing and that, on the other, I've been handed a master treatment plan by Dr. Wilbur, with which I will manipulate her.

I think I need to retreat to a less confrontational stance and concentrate on building trust between me and the various personalities.

. . .

12

August 28, 1981

I am gaining more and more confidence in my own instincts for treating Jo and the other personalities. With her, as with my other patients, I find that my therapeutic approach works only when I really believe in what I am doing.

I am honestly fond of all of the personalities I have met, and I respond to each of them sincerely. I treat them as individuals. I am well aware that each personality is struggling in her own attempt to trust me.

Little Missy cuddles with me and sometimes whispers, "You love your new friend" (she still refuses to use the first person in referring to self), but she is occasionally afraid that I tell her mommy her secrets.

I've developed a friendly "acquaintanceship" with Renee. She protects herself against deeper involvement with me by focusing on the therapeutic nature of our relationship. Renee said to me, "When you think you've done your job, you'll just go on your way and never think of me again. But that's OK. It's supposed to be like that."

Joan Frances is so helplessly trapped in her desire to please Mother that she still refuses to consider the possibility that she may be multiple.

I'm more frustrated with the Jo personality. Jo, even with her ever-growing dependency on me, is always holding back, afraid to admit that she cares for me at all.

As usual, I've taken my problem to my best colleague. For the past few weeks, Gordon has listened patiently as I've searched for a way to let the personalities know that my feelings for them are genuine.

Last weekend, Gordon and I were at our cottage and I was talking about the personalities. "They'd love it up here. It's so beautiful," I said. Then, on impulse, I cut drying flowers and weeds and arranged a bouquet in an old beer bottle.

I presented my gift to Missy during our next therapy session. I said that when she gets scared at night she can look at the flowers and think of me. Once Missy was sure that I still wanted her to come back and see me in my office, she was happy with her gift. Jo and Renee were both amazed that I would do something like that for them. The next day, I even received a carefully worded thank-you note from Joan Frances.

Five months into treatment and I feel as though I am still at the first stages of developing trust. Yet both life and therapy go on for the personalities. Last week, Renee's dream came true: after a year of waiting for an opening at a suburban school district, she started her job as a high-school social-studies teacher. Both Renee and I think that her self-esteem will only improve with her change in jobs. I am sure that she is a great teacher. And yet I know she is quite ill.

I think I have never had a patient who was, at once, so functional and so needy. On the same day that Missy is huddled in a fetal position in my office and sobbing, Renee has taught a full day of high school and Jo has attended a class toward her master's degree in political science.

After a session, one of them will cook dinner and respond appropriately to the boyfriend, Steve. I am determined both to preserve her ability to keep going with life and to keep her focused on treatment. And I worry about when these two therapeutic goals will come into conflict. Renee is able to form excellent and helpful, though limited, relationships with the high-school students she teaches. But, aside from Steve, she is not able to maintain a close relationship with any adult. And even the relationship with Steve seems based on his ability to deny the reality of the disorder.

The other personalities appear less concerned about interpersonal relationships. For example, Jo's studies allow her to use her obviously superior intellect, and she doesn't care that she has no friends among her graduate-student peers.

Since as a whole she is clearly able to give to others and is just as clearly uncomfortable about understanding that other people would like to give to her, I will continue to find nonthreatening ways to do just that. Jo has a birthday in a few days, and I will bring in a homemade cake to celebrate.

. . .

September 1, 1981, Jo's twenty-sixth birthday, was another good day for me at school. I still could hardly believe that I had landed a high-school teaching job in the best school district in the Chicago area. Ever since my internship with the legislature, assigned to a child-advocacy task force, I had known I wanted to work for and with children. Their rights were so often ignored that I felt they needed me fighting in their behalf. I had completed my teaching certification through night and summer classes the year before I met Lynn but had no real hope that a job would come through.

So I was surprised this summer to find that I had my choice of jobs in a market glutted with social-science teachers. I interviewed well and, lacking teaching experience, I was cheap.

Being the "people-pleasing" personality meant that I was the one in the group who handled job interviews. The other personalities seemed content to have me handle the job as well. That suited me. I liked teaching, and liked feeling that I had found my niche. The Jo personality attended late-afternoon classes at the University of Chicago, working on her master's, and she also reserved some time during the week to read and study for class. Any personality who wanted to was welcome to spend time with Lynn during the daily sessions, but the teaching and preparation time were mine alone. Life was hectic, but I was happier than I had ever been.

I loved my students, genuinely and openly. "In my class," I said, "you'll learn to think like citizens." And they did. I was particularly proud of the strides I had made with my class of "underachievers."

During the first week of school, I had worked to convince these cynical kids in my "slow" class that the school system was wrong in calling them slow. The only problem they had was that they had begun to believe they were failures. I tried to get them to see what happened when society made certain groups of people (children, Blacks, and women) think they had nothing to offer within the political system. I told them that they had important things to do and say. I believed in them and I respected them. Soon, I promised, they'd begin to believe in themselves.

"Eight a.m. is no time to get excited about the Civil War," I thought one morning. I taught best by getting the kids fired up about some topic and then stepping back to facilitate a robust group discussion. But, despite my distribution of orange juice at the beginning of the hour, and my purposefully provocative statements about slavery and utilitarian ideals, twenty-two bored students sullenly observed my attempts at discussion.

I walked away from the circle of students, thought for a minute, and then closed the classroom door. I returned to perch on the edge of my desk. "OK, troops," I said, "true-confessions time." Some of the students looked interested; perhaps they were relieved that I had given up talking about some old war.

"Do you folks remember that the other day I said our class had to become a community?" I began. "Classroom-as-community means that, once we begin to trust one another, we can take risks and say things that we might not say in other situations. I am about to take that kind of risk with you now."

I saw I had their attention, and continued. "I have a guess as to why our discussions are less than stimulating, and I want to check out my hunch with you. Could I please see the hands of people who have smoked dope since ten p.m. last night?"

As I expected, no one moved, but I watched their expressions with amusement. Some of the students scowled, wondering if I was going to have them busted, and some grinned, guessing that I had had some drug experience myself.

I smiled in what I hoped was a noncommittal way. "OK," I said, "you don't have to answer yet. Let me tell you what I've been thinking. I think that a lot of you walk in here after getting high. My guess is partly based on the joints that I see passed outside my classroom window. But I am also basing my hunch on how badly our discussions are going. We all know that pot inhibits the ability to make logical connections, but I'm wondering if you know that this effect—the effect of THC—lasts for a full eight hours after smoking. Now, I'm not going to turn anyone in. I'm just testing out a theory—and that's what learning's all about, by the way. So, how many of you got high this morning?"

One hand raised; a finger waved from the next desk; one guy grinned and nudged his neighbor, who nodded his answer to me; and so on around the room, until ten kids grinned sheepishly at me.

"And how about last night?" had most of their classmates joining in the nods and hand gestures. I nodded back in mock dismay, enjoying their conspiratorial confessions and their trust in me.

"Well, here's the point," I continued in a more serious tone. "If you come here under the effects of THC, we cannot share and grow and talk in a way that can make this experience learning and fun. I'll end up spending the semester talking *at* you, and we'll all be frustrated and bored.

"Now, I'm not going to tell you that marijuana will make your eyes fall out, but I will ask you not to smoke dope for eight hours prior to coming to my class. So, your homework assignment is to stay straight tonight and tomorrow morning. What you do after class tomorrow is your own business. By the way, I'll be checking to see that you did your homework."

The bell rang on cue and the students drifted out, laughing at my bizarre homework assignment and whispering among themselves about this unteacherly conduct. I knew they weren't sure what to make of me, but I also knew that I'd have a brighter, more alert group in the morning. I waited until the last student left before depositing in the trash can a joint that someone had left on the corner of my desk. No one would know what had become of the gift, and I didn't have to know the identity of the giver to perceive the thought behind it. Someone had acknowledged what I gave to the class—my trust, my understanding, my respect—and I accepted the gift as a token of appreciation and connection, although I was pretty sure my supervisor wouldn't have interpreted it in the same way.

I couldn't wait to tell Lynn this latest victory. Being with kids made me feel so good about myself, and sharing my school day with her had become an important part of the experience. She appreciated my motivations, applauded my attempts, and suggested alternatives to problems that had me stumped. But, most important, I knew that Lynn agreed with me that even the most damaged and disenchanted teenager was only waiting for someone to see the real person beneath the defense and respond with genuine caring. Lynn supported my feeling that I was a natural teacher, eager for the opportunity to show what I could do.

I strolled happily into the mental-health clinic that afternoon, not worrying about the session that was to come. After I talked with Lynn about my teaching, the treatment hour was not my concern. I was celebrating the day and thinking about the restaurant where Steve and I would have a birthday dinner. I swapped favorite restaurants with the receptionist while I waited for Lynn to finish with her earlier patient.

"Happy birthday!" Lynn said and greeted me with a hug. I hugged her back and thanked her, but reminded her that it really wasn't *my* birthday. Jo was twenty-six today. I was quite happy to remain nineteen or twenty, thank you. That's the nice thing about having a lot of personalities, I mused: no one inside seems to care much about age. Missy was five no matter how old the body got, and I was always right around twenty.

When I walked into Lynn's office, my smile faltered and finally slipped. A birthday cake sat on the little table next to the patient's chair. I knew that Lynn had thought this would be a nice gesture, like the bouquet of dried flowers she had given to Missy. I hated to hurt her feelings, but I knew that Jo wasn't going to handle this well.

"Lynn," I said, "I don't mean to sound ungrateful. I think it was really sweet of you to bake the cake. But Jo hates birthdays. I've been celebrating them for her for years."

With that, I slipped inside so that Jo could come out and receive her present. Within a few seconds, Jo came out, registered where she was, saw the cake, realized that Lynn had baked it for her, blushed deeply, and raced deep inside our collective mind. I came back, shrugged "told you" to Lynn, and accepted her offer of birthday cake and tea.

Not surprisingly, Lynn's choice of conversation was Jo's problem with birthdays. "Well, you know Jo hates being the center of attention," I began, "so I'm sure that that's part of it. But there's something more. Jo felt that the only reason her parents loved her or ever gave her anything was out of a sense of duty. They were stuck with her and had no choice. When other people are nice to her, Jo feels guilty, sure that she must have manipulated them into responding to her. She's sure no person would come to love her or want to give her something out of genuine affection."

Lynn became thoughtful. "The dried flowers recognized no special day, only a special feeling that Jo could not have manipulated into being," she proposed, "but birthdays are different. Birthdays are something that Jo thinks people HAVE to respond to."

"Bingo," I said.

Lynn sighed and smiled wearily. "Oh, Renee, how am I ever going to break through all of Jo's defenses?"

"Well, you don't have to worry about that now," I reassured her. "Jo won't be back this afternoon. Let me tell you what happened today at school!"

Jo didn't reappear during the hour, but Missy popped out, as she often did, for a few minutes with her friend. Missy spied the cake and fled from the chair to a corner in Lynn's office as soon as she realized it was her birthday. Refusing to talk, she huddled in the corner to suck her thumb and rock, eyes closed, somewhere far beyond Lynn's touch.

All of us felt uneasy about birthdays. If it weren't for the social expectations, I would have given up the birthday altogether, but I knew that that reaction would have been harder to explain than my pretending for the people around me that the day had some special meaning.

When Jo returned—at the next appointment, with all traces of the birthday fiasco gone—it was clear that Lynn considered Jo's inward flight more than just a social faux pas.

"Jo, we've got to talk about this," Lynn said firmly, and Jo realized that she was probably right. "Let's talk about some of the birthdays you remember."

Jo took a deep breath and thought back. Talking about birthdays past would probably be easier than finding out how she had manipulated Lynn into doing something nice for her.

"When I was a child," Jo said, "I did have one positive feeling about birthdays. Each birthday meant I was getting closer to being an adult. I really was a terrible flop at being a child. I was never the kind of child people expected me to be. I was too sensitive, too smart, too something. I never lost hope that I'd do better at being a grown-up."

"Do you remember any specific birthdays?" Lynn prodded. Jo said yes and then was silent. "Jo?" Lynn said gently, but with a touch of warning in her voice.

Often when her memories were too painful for her to want to discuss, Jo slipped away and another personality came out. "It's still me," Jo said, "I'm just afraid that if I tell you the truth, you'll laugh at me."

"Why should I laugh?" Lynn asked.

"Sometimes," Jo faltered. She bit her lip and tried again. "Sometimes I remember things *too* well. I can't help it. Maybe it's because I've lost so much time in my life, but I have some very early memories. I really do."

"I won't laugh," Lynn promised again. "When is the first birthday you remember?"

Lynn didn't look surprised when Jo confessed, "My first."

Jo remembered the scratchy dress and high white shoes her mother dressed her in for her first birthday party. She remembered the feeling of all those people—aunts, uncles, cousins, family friends—staring at her. "My mother—her hair was long and brown then—held a cake with one candle. Her mouth smiled for all the people, but her eyes warned me to behave. I screamed and cried and twisted in my high chair, wanting only to get away, to hide myself."

"Hide yourself from what, sweetie?" Lynn asked.

"The people, all the people," Jo murmured, lost in memory. Then she looked up, at Lynn. "You see, I've never been able to filter out the images and emotions that come from being in a crowd of people. The more people, the more constant the outpouring of vibration and energy of thoughts and feelings from them. That first birthday, I wanted only to get away from the people. Since my mother couldn't tolerate my crankiness, I soon got my wish."

"Go on," coached Lynn.

"I remember my second birthday too—not the celebration, just the accident. You might have noticed my scar." Jo touched her left eyebrow, which was split by a small piece of scar tissue. "I got that the day I was two. It was all because of those horrid little plastic-covered bells that people put on babies' shoes. I didn't have a name for them, of course, but I hated the noise the bells made whenever I moved my feet.

"My mother put those bells on my feet and then moved away from me. She crouched down by a chair and called me over. I moved my feet, and the bells made noise. I stamped my feet as an experiment, trying to make the jingling stop. I remember that my mother and sister thought my attempts were all pretty funny. But I was so busy concentrating on preventing the noise and walking at the same time that I lost my balance and hit the sharp wooden leg of a chair. I spent my second birthday having my forehead sutured.

"I don't remember my third birthday," Jo said with a rare grin. "I don't have perfect memory, you know," she added, teasing. Lynn smiled back. "But I do remember my fourth."

Lynn chuckled at Jo's playful manner and replied grandly, "Well, please go on."

"My parents took my sister and me to a restaurant for my fourth birthday. They said that I could have anything I wanted since it was my birthday. I wanted a hot dog. But for some reason that was impossible in this restaurant. I felt betrayed, and must have made quite a scene.

"On the way home, I sat in a corner of the back seat, listening to my mother tell me that I was a selfish, greedy little girl and that I had ruined the evening for everyone. I wasn't troubled by my mother's scolding. I wanted to figure out what had gone wrong.

"I thought carefully about the events of the evening and decided that there must be limitations on desires. It wasn't true that I could have anything I wanted. Not all restaurants served hot dogs. I felt good about understanding that, but I still didn't know how people figured out what it was safe to want. I did know, from my mother's scolding, that 'wanting' was a problem. If the desire could not be filled, then I was greedy and selfish. Since I couldn't figure out how to judge the possibility of fulfilling a desire, I decided on my fourth birthday that it was safer not to want anything at all."

Jo paused. "You know, I really wish I had been better then at making sense of things. I mean, I had been reading for almost a year by my fourth birthday. If I had thought it all through a little more carefully, I would have figured out that the restaurant menus tell people what is possible to want and what is not."

"My sixth birthday also stands out for me, because it was then that I figured out why my mother always opened gifts on my birthday. Her birthday was the same day as mine.

"About a week before my sixth birthday, my father showed me the gift I was to give to my mother. This was new, and I felt very grown up. I watched him wrap the gift and didn't think about it again until the night when my mother and I opened our presents.

"My father handed her the package and said, 'This is from Jo.' I smiled proudly, feeling very wise. My knowing what was in that box made the gift *really* from me.

"My mother fingered the package and then began to unwrap it. She said, 'I bet I know what this is. I bet it's a record album to go with my hi-fi.' I nodded and smiled with pleasure that she had guessed *my* gift.

"My sister, who was fourteen at the time, was horrified by what I had done. 'You told! You're not supposed to tell, you little brat!' Carol yelled, and ran from the room.

" 'Now look what you've done,' my mother said, and went after my sister to comfort her. The special record lay forgotten on the floor, and I looked at my father with tears in my eyes. 'You ruined her surprise.' He sighed and gave me a hug. He didn't know how to please her either," Jo added as an aside.

"My seventh birthday was very special," she said, "and I'm just now beginning to understand how special it was. Although I didn't interpret it correctly then, it was around that birthday that I knew that time was different for me."

"Time?" Lynn shook her head in confusion. "What do you mean, time was different?"

"I had wanted a watch ever since I was five years old, but for two years my father said I was too young. Watches were not toys." Jo looked up, and her face showed little-girl disgust. "I knew watches weren't toys, and

I thought my father was putting me down when he implied I didn't know that. I knew watches, clocks were powerful and important. That's why I wanted one.

"My father was right in saying when I was five that I 'couldn't even tell time yet.' So I learned. And once I had learned, clocks began to tell me how many blank hours had passed. They counted off the agonizingly slow minutes until my father came home from work. Finally, two years later, on my seventh birthday, my father gave me a watch.

"I remember being astonished, overwhelmed by the power I had been handed. I know that sounds silly, but I completely misinterpreted the concept of time. When I was seven, I reasoned that if I owned a watch I could make the time move slowly or quickly at my command."

Lynn shook her head again. "Wait, Jo, I'm not following."

"OK," Jo said slowly, "let's try an analogy." She wanted to go slowly enough to make Lynn understand, but was trembling with excitement as she sorted out this childhood experience.

"Let's say you worked on an assembly line. The movement of the line would control how quickly you would have to move to do your job. Now, if you suddenly had the switch at hand to slow down or speed it up, the line would be in your control, right?" Lynn nodded. "Well, that's how I felt about time!" Jo said. "I thought that if I owned a watch I could control the speed at which time passed. If I wanted to slow time down, I could set my watch back. If I wanted time to move quicker, I'd set it forward."

Lynn was silent, so Jo returned to her memory. "I exercised my new power cautiously. When I couldn't wait for my father to get home, I set the watch a little forward—no more than fifteen minutes. When I wanted more time for reading before bed, I gave myself no more than thirty extra minutes. My parents' annoyance that I wasn't yet asleep didn't bother me. When they asked, I looked at my watch and dutifully read off the time."

Jo grinned. "It took my father weeks to realize that the watch wasn't slowing down or speeding up of its own accord. He was furious and took the watch away from me, angry that I had treated my watch as 'a toy.' I kept trying to explain how subtly and carefully I controlled time— I never moved it impulsively—and he grew more and more bewildered, until I finally stopped, a new recognition blossoming in my mind. I felt stupid and humiliated by my ignorance."

Lynn waited, looking puzzled. "I know differently now, of course," Jo said, "but in that agonizing talk with my father I realized that I was wrong in thinking that people controlled time. People didn't control time by owning a watch any more than they controlled the seasonal cycle of leaves by owning a tree. I knew suddenly that I had had the metaphor all wrong.

"So I started thinking that time controlled people. Time seemed to me to be like an untamed horse—galloping crazily ahead when it desired, or grazing quietly at will. Sometimes it moved fast and sometimes very slow. When I had wanted a watch so desperately, I had thought that timepieces were like bridles, controlling time's passage. Then I thought I understood that clocks were only flecks on time's back, recording its erratic movements."

Jo looked at Lynn. She was surprised at how sensible all of this seemed and felt a little triumphant that her understanding of its significance preceded that of her therapist. "I guess I knew even then that I still hadn't quite gotten the concept right," Jo said, "and maybe I'm still confused about its seemingly relative nature. I mean, if you think about it, time really is longer for a child than it is for an adult."

"Slow down, Jo, I'm not following," Lynn said again.

"A day is a much larger percentage of a child's life than it is of an adult's life, right?" said Jo. Lynn nodded. "The only sense we have of time is in relation to the amount of time we've experienced, so it's always relative to the individual," Jo finished. She chuckled both at her own understanding and at Lynn's confusion. "I think I'll take a course in the philosophy of physics and see if I can do a better job of clarifying the concept of time."

"Let me know if you do," Lynn responded. "I never thought of time as so complex before."

"There's more," Jo said excitedly, then looked to Lynn in an aside. "I only remember one more childhood birthday, but I think it provides some evidence that I was losing time even when I was young."

"Tell me about it," Lynn said, listening with new interest.

"On my tenth birthday, I suddenly 'woke up' in my family room. There were lots of girls there, girls that I recognized from my class at school, girls who hated me. They teased me, threatened me, and even blackmailed me—in exchange for my lunch money, they wouldn't tell the teacher that I had been talking when she was out of the room. They terrorized me so much that I paid up even when I had done nothing wrong.

"These were the girls who threw the ball especially hard to hurt me when I dared to play with them at recess. These were the girls who taunted me when I didn't. Even Courtney Myers, the ringleader of the gang, was there, controlling the other girls with a twitch of her innocent-looking smile or with a swish of her long blond braids."

Jo was lost in her memory of pain and surprise. "When I finally decided I wasn't imagining the scene, I walked upstairs and found my mother in the kitchen. 'What are those girls doing here?' I asked her.

" 'You know perfectly well that they are here for your birthday,' she answered. Then I understood. They were with me to make a bad experience worse."

Jo brightened. "But there was some comfort associated with that particular birthday. Later, when I was alone, I realized that I was a full decade old. A decade sounded like a significant span of time. It meant to me that half of my waiting period was over. When I got through another decade, I'd no longer be a child. I wanted so badly to be an adult, so that I'd understand everything and be able to get away from all of the people.

"I guess that birthdays always have been horrible times of tension for me. A lot of that tension revolved around my mother. I ached for my father as he tried year after year to find a way to please her on her birthday. He wanted so badly to please her. The year he bought her a fur coat, both he and I were sure he had it right this time. But my mother burst into tears when she unwrapped the gift: she didn't want mink.

"No wonder you don't like birthdays," Lynn began, but Jo cut her off.

"I mostly hate birthdays because I know I was supposed to be my mother's birthday gift. That's what my mother said. Carol was born December 22, her Christmas present, and I was her birthday gift. I think I always felt that I was the worst birthday gift my mother had ever received. Getting me for her birthday was far worse than getting the wrong fur. The coat was returned, but I couldn't be."

Jo looked at Lynn, face drawn and bitter. "My mother was never particularly good at handling disappointment."

Jo stopped speaking and finally, for the first time, cried in front of Lynn. She cried with guilt and resentment that she had never been able to celebrate her own birth. Jo sobbed at the injustice of it all, and let Lynn comfort her.

When I resumed control to take the body home, I noticed that Lynn looked a little drained by the ordeal. "Well, Renee," she said, "the birthday cake didn't work, but focusing Jo's attention on birthdays sure did."

I couldn't help agreeing.

A few months later, Missy, Isis, and I held a rare internal discussion about what to get Lynn for Christmas. Jo didn't have internal awareness of us, Joan Frances turned her back on us, but Missy, Isis, and I could talk together if we chose. Christmas-gift giving and receiving were almost as frightening for Jo and the others as birthdays.

The Jo personality was consumed with finding Lynn the perfect gift, even if she couldn't discuss it with us. Joan Frances wouldn't consider it. Missy, Isis, and I decided we would follow Jo's lead and then add some touches of our own.

"Something living and growing," Jo thought.

"She has an officeful of plants," I grumbled, but didn't interfere as Jo walked through a nursery and picked out a small Norfolk pine.

"You can make things to put on it, decorate it like a real Christmas tree," Missy said excitedly.

"The decorations must be significant," Isis added.

Over the next week, Missy worked carefully with an art knife held in her left hand, sculpting intricate paper snowflakes. Isis helped with the design, so that each tiny flake was unique but as exquisite as the last. I tied the paper snowflakes to the branches with slivers of red ribbon, and Jo sat back, embarrassed but pleased with the improvements her "unseen elves" had made to her gift for Lynn.

Lynn openly admired the tree's beauty and the deep meaning of the gift. "I want to give you all a big hug," she said, but as she reached, she saw the body flinch. She moved back. "I also don't want to scare anyone."

She gazed thoughtfully at the tree. "Renee," Lynn said slowly, "there are an awful lot of snowflakes on that tree."

I shrugged. Isis had decided on the number. (I was the one who gave Lynn the tree, because none of the others dared to be out for the presentation.) Lynn was right. I counted twenty-four snowflakes on the tree. Isis's message was clear. There were more personalities, each unique and important to the design of the whole.

BOOK II

13

At every session since the holidays, I have been meeting and hearing about more personalities. The new level of trust has allowed out personalities who have mostly remained dormant during the adult years. Renee now seems more intrigued than frightened by the appearance of personalities she didn't know existed. She's thinking about them actively, using her talents to make sense out of a system that was first denied, and then seemed terrifying and chaotic to her.

The first group are what Renee calls the autonomous personalities—Jo, Missy, Joan Frances, Isis, and Renee—who are truly well defined and complete enough as individuals to be able to function autonomously, without the assistance of the others. Each appears to have as full a range of dispositions and capabilities as any individual person. They seem to me also to be competitive with one another. Each is worried that they (or I!) will make a final determination of which one of them gets "total control of the body."

Then there are the special-purpose or "single-motive" personalities, who have clearly defined tasks—such as organizing files, cooking, or cleaning house—and seem to have no interest in holding the outside consciousness after they have completed their tasks. Nor do they seem to have the capacity that the autonomous personalities have for individual growth and change.

The third group Renee describes as "past-keepers," personalities who hold some experience or knowledge from the past. They fit into the system, she says, by hiding memories that might prevent the autonomous personalities from functioning.

The Robin and Reagan pair of personalities, who filled me in on some *family background and early-infancy events, were only a precursor of the many past-keepers I have met in the last few weeks. Robin and Reagan are unique in that they date their creation not to a single traumatic event but to the need of the group to maintain a nonconflicted, nonabreactive memory trace.*

The other past-keepers are both reactive and information-providing personalities—they appear in my office to give me information the system seems to think I need, or in response to my touching a critical nerve in the Jo, Missy, Joan Frances, or Renee personalities. Renee tells me that they sometimes come out outside my office, when something triggers an abusive memory.

The past-keepers often seem "frozen in time." When a past-keeper surfaces, it usually relives or abreacts a situation before my eyes. I don't have to worry that the actual situation being relived isn't as clear to me as the emotions involved. Renee is able to watch the personality's memory-come-alive from a safe distance. "It's as though I'm sitting in the audience, caught up in a well-made film," she says.

Renee invariably pops out after one of these emotionally draining scenes and describes in detail for me what the past-keeping personality was experiencing. Interestingly, Renee is now spontaneously offering some analysis from her protected "outsider's" position. I am encouraged to hear Renee cluck sympathetically, "That poor kid," or "No wonder she felt so bad."

Some personalities are difficult to classify. Little Joe, for instance. Renee says he's a past-keeper, but he doesn't seem interested in sharing what he's kept. He appeared for the first time just last week.

Missy had come out and instead of engaging me in conversation announced that "you wanted to be in your corner." I reminded her that it was safe outside, too, but let her retreat to what she called her "inside place."

I stroked her back as she huddled deep within herself. After a few minutes, I noticed that she was staring intently at my hair.

"What is it, sweetie," I asked.

"Hair," said a voice that wasn't Missy's. It was Little Joe, a two-year-old personality, and his fingers played in my waist-length hair just as my own babies had many years ago.

My skin prickled as I realized how complete my experience was of being touched by a toddler.

Little Joe told me nothing, nor did he demand much in return. In response to his plaintive "Twuck?" I brought in a red-and-yellow toy dump truck that sat on a low shelf awaiting his visits.

Little Joe rolls the truck back and forth across the rug with plump, uncoordinated hands or touches my hair and stares at my face. Renee says that Little Joe thinks I'm his mommy, who, twenty-five years ago, also had long dark hair. I'm happy to give this baby boy the nurturing he needs.

. . .

The Jo personality had no early-childhood memories of her mother, although she could recall happy hours spent with her father when she was very young. Ray's companionship and affection had been freely given and gratefully accepted.

The little girl's dependency on her father made Ray's abuse more insidious. From the time she was three, Daddy took her along when he ran errands. Once they drove away from the house, Daddy picked her up and placed her on his lap so that she could hold the steering wheel and "drive the car." Daddy's hardness under her buttocks and the hard steering wheel in her hands were equally part of the experience.

Still, Ray provided security and certainty. The personalities knew where Daddy stood on most issues and could usually predict his reactions. Mother's expectations were never so clearly stated or understood. More than one personality was created in the hope of being the daughter Nancy could consistently love. More than one new personality was created in response to Mother's unexpected fury.

After the initial personality split at six months, the Missy personality had no interest in pleasing Mother. When Missy wasn't doing what she liked—drawing, playing outdoors, or spending time with her daddy—she retreated to her "inside place" and left the outside to "that other girl," as Missy called most of the other personalities.

Nor did the Jo personality care about pleasing Mother. Ray spoke of Nancy with disdain, and Jo learned to look at her mother with pity and feel proud that she wasn't, in her father's words, "anything like your mother or her side of the family." But the Joan Frances personality wanted desperately for Mother to love her and always felt guilty and unworthy of Nancy's approval.

Nancy was as proud as she was critical of her younger daughter. She spoke glowingly about the precocious little girl who said her first sentence at seven months and walked at ten months. She boasted that Joan Frances had taught herself to read when she was three and began reading music and playing the piano at five. Unfortunately, Jo—the personality who accomplished all of this—did so for her own pleasure. Jo cycled inside her mind whenever Nancy tried to show her off to company.

The Joan Frances personality cringed in embarrassment when Mother demanded that she perform tasks of which she was incapable. Joan Frances didn't have access to Jo's learning in the early years, and no amount of maternal anger could summon it forth. The only solution available was to create yet another personality—one who loved performing for Mommy's friends and who had the additional ability to skim off Jo's learning.

Dear, the young "performing" personality, sat primly on the chair in Lynn's office the day they met, her hands folded on her lap. Lynn watched the legs shorten as Dear took control. Soon only her toes scuffed the carpet. Dear's recitation of all that she did was so vivid that Lynn said later she could almost see the inevitable white anklets and black patent-leather shoes. "I know how to be a little lady," Dear explained with her five-year-old confidence. "I like doing all of the things I'm asked, so that Mommy will be proud."

Joan Frances, who often heard Nancy extol the virtues of the Holy Sisters, wished that she had "the calling," because Mother would like her then. And so Theresa, the personality who wanted to join the convent, came to be.

Nancy smiled with reverent pride when she walked by her daughter's room and found the seven-year-old on her knees, eyes closed in prayer. Jo, however, was annoyed to find that her allowance had been spent on holy cards and religious statues for the altar *she* had supposedly created in the corner of her bedroom. Even at that age, she chafed under the dogma of the Catholic Church and the strict discipline of the parochial school she attended. Jo decided it was pretty dumb for a religion to connect wearing hats to church with getting into heaven. The religious fervor soon abated, but Theresa, full of guilt for her sins, remained.

The Karen personality was created when Jo was nine and her mother said once too often, "Why can't you be like your cousin Karen?" Jo's internal Karen was the perfect mimic of her cousin, and fulfilled Nancy's demand that the child be neat and organized. Unlike such past-keeper personalities as Little Joe and Dear, who stayed frozen in time with their bits of childhood experience, Karen grew and developed into a "special-purpose" personality for the group. The group had a continuing need for her organizational abilities.

Mother seemed never to be satisfied. Tracy came at age ten to appease Nancy's demands that the child remain in view. Unlike Jo and Missy, who liked to hide themselves away, Tracy was content to read or play quiet games in her mother's presence.

Tracy didn't mind being observed because she had a magical, invisible bubble that wrapped around and protected her. Sure enough, when Nancy came close enough to touch Tracy, Tracy disappeared and one of the other personalities was forced out to deal with Mother.

Other "past-keepers" weren't nearly as sweet as Little Joe, Dear, Theresa, or Tracy: they weren't at all what Mommy wanted. But they were created by Nancy and her anger.

One day, when Nancy screamed in rage at her two-year-old daughter, Josie found herself propelled against a wall. Josie, created in that instinctual certainty that she was about to die, remembered her terror and then a wonderful blackness that brought peace. It was Jo who woke up in the emergency room, having her head X-rayed because she had "fallen out of bed," but there was now a personality who would be called forth by an overwhelming panic in the system. When Josie resurfaced through therapy, she seemed to Lynn terrified and impulsively self-destructive. But all Josie ever wanted was peace, the lovely black unconsciousness that came when she hit her head hard enough against the wall.

Sissy too was created in terror and anger. But, unlike Josie, she sought the help of others rather than unconsciousness. She wanted people to know about her anger and pain. She first came one day when three-year-old Missy was practicing her drawing. Missy loved when big sister Carol gave her drawing lessons. But this Saturday morning Carol was playing with friends and Daddy was at work, so Missy started a picture to show her sister later.

Missy drew her cat carefully, in short, controlled strokes, with her crayon. Carol always placed the crayon in her little sister's right hand, but Missy knew that her left hand was better for precise work like this. She concentrated so completely on her task that she didn't hear Nancy enter the room.

Suddenly Mommy was beside her. She grabbed Missy's left hand, and a long jagged stroke ran the length of her nearly completed picture. "How many times do I have to tell you to use your right hand?" Mommy shouted. "That's bad, to use your left hand!"

Missy quickly slipped away to her inside place. "I've had enough of this," Nancy stormed as her daughter got that "blank" look. She raced from the room and returned with a pitcher of cold water, which she threw at the still-expressionless little girl.

That certainly did the trick. Her daughter's eyes opened wide and full of hate. "Out!" the child screamed and ran for the window, her tiny fist clenched to beat through the glass. "I want the people, the people!" Nancy pinned her daughter's arms behind her back and carried her kicking and screaming from the window. The tantrum subsided, but Sissy remained and held her rage, sure that one day she could make the people see.

School was a refuge, Lynn and I learned, and at first an enjoyable experience for Jo. Jo started the first grade a year early, when she had just turned five. Since she could already read, the schoolwork was easy. She was so quiet and polite that she never received negative attention from the nun who taught her class of forty children. In fact, in a class so large, Jo was mostly left alone.

Jo, the personality who started school, was the best student in her class. She was challenged by the independent work Sister gave her and quietly made her way through third-grade math problems and the fifth-grade reader after she performed the first-grade classwork with dispatch.

One day, some new adults came into the first-grade classroom to give the children IQ tests. Jo worked happily through all of the easy little tests, careful to listen and follow directions. Then she noticed the testers nudging one another and watching her as she completed page after page at twice the speed of the other children. Afraid of any attention, Jo began pacing herself with the little boy next to her. Over time, she learned that she attracted even less attention if she purposely made a few mistakes.

In this strict Catholic school, where all children learned to use their right hands, Jo's natural left-handedness caused problems for her as well. She was obedient even when she thought the rules were stupid, and during writing practice calmly worked at making her letters with her right hand. It didn't surprise her that her writing was worse than the other kids', nor was she distressed by the low marks in penmanship on her report card.

Jo received the top marks in every other subject, and the nuns wrote glowing comments about her school performance.

But when it came time for art period, Missy took over. Art was her favorite activity, even if her mother said she didn't have her big sister's talent. Art demanded a steady hand, whether Missy was drawing, coloring, or cutting paper, and Missy knew her left hand was best for that. Why should the nuns care which hand she used if a pretty picture was the end result? But the nuns did care, and after her left hand was smacked with a ruler, Missy gathered her artistic ability and nestled it safely in her inside place, where people didn't hit her hand or call it bad.

At home, the sort of frustration Missy felt might have brought forth Sissy, who would try to get through a window, or Josie, who would fling herself against the wall. But the personalities were frightened by the imposing nuns in their black flowing robes and heavy crosses. A new personality was created, a little girl named Veronica, who could express frustration without being noticed. Remembering to use only her right hand, Veronica drew a squiggly border around a sheet of paper, each loop and twist representing the turns she made as she ran away in her mind. She filled the center of the page with the words "run and run and run and run . . ." until the frustration was spent and another personality could resume control.

But not all of the childhood memories were bad. She received an abundance of love from her extended family—Ray's siblings and their children.

Two of Ray's sisters, Marie and Christine, lived nearby with their families. Ray loved his family passionately and took every opportunity to get them all together. While Jo was growing up, weekends meant a Saturday or Sunday visit with her cousins that usually stretched far into the night as the six adults played cards. The cousins were playmates and conspirators. These were the only children that Jo really enjoyed. Of the nine cousins who came to play, she felt particularly close to Christine's son, Matthew, who was only ten days older than she, and to Marie's daughter Karen, who was six months older.

After a long day of closeness with her aunts, uncles, and cousins, Jo sometimes fantasized that a call would come from the hospital where they had all been born. A mistake would be reported and Matthew would be given to her parents, who so badly wanted a boy, and she would be given to Aunt Christine, her real mother, who didn't mind if kids were messy and noisy.

Jo and her cousin Karen were together on more occasions than the large family gatherings. When the two girls were five years old, they made a pact to be best friends for life. From then through high school, they talked on the phone two or three times a week and spent many nights and a large part of summer vacation together.

Sometimes Karen stayed at Jo's house, but neither of the girls much enjoyed that. Karen felt uncomfortable around Aunt Nancy and Uncle Ray, who insisted on being addressed as "ma'am" and "sir" and who expected perfection from all children. And she didn't like it when Aunt Nancy held her up as a model for Jo. She thought Jo was just fine the way she was. She particularly hated it when Jo started acting like Karen for Nancy's benefit. At first it was funny, but then Karen realized that sometimes Jo couldn't stop pretending after her mother left the room.

Life was much better at Aunt Marie's. The cousins were both more relaxed with Karen's parents. At Aunt Marie and Uncle Jack's, Jo felt that she was part of a real family. She never felt that at home. Mom and Dad and Carol and she were just four people thrown together by fate. There seemed to be tension whenever more than two of them were in the same room.

Aunt Marie's house was different. Even though her cousins Ann, Karen, and Bob sometimes yelled at one another or got mad at their parents, it was clear that they all loved one another.

All the kids had daily chores at Aunt Marie's and Jo loved seeing her name and chores on the list right along with the other kids, as if she really belonged with them. Doing chores at Aunt Marie's was fun. There was sometimes a lot of work—weeding the garden or picking fruit from the trees—but everyone pitched in. And at Aunt Marie's the kids knew they were done when they had completed the list. At Jo's house, children were perpetually on call, expected to drop whatever they were doing instantly to meet parental demands.

Aunt Marie didn't get mad if things weren't perfect. Unlike Jo's mother, Aunt Marie never said, "You will redust every piece of furniture in this house because you missed the table leg." Aunt Marie never forbade her to read for a week because she had forgotten to take out the trash. Aunt Marie just said, "Let's make sure this place doesn't get condemned," and everyone worked together without fear of punishment.

Aunt Marie and Uncle Jack didn't seem to mind her being at their house, no matter how long she stayed, and Jo knew that her mother preferred for her to be gone. But when she asked her father if she could live there all the time, maybe just for a year or so, he shook his head sadly and said, "I'd miss you too much, cookie. I need you with me. How come you want to leave your old man?" After that, Jo's sadness at the end of every visit to Aunt Marie's was balanced by the knowledge that she was important to her father.

All of the personalities who experienced bits of childhood added their pieces to the patchwork quilt of childhood memories. Tracy, Veronica, Dear, and many of the others had rich descriptions. But I had nothing to add.

I could monitor what happened after age fifteen, but could get nothing from before. I learned what early life was like for Jo and the others as the personalities shared their stories with Lynn. Sometimes I felt guilty that I couldn't provide more information for Lynn, but otherwise I was glad she was there to help.

I had done really well for ten years, but now I was happy to have Lynn's observations. She helped me accept the finality of my divorce. When Keith moved to California, I had to give up my hope that we would get back together. She helped me see that Keith's rejection was attributable to his own problems as much as it was to mine. That was a new idea for me, and for the other personalities as well.

Neither Nancy nor Ray had ever admitted to having a problem. If they were angry or frustrated or depressed, it was Jo's fault, or Carol's fault, or their bosses' fault. I had never before considered that someone near me might have problems that were not caused by me. I had been created to please people. If the people around me weren't happy, I must be doing something wrong. Lynn helped me see that I lacked the power to make other people feel anything.

Though I appreciated the insight and revelations Lynn offered me, I needed to escape from them as well. I was glad to be living with Steve. His denial of the disorder brought freedom. I didn't want to think about MPD outside Lynn's office, and I didn't want Steve to decide that I was crazy. None of the others interfered. The personalities were all used to being treated as a single person.

We accepted Steve's conclusion that Jo was just "moody," and he tacitly accepted periods of amnesia and variations in behavior. Though he called all of us Jo, he liked me best, because I was good socially and attentive to him. But he was a mentor to the Jo personality as she worked her way toward a master's degree. Steve was even tolerant of Joan Frances when she called her mother and all but crawled to win Mother's approval.

14

Jo didn't have more than two or three hours of awareness on any given day. When she wasn't doing work for her graduate classes, Jo thought about, or wrote about, getting well. Jo's goal was no amnesia. She wanted all of the time.

Jo didn't have my ability to monitor what went on when she was "inside." Her life was a slide show of fleeting moments. She wasn't sure what she'd do with twenty-four hours of a day, but she knew she wouldn't spend an afternoon coloring, as Missy sometimes did. She certainly wouldn't spend precious minutes playing with a toy dump truck in Lynn's office, as Little Joe did. She confided to Lynn one day, "I might even quit that teaching job of Renee's."

Jo wanted to be well, didn't know how to get there, but was sure that it wouldn't happen without her hard work and focused attention. She was slightly annoyed when Lynn said sympathetically, "I wish I had a magic wand to make things better, but therapy doesn't work that way." Jo knew that much, but she couldn't figure out how therapy *did* work and was frustrated by her uncharacteristic inability to understand.

Jo felt let down by her mind, by her extraordinary analytic abilities. She had always thought she was smart and had approached any intellectual challenge with glee. When presented with the philosophical hypothesis that people could be nothing more than minds in a vat, hallucinating reality, Jo wasn't perturbed or perplexed. Amnesia and the familiar feeling of "I just got dropped in here somehow" enabled Jo to see how this improbable hypothesis served as an analogy for her life. She figured that she could be a very contented mind-in-a-vat, but Lynn had forced her to accept she wasn't alone in a vat or in her body. This was a problem that she could not puzzle out.

Jo's natural tendency, when faced with her ignorance, was to read everything she could on the problem at hand. Jo's library included over five thousand books and ranged over a mind-boggling array of topics. "The only thing still catholic in my life is my library," she sometimes joked. Nevertheless, Jo now avoided literature on mental illness.

Jo knew she was suggestible. Her parents had always told her she was a very impressionable child. And, after all, Jo knew that she had somehow unconsciously created all of these different personalities. If she scoured the medical journals for clinical reports, Jo was afraid that she would contaminate her own treatment. Lynn endorsed Jo's avoidance of the literature: Lynn said that they needed to do this in their own way. But a year had passed since Jo had made this agreement with Lynn, and now she felt trapped by her ignorance and suspicious that Lynn wouldn't tell her how to get well. The only suggestion Lynn made was one that Jo couldn't tolerate. Lynn had been tape-recording the sessions for the last six months, and when Jo appealed to her for help, Lynn gestured toward the growing mound of tapes in her file drawer.

Jo resisted. She didn't want to listen to the tapes. Because of remarks casually dropped by family and friends, she suspected that at least one of the personalities sounded like her older sister and that another sounded like her mother. From Lynn, Jo learned that one of the personalities sounded like a little girl, and yet another like a small boy. She couldn't imagine why Lynn would want to humiliate her by making her listen to those voices.

Jo thought that, even if she screwed up her courage to try, the experiment would end in disaster. Every time in the past when Jo had tried to watch herself on videotape, tried to look at a photograph of herself, or even listened to her own voice on tape, she had lost time. What would Lynn do when Jo lost time listening to the treatment of the other personalities? If she tried and failed, maybe Lynn would say that she wasn't trying hard enough. The way Jo figured it, Lynn would stop treating her if she thought that Jo wasn't working at getting well.

"Besides," Jo decided, "Lynn has already told me what the other parts of me have said. Why should I want to hear those lies again?"

DIARY *March 8, 1982 (A year into treatment)*

I've certainly made some progress: I've learned a great deal about Jo's abuse and have met seventeen different personalities (although some of the past-keepers are more fragments than real personalities), and I've begun to conceptualize the structure of this particular multiple. But treatment seems to be at a standstill. I think they have all grown to trust me and are unlikely to terminate treatment prematurely; still, I feel a need to push beyond our present plateau.

Renee clearly values our relationship but is wary of acknowledging this and attempts to stay uninvolved in what she considers "therapy." The label aside, she has become quite adept at using me to problem-solve about relationships and situations at home and at work.

Missy, the most complete child personality, has been able to establish an unconflicted relationship with me. She enjoys hours of sitting on the rug, encircled by my arm and talking. She doesn't care if it is "therapy." She knows I listen to her and care about her. Missy unabashedly soaks up my nurturing. This may be safe because Missy knows I care about her even though I know that her father molested her. Even at an early age, the personalities had too much guilt to allow this to happen with Nancy.

Jo, who is the most aware of being involved in "therapy," is both the most intellectually defended and the most emotionally infantile of the group. She is completely unable to modulate emotion. She has an intense desire to master the process of treatment but can't let herself get emotionally involved. Not surprisingly, she's left frustrated, thinking that I have the answers but won't share them.

Jo is so bright, so persistent, and in so much pain that both of us are drained by the work I do to evoke emotional response while she defends intellectually. The task of feeding bits of digestible emotion to a being so capable and so guarded is excruciatingly slow. I insist on relaying the tales of abuse that the other personalities have shared, and she refuses to believe that she was hurt. Jo listens politely, flinching only a little when a particularly strong accusation has been made against her father, and then calmly explains why things couldn't have happened that way. She'd much prefer that I perceive the personalities as lying rather than abused.

As I write this, I see that it is really with Jo that I am stalemated. We seem to be locked in a circular pattern that must be broken. Although Dr. Wilbur cautioned me that Jo's fear of reading literature about MPD was justified—because of the extreme suggestibility of any multiple—Wilbur also said that the book Sybil *has been successfully used in the treatment process by some therapists.*

My sense of Jo is that she may become troubled by how she is different from Sybil, but reading the book should at least reopen dialogue for us. Listening to tapes of the personalities is far too emotionally laden to be of any use to Jo now; it may be that she can maintain enough distance from Sybil *to benefit from it.*

.   .   .

When Lynn raised the possibility of Jo's reading *Sybil,* many of the personalities were intrigued by the idea. Years ago, Carol had recommended *Sybil* as an interesting book and I had tried to read it. But it didn't engage me at the time. I got bored and finally put it aside. The book made me uncomfortable.

I also managed to avoid seeing the movie based on the book. When I was student-teaching, the year before I met Lynn, *Sybil* was a movie often shown to high-school psychology students. I hadn't taught psychology, but my office had adjoined the school's viewing room. The haunting music and bits of dialogue that seeped through the walls bothered me. As with all my phobias and "uncaused" fears, I avoided the movie. Since I couldn't tune it out, I found other places to work whenever *Sybil* was being shown.

Now Jo was taking up the challenge. She decided to approach *Sybil* analytically and not get caught up in the story. She would read it with a purpose. She would abstract useful treatment techniques from the book. Finding out how another multiple had been treated would give her some clue as to how she herself could get better.

Every evening, Jo pounced on the book as she would upon any intellectual puzzle. She skimmed the pages she had read the night before so that there was no chance of misinterpretation, no chance that she might forget some aspect of the treatment process. And, every evening, Jo put the book aside, choked by her own feelings of hurt, anger, and despair. The book made her feel empty and aching; Jo longed for something she could not name. She decided not to mention to Lynn how she felt; Jo didn't know how to talk about feelings.

Instead, during her sessions with Lynn, Jo concentrated on how she and Sybil were alike and how they were different. "I guess I'm like the Sybil personality," Jo said, "the core personality of my group. My Renee is like Sybil's Vicky—the personality who knows everything about everybody."

Lynn didn't think the comparison quite fit and told Jo that she found it difficult to think in terms of a core personality who had more centrality than the others. "And Renee certainly doesn't know everything about everybody in your group, Jo," Lynn said, "although she does play a very important part in getting you through each day.

"I have real relationships with many of your personalities," Lynn concluded, "and I can't place importance on only one part of the totality. I think it's better to help every part become stronger and healthier than it is for me to play favorites."

Jo didn't like what she was hearing, so she changed the topic. "Hypnosis was an important part of Dr. Wilbur's treatment of Sybil," she began again. "Are you still planning to take courses in that?"

Yes, Lynn was now learning to be a hypnotherapist, although her instructor didn't know anything about using the technique with a multiple. "I don't think we'll use hypnosis for a while yet," Lynn said.

Jo was pleased to hear it. She was secretly terrified of hypnosis and believed that Lynn would interpret her fear as a sign that Jo didn't want to get well.

Jo finally ran out of ancillary issues to discuss and tried to tell Lynn what was really on her mind after reading *Sybil*. "Sybil and Dr. Wilbur seemed to care about each other as friends," Jo said.

"I care about you very much," Lynn quickly reassured Jo.

Jo sighed and tried again. "I know you care more about me, in a way that's different from what you feel for your other patients," Jo said. "You let me call you at home; you see me five days a week; it usually doesn't matter if we run over the hour." Lynn nodded: all of this was true. Jo hesitated and looked down at her hands. "But Dr. Wilbur saw Sybil outside their office time. Their relationship wasn't . . . It wasn't just professional."

Jo's reading of Sybil *certainly has borne out my theory that her problem would be not fitting into that model. What I failed to foresee was her concern about my not fitting the model of Dr. Wilbur as therapist. She clearly wants me to see her outside the office, as Dr. Wilbur did Sybil.*

I specifically asked Connie Wilbur about this when I saw her on consultation, and she told me that that aspect had been overplayed in the book. There had actually been little contact outside the office. Telling this to Jo, however, made her feel that I was being manipulative, using the book selectively.

I have certainly seen patients outside my office in the past, particularly when working with delinquent teenagers. But this is different.

First, I am working in an office rather than in a field setting, and presumably doing a different kind of social work.

Next, I am really feeling my way with Jo. As she has pointed out, I spend more time with her than I do with anyone else. What would happen if I opened the door to outside time? I already have to deal with strange looks from some of my colleagues because of the attention and techniques I use with Jo. What would they say to even more "overinvolvement"?

Finally, Jo has been abused over and over again by professionals. Some shared with her mother information she had given them in confidence. Still others seemed to care and then precipitously abandoned her. It is mandatory that I not get into a situation where I promise more than I can give.

. . .

Jo felt sure that Lynn was refusing to see her outside the office because she didn't love Jo the way Dr. Wilbur loved Sybil. Lynn said, "We can be friends, if you like, when the therapeutic part of our relationship is over." Jo decided that this was a delaying tactic designed to give her empty hope. Jo thought that she was not worthy of anyone's freely given affection, and now felt deceived whenever Lynn said how much she cared.

"I wish you wouldn't say that," Jo told Lynn. "You wouldn't care if I stopped coming to see you. You'd use all the time you now spend with me in some more productive way." If Jo stopped therapy, she was sure that Lynn would chalk it up as an academic failure and go on with her life without a backward glance.

Jo had fought knowing that the aching she felt when reading *Sybil* was her desire to be loved by Lynn. She knew she was too old for a mother and hadn't wanted to discuss it with Lynn. But once the feeling was out, once Jo had ripped open the wound, she couldn't leave it alone. She tried hard to accept intellectually Lynn's reasons for not seeing her outside the office, but felt miserable about what she now perceived as Lynn's rejection.

Lynn's talk of Jo's "splendid strengths" and "all you have to offer the world" was empty. Lynn wasn't interested in Jo in any meaningful way.

"What's the use of trying? The only person who ever loved me is dead; I might as well be dead too," Jo thought. It was too late for regrets. She couldn't think, couldn't work; all she could do was hurt. She wanted to die.

Soon she'd be going home to Richmond to visit her family and to visit her father's grave. She decided to slash her wrists in the cemetery. She'd join the only person who could love her.

DIARY *May 10, 1982*

For a month now, I have been dealing with the issue of outside time with Jo and trying to put it to rest. I know that she is infuriated and feels powerless. I know she totally misunderstands what I am saying to her. Perhaps I need to re-evaluate what is going on. It is obvious to me that Jo's anguish is real and that she seems to be fast approaching some crisis point.

Jo is leaving on Friday for a visit to Richmond. Before she goes, I will make one last attempt to confront and work through this problem. Renee said today, "I don't see why this is such a big deal. Jo isn't asking to live with you, for heaven's sake. She's just asking for an hour outside the office."

Maybe I am making too much of this. If a visit outside makes her more comfortable now, perhaps I can deal with the other issues later as they arise.

. . .

At the next session, Lynn started out, "Jo, tell me again why you want to see me away from the office."

Jo took a deep breath. Though she hated discussing her feelings, she knew nothing would matter after this weekend. "I'm afraid of what you're really like outside the office," she said. "I don't know if you are real with me in here.

"If you did spend some time with me outside the office," Jo said, "I think I'd know that you care about me in a real, nonprofessional way. You've been trying to convince me for a year that I should have more of a sense of my worth, but how can I believe that people could really want to be with me if you aren't?"

Lynn looked directly at Jo and said, "OK, why don't you come to my house for tea next Monday?"

It was more than Jo could have asked for. Her fondest hope had been that Lynn might capitulate and agree to have coffee with her in the campus cafeteria. But Lynn was inviting her to her home! "Oh, Lynn, you don't have to do that," Jo said, feeling guiltier than ever about her desire. "I don't want to intrude on your privacy."

"No, Jo," Lynn said firmly, "if you're going to see me outside the office, you're going to see me in my natural environment. Come and see how I live."

Jo was confused by Lynn's turnaround. "I think I changed her mind," she thought with a shiver of delight. Throughout the weekend in Richmond, Jo mulled over her old fears and new feeling of power. Her plan of suicide was forgotten.

Jo arrived at Lynn's house a few minutes early and sat in the car, wondering if this would be yet one more experience that another personality would take away from her. When, five minutes later, Jo was still herself sitting in the car, she realized that she had been half-hoping that a less socially awkward personality would seize control. This was not to be.

Though many of us watched through Jo's eyes, this was to be her experience alone. Lynn had acquiesced to Jo. She had invited the Jo personality to her home. The rest of us wondered why anyone would want to socialize with a personality as inept as Jo, but we agreed to keep out of the way.

Lynn seemed to anticipate Jo's discomfort. "Come in, come in," she greeted Jo's knock at the door. "Sit anywhere," she said, gesturing toward the living room, and went into the kitchen to make tea.

Jo felt a little less anxious as she had a chance to take in her surroundings alone. She patted the scruffy dog, sat on the sofa, and felt calmed by the tinkling of wind chimes in the window. She had heard that sound when she talked to Lynn on the phone. In the future, she'd be able to visualize the brass chimes in the living room.

Then she noticed a curious drawing framed on a table in the corner. Jo had the odd feeling that she ought to know the picture. Brightly colored flowers sprang from a dark box. A sense of upward motion filled the center of the drawing. Lynn returned with tea and retrieved the picture that had captured Jo's attention. She sat next to Jo, the framed drawing on her lap.

"I guess you didn't see this, Jo," Lynn said. "This was Missy's Mother's Day present to me. Well, actually, Renee gave it to me. Missy was brave enough to make it, but not brave enough to hand it to me herself."

Jo blushed deeply. This wasn't the first time she had been confronted with the activities of unseen others. As usual, she apologized. "I'm very sorry, I'm sorry that you had to deal with that." She shrugged helplessly. "I just didn't know."

"You're sorry?!" Lynn said sharply, then carefully modulated her tone when Jo flinched. "I thought the drawing was lovely and meaningful. Missy's telling me that I'm like a mother to her, and she's showing that she feels free enough to do artistic work. Don't you see the significance of this picture? That box has hidden your secrets for years. Now beauty is coming out of it." Jo nodded at Lynn's interpretation. Still she felt ashamed.

"You know," Lynn said, "the Missy part of you has artistic talent. She just hasn't had much time to let that talent mature."

Jo brushed this aside with even more embarrassment. She didn't know how to deal with positive reactions to her own accomplishments; how was she supposed to feel when something nice was said about the personalities who stole her time?

"I like your room," Jo said, changing the subject. "Everything seems soft and quiet." She surveyed again the muted colors and nubby textures, committing it all to memory.

"I wasn't allowed to sit in the living room when I was growing up," she said, "but I wouldn't have wanted to anyway. It was all so stiff and formal.

"I like this room," she said again. "It looks like you."

The first appointment after my visit with Jo at home—and we are all far more relaxed. Gone was Jo's terrible tension of these last few months. And Renee finally told me today how despairing Jo had really been. Just before my capitulation, she said, Jo had made plans to kill herself on her father's grave. "My visit to Richmond went a lot smoother without that little complication," Renee said, laughing.

I felt a lurch in my stomach at this revelation, but I also felt totally vindicated in my decision. No one in the group had attempted to manipulate me by telling me Jo's plans beforehand.

This was truly a milestone for Jo. In a last, desperate attempt, she had pleaded her case, fought it through, and won—thereby showing far more trust in herself and in me than she realizes even now. And I, seeing my action as an appropriate response to genuine need, also trust both of us more. That need has been satisfied in an open and direct way. Now we can get on to other issues. Whether or not we do more outside the office is secondary. I can't help thinking, though, how healing it might be to have a weekend of therapy at the cottage.

· · ·

15

Jo's visit with Lynn had an effect on all the personalities. Those personalities who had some internal contact all agreed that we would help Lynn help Jo if we could.

None of the personalities ever expected that the opportunity to enjoy Lynn's company outside her office would be repeated. Even Jo and Missy understood that their longing for more of Lynn's time was unreasonable. No person could fill twenty-six years of lack. And each personality had learned from experience that it was less painful to set limits than to have some external person set limits for us. We would not ask for more from Lynn.

One afternoon about a month later, the receptionist's area outside Lynn's office became unusually noisy. End-of-semester revelry erupted as the social-work and psychology students shouted down the hallways that freedom was theirs at last. Missy was terrified by the unexpected sounds and voices. Lynn's reassurances failed to calm her.

I apologized for Missy's reaction. "I know it's crazy," I confided to Lynn, "but Missy still thinks that her mother might come storming into your office. She just flips out every time one of your students ignores the 'in-session' sign and comes in to say goodbye to you."

"I've got an idea," Lynn said suddenly. "Why don't I take Missy to the park tomorrow?" I was stunned by Lynn's suggestion. Not only was she once again proposing to spend time with us outside the office, but she was apparently willing to be seen with Missy in public.

Missy reveled in the relaxed visit with her friend and did nothing to embarrass the rest of the group. She enjoyed exploring the large quiet riverside park, feeding ducks and watching great freighters maneuver through the port.

"Your daddy drove big boats like that," Missy said. It had been a long time since she had seen her daddy, and she always visualized him on the deck of a ship, one day coming back to find her. Missy scanned the ship reflexively and then looked at Lynn. For the first time, she didn't ache for Daddy's rescue. Lynn and the "other girls" inside her took care of her now.

A memory flowed over Missy. A large wooden casket, covered by a spray of gardenias, her father's favorite flower. "He died," Missy said softly, tears rolling down her cheeks. She put her head on Lynn's shoulder, watched the ducks, and felt sad but safe.

Jo knew that Lynn saw and celebrated the new strides she was making. Now, whenever Jo became aware in Lynn's office, she was glad to be there and had no worries about what the others had done in her absence. She accepted that Lynn would continue to know her and love her for her own self.

Jo strove harder than ever to cooperate. She agreed to let Lynn hypnotize her, although she wasn't sure she was ready for it. The very thought of hypnosis made Jo feel clammy. Nevertheless, she was willing, in theory at least, to put irrational fear aside. She trusted Lynn now.

Lynn welcomed Jo's brave decision, but said they should try to work through her concerns first. Lynn spoke glowingly of the hypnotic experiences she had in training. "I felt terrific both during and after the hypnosis," Lynn said. "I felt calm, relaxed; and the hypnotic suggestions helped me lose some weight."

Jo reasoned that, in her case, hypnosis would allow Lynn to communicate with the single, solid unconscious self that was her core and the core of the other personalities as well. The sooner Lynn gave her unconscious the message that she didn't need other personalities, the better. Yet Jo remained frightened by the idea of hypnosis.

As usual, the fear felt by the Jo personality bounced through the system and affected the other personalities. Though the group agreed not to interfere with the hypnosis, many of us felt trepidation. I searched for the meaning of the uncertainty but came up empty.

"Have any of you ever been hypnotized before?" Lynn asked.

"Not that I'm aware of," I said. "Maybe it's just a control issue. We all know that hypnosis means letting go to you. You know that I can usually take over the outside awareness when I want. Maybe I'm afraid that when you hypnotize Jo I'll be stuck inside."

"I do trust you," I added with a smile, "but you know I've been the personality running this show for a long time." I also explained that some of the other personalities might still be afraid that Lynn would destroy them while they were hypnotized and powerless.

Lynn reminded me that she didn't want to dispose of any personality. Integration, if it ever happened, was a process of everyone's deciding to join together. No personality would be sacrificed.

"Jo thinks we'll all be gone someday, and she'll be the only one left," I said.

"Jo still has a lot to learn, doesn't she?" Lynn answered. I promised Lynn that we would all do our best.

The next session, Jo stretched out on the rug, trying, but trembling. Lynn began speaking softly, her voice modulated to Jo's breathing pattern. Jo's trembling gave way to nervous giggling. She sat up. "I just can't do it," she said. "The way you are talking is so out of character. Usually you're so quick that it scares me. This change seems ridiculous."

"Resistance!" said Lynn, and the word was enough to silence Jo's friendly criticism of her technique.

After a few more tries, Jo relaxed. Behind closed lids, she began to envision the lovely scene Lynn was describing.

"You're at the edge of the ocean," Lynn said, and Jo imagined the sound of lapping waves.

"You're walking with bare feet in the sand," Lynn murmured, "and feeling the water on your toes." Jo could feel the sun on her back and the wonderful expanse of the sea at her feet.

"This is real! It's working," Jo thought with disbelief, and then slipped peacefully into the scene in her mind. She no longer needed to concentrate on what Lynn was saying. The voice grew more distant. Peace.

Then, suddenly, Jo felt slapped down by an icy wave. She fought to regain her hold, but the panic was stronger than she. She felt herself being dragged helplessly, ebbing away. "Help! I'm drowning," Jo thought wildly, "I'm drowning in my self."

The Josie personality sat up, quick and tense. She felt the panic surge through her and looked for the only release she had ever known. "THE WALL!" Josie scrambled across the room and began hitting her head against the wall before Lynn had a chance to react.

"Renee! Jo!" Lynn called, hoping that the system was sufficiently hypnotized that she could indeed call out another personality. But as Lynn pulled Josie from the wall, she realized that the other personalities were blocked by panic as usual. Josie struggled against Lynn's embrace until the wild fear was gone and Missy could lean, exhausted, into the therapist's arms.

Jo knew that she had tried her hardest to cooperate with the hypnosis, and Lynn believed that. Lynn reassured her that what had happened had nothing to do with clinical resistance.

"We have to figure out why you became so overwhelmed with fear," Lynn said. "Let's start at the beginning. Have you ever been hypnotized?"

"No, never," Jo said with certainty.

"What was it like when you were going under?" Lynn asked.

"I felt calm, at peace, and, at the start, a little amazed that the seashore scene felt so real," Jo said, "and then there was this incredible fear and I was gone."

"What were you afraid of?" Lynn asked.

Jo, her brow wrinkled, became lost in thought. "I know this sounds crazy," she said finally, "but I was afraid that you might do something to hurt me."

"I don't think that sounds crazy at all," Lynn said. "How did you think I might hurt you?"

Jo flinched. "I know you'd never hurt me."

Lynn wasn't about to give up that easily. "Don't worry about reassuring me," Lynn said. "I know *you* know that you are safe with me, but in what way did you fantasize that I might hurt you?" Jo shook her head in response, but could tell that Lynn would not let it drop.

"Let's free-associate," Lynn said. "What does the hypnosis bring to mind?"

Jo relaxed and let the responses come uncensored. "It makes me think of the ocean; you know I love the sea."

"Listen to my words," Lynn said, and repeated key phrases softly, as she had done during the hypnosis. "Listen to my voice. You're safe here."

Jo stiffened. "Larry!" she cried out, pleased that a memory had been evoked, but more perplexed than ever. What did her high-school psychology teacher—her favorite teacher—have to do with this?

"When did Larry say those words?" Lynn asked. Something in the therapist's weary tone made Jo think that Lynn had some idea of the answer. Jo ignored this for the present. Discovering and tracing a memory was a new experience for her. She didn't want to lose her train of thought.

Jo considered the possibilities aloud. "In class? No, I'm sure that Larry wouldn't have conducted hypnosis in a high-school psychology class."

Lynn nodded, but added nothing to help.

"I guess it makes sense, though, that he might have known hypnosis," she speculated. "He told me that he had been a therapist in Sweden."

"When did he say those words to you, Jo?" Lynn asked again.

"Well, I'm sure he wasn't trying to hypnotize me," Jo responded.

"When, Jo?"

Jo licked her lips. "I guess it was over at his apartment. I went there one time. But Larry was only trying to make me feel better."

Jo stopped. She brushed away the shiver she felt then, knowing that it was irrational to be concerned about Larry or about her memories of him. "I was over at Larry's apartment during that time when my parents were living apart and so involved with their own problems. I was confused and scared. Larry was the only person I could depend on."

"What did Larry say to you when you were in his apartment?" Lynn prodded.

Jo answered, struggling to keep her voice calm. "Oh, he just told me to let my muscles relax and listen to his voice and I'd feel better."

Lynn pressed further, but Jo now resisted getting near the memory that pulsed with warning. She couldn't discuss it.

Lynn backed off, and the session ended. As Jo walked from the clinic, she realized that Lynn had, uncharacteristically, not offered any information from the other personalities. Nor had she shared her own speculation.

That was OK. Jo was sure that she had no interest in what Lynn had to say.

DIARY *June 2, 1982*

The pattern is astounding. It seems that the sexual abuse by her father set her up as a continual victim, ready to be lured by other abusers with other pathology. From what the other personalities tell me, I think Jo was raped by her high-school teacher that day, and that he used hypnosis as part of his seduction.

I have been given a batch of jigsaw-puzzle pieces from the various personalities, and these pieces suggest a particularly devastating adolescence. But the pieces have been handed to me in many different ways. Sometimes the abuse is presented in a straightforward manner, as when Isis told me about Ray's sexual excitement in hugging his thirteen-year-old daughter. More often, the pieces appear as transference, like Jo's reaction to my "professionalism" or to my attempts to hypnotize her. Still other times, the pieces are tossed my way without emphasis, so that it is up to me to separate what is relevant from what is not.

It's time that she started helping to put some of the pieces together.

. . .

16

The next time I went in, Lynn had a plan. "Renee," she said, "how would you like to do some detective work with me? I want to try to construct a whole time frame in Jo's life."

I thought it sounded like an interesting project. Although I myself hadn't experienced any of the time that Lynn wanted to talk about, I had monitored what the other personalities had told her so far. I agreed with Lynn that all the pieces supplied by the separate personalities seemed pretty jumbled.

Lynn prescribed the end of the sequence we would piece together. "Now," she said, "we know when you were born, right?"

"Right," I answered. "I became a separate personality when Jo went to bed with her psychology teacher. But I really didn't know that he had hypnotized her until recently."

"That must have been a horrible experience for Jo," Lynn said.

"I never thought about that," I said, then laughed when I considered the outcome. "It was sure a wonderful experience for me."

"Well, we'll come back to that later," Lynn said. "Now let's figure out where to begin. How about when Jo's parents separated?"

"Let's see, she would have been twelve or thirteen then," I said, "but no personality has had much to say about Nancy and Ray's splitting up."

"We'll hear about it when they're ready," Lynn said. "Let's start a little later. Let's begin with Jo's first memory of high school."

Jo leaned back to rest her head against the bathroom wall. Startled to find no support behind her, she opened her eyes to an entirely different world. She wasn't in a school bathroom, as she had thought. She was sitting at a desk in a classroom.

She clutched the book in front of her in an attempt to hold on to *now.* The psychology textbook lay open to page 72. A colored illustration in the book identified parts of the human brain.

Jo saw that she was sitting among other students in a classroom. From the front of the room, a man in his late thirties glanced curiously at her through black-rimmed glasses. He stood behind a table that held a multi-colored plastic model of a human brain, at which he gestured while describing the name and functions of each part. A laboratory area with tables and high stools filled the room to her right. To her left, she saw other students and a cinderblock wall. Some of the students watched the teacher; others just looked bored. The door leading from the classroom was behind Jo on her left.

"Escape," Jo thought, but where? If she ran from this room, where would she go? She didn't know where she was. Since there were no windows, she couldn't look outside for a clue. When she tried to remember what day it was, she realized she didn't know.

The confusion felt like internal quicksand, sucking her into panic. Jo shook her head and searched the room again. She noticed, above the man who was speaking at the front of the room, a yellow placard pinned to the bulletin board. It said "Mr. Dunlap." "Mr. Dunlap," Jo thought, testing the name with her tongue.

Jo looked around the room again, searching for familiar faces among the students. She didn't see anyone she knew, and the girls looked older than she and more sophisticated. They looked like high-school students.

Bewildered, Jo looked down at her textbook. Maybe her memory would click once she found her place in the reading.

Sheets of notebook paper next to the book drew her attention. There, in neat rounded script so unlike her own sloppy, jagged writing, Jo saw the date, "Oct. 24, 1971."

"Oct. 24!" Jo felt herself grow cold and sweaty all at the same time. "It can't be. It's April. It was just April."

She took a deep breath to calm her panic. "Remember," she told herself severely, "stop being so stupid. Just try."

She looked down at the floor and spotted a purse sitting next to her feet. It must be hers. Surely something in there would jog her memory. Trying not to be conspicuous, Jo snapped the point of her pencil. She glanced at the teacher, but he didn't seem to be watching her.

Jo pawed through the contents of her purse. She dug frantically, hoping she looked as though she was searching for a pencil, desperate to find something familiar—something to connect her with now.

She raised her hand from the purse in surprise. She had lifted out a small plastic bag containing marijuana. Where had this come from? She didn't use drugs.

Jo glanced at the front of the room again. The teacher was still talking, but now he was also watching her and looking at the bag in her hand. Jo dropped the bag back into her purse and put her head down on the desk, hiding her face in her arms.

Jo closed her eyes and concentrated on her most recent memory. "Wasn't it a minute ago?" she thought. Maybe it was yesterday.

Yesterday, Jo had been a ninth-grader at East Junior High School. It was a morning in April. She remembered going to her first-hour class, Spanish with Mr. Hahn. When the class had started that morning, Jo had shifted uncomfortably in her seat at the front of the row. The students on either side of her recited along with the rest of the class while Mr. Hahn gave instructions in Spanish. Although Jo was an A student, she couldn't understand what the teacher was saying. "Why can't I remember?" Jo wondered in panic. Before she really thought about what she was doing, she bolted from the classroom.

Now where? Jo slipped into the girls' bathroom and splashed her face with cool water. She held her hands to keep them from shaking.

Now what? It wasn't safe to stay in the bathroom for long. Soon a teacher on hall duty would come in. "I'll tell her I'm sick," Jo muttered, and leaned against the cold tile wall. She felt caught in swirling confusion. "Maybe I *am* sick," she thought, "maybe I should go to the nurse."

Jo liked the school nurse. Many times this year, the nurse had hugged her while Jo sobbed, hating her father for leaving, hating her mother for wanting to live away from him. While Jo cried, the nurse stroked her head, saying, "Poor little chickadee." But last week, when Jo again arrived at the nurse's office in tears, she was sent to her guidance counselor.

The counselor had looked at her over a stack of achievement tests and had asked if this was important. Jo had replied that everything was fine.

No, she couldn't go to the nurse and be sent away again. Afraid to move, afraid to stay, Jo pressed her head against the cold tile.

A screaming bell jerked her back to the present reality of Mr. Dunlap's psychology class. "I won't move," Jo decided, "I'll pretend I'm asleep."

The room became silent as the last students filed out, laughing and talking with one another. When someone unexpectedly touched her arm, Jo jumped upright and stared, terrified, into the eyes of her psychology teacher.

"Jo, it's my free period. Let's go back in my office," he said. She gathered her books and followed him. Mr. Dunlap sat at his desk and motioned for Jo to sit in a chair at its side. He leaned back in his chair, tapped a pencil on his teeth, and watched her. Eventually he leaned forward. "OK, Miss Casey, what's going on here?"

"Wh-what do you mean?" Jo asked haltingly.

"The marijuana," he said.

"It's not mine," she responded.

"Give me your purse," he said, and she clutched it tighter, not knowing what else he might find in there. Finally, Jo reached into her purse and handed him the plastic bag.

"So, what do you think I should do with your ounce of grass?" he said.

"Keep it," Jo said, relieved to have a question that she knew how to answer. "I don't want it."

The teacher studied her for a minute. "You seemed pale and upset in class today," he said. "Is something going on at home?"

Jo sat mute. She didn't know.

"Did you have a fight with your mother? With your father? Do you have any older sisters or brothers?"

She relaxed slightly. "I have a sister, but she's mad at my mother and won't tell us where she's living. My father won't tell me where he lives either, but sometimes he calls or comes to see me." Jo trailed off, wondering now if any of this was still true. Things had been this way in April, but now it was October.

The teacher looked at her thoughtfully. "You really don't have anyone to talk to, do you?" he asked gently. Jo shrugged, knowing that it wasn't safe to talk about her problems. They told her mother what she had said, asked questions she couldn't answer, or simply sent her away.

He wrote something on a slip of paper and handed it to her. It said "Larry Dunlap" and had a phone number. "This is my home number," he said. "Don't tell the other kids that you have it, but you can call me if you need to talk. OK?"

Jo took the paper and nodded. She didn't want to think about talking to him; she just wanted to get away before he discovered that she had lost her memory.

"Now, let me give you a pass to your next class," Mr. Dunlap said. "Where is it?"

"That's OK," Jo said, standing up and edging out of the office. "I don't need a pass."

The teacher smiled reassuringly. "Don't worry," he said, "the marijuana is our secret. Really, you can trust me. This is a safe place for you to be."

Jo walked into a large unfamiliar hall. She picked a direction at random, and hoped that her memory would return soon. It had to.

As she walked, Jo pieced together what she could. This was a different school from East Junior High. Psychology was a high-school subject, and the date on her paper had been October 24, 1971. She must be a tenth-grader now, and this must be John F. Kennedy High School. Of course. Entirely logical.

"Is it really October?" Jo wondered.

The hall she had chosen finally ended at a set of double doors. She looked through the screen-meshed glass in wonder. The trees, the wonderful forest just outside the building confirmed it. October.

She slipped out the door and sat on the concrete step. Jo inhaled deeply, breathing in the smell of the dying leaves.

She opened her large blue three-ring binder, looking for something that might jog her memory. She found her semester schedule, printed in precise letters and carefully taped to the inside cover. Period 1: English, Mr. Smith; Period 2: Spanish, Mr. Walker; Period 3: Geometry, Miss Hernandez; Period 4: Journalism, Mrs. Adams; Period 5: Psychology, Mr. Dunlap; Period 6: Gym, Miss Maloney. A list of room numbers ran down the right side of the sheet. Jo figured that she must have made out the schedule for occasions like this.

So she was supposed to be in gym class. Jo hated gym. She was awkward—"clumsy," her mother said—and always the last chosen when teams were picked. And then she had to endure the junior-high locker room, where the other girls had made fun of her underdeveloped figure.

"Maybe I'll stay here until the end of the day," Jo thought. It was cool and peaceful near the trees, and Jo was much calmer than she had been earlier. Soon she'd be calm enough to remember everything.

Suddenly a woman rounded the end of the building. "Hey, what are you doing here?" she called. Jo froze in panic and felt darkness descend once again. Another personality took over.

"I'm just on my way to class." Isis smiled at the teacher and rose gracefully to her feet. "My psych teacher kept me after class, and I stopped outside for some air. I'm going, I'm going."

Isis slipped back into the building before the teacher could protest. She hurried down the hall.

Isis was one of the personalities who had been active during Jo's six-month absence. She was the one responsible for the marijuana, and regretted losing it. She didn't worry that Larry would report her; he'd probably smoke it himself. Maybe she could find a way to get it back from him. But right now she hurried to her favorite class.

Isis walked confidently into the gym, knowing that Miss Maloney would not be upset by her tardiness. The teacher listened to Isis's explanation—"Mr. Dunlap gave me the old 'you-better-study-harder' routine"—while continuing to referee the class's basketball game.

Finally, she turned to Isis. "It's too late now for you to get into the game," she said. "Why don't you go into my office and wait for me?"

Isis lounged in the office and thought briefly about what had happened an hour earlier, when Jo had awoken from her six-month-long sleep. "The glass box," she murmured.

Sometimes Isis felt trapped inside, watching through a glass box, while her body did things beyond her control. Other times, like now, she could do what she wished.

What Isis wished was for the body to move gracefully. She was an asset to any team when the students divided up in gym class, but the team captains never knew what to expect when they chose Jo Casey for their side. Sometimes she was a star player; other times she tripped over her own feet. Isis felt bad when that happened, but it couldn't be helped.

When trapped in the glass box, Isis could only watch her body in dismay while it stumbled, muscles so tight that the body tripped itself. But when she was out, she made up for it. Isis loved ballet dancing and was now working to develop the complex control and skills needed for gymnastics competition. With Miss Maloney's private coaching, she hoped to make the gymkhana team in the spring.

Some of the students said that Isis was psychic. It was true that she was pretty good at guessing what other people had on their minds, and sometimes she could anticipate what people were about to do or say. Isis herself consulted mystical literature and decided that she must be some sort of roving spirit. She figured that her "glass-box" periods proved that her powers were limited and that she was a visitor within this body, not an owner.

Nevertheless, Isis enjoyed her visit, amused that so wise a spirit would find herself in the body of a gangly high-school girl. She wrote melodic poetry that pleased the English teachers, and she had some admirers among the students as well. Some of her classmates were a little afraid of her, but that was fine with Isis. She didn't want many people close to her, choosing instead to maintain a spiritual distance.

Miss Maloney entered the office as the students rushed to shower and dress before the final bell. "Well, kid, I don't have much to clear away here, so we can leave as soon as the bell rings," she said.

Isis was pleased that Miss Maloney now took it for granted that they'd be driving home together. "Ready when you are," she said.

When Nancy and Ray separated, Jo and her mother moved into the apartment building in which Miss Maloney lived. The teacher provided rides to and from school and seemed to enjoy the company of at least this one personality. And Isis loved being with Miss Maloney.

She liked watching the teacher drive. When Miss Maloney was busy maneuvering her little sports car through the traffic, Isis could study her with frank interest. She knew, with nothing said, that Miss Maloney was a lesbian. Isis knew she too was attracted to women rather than men, and longed to talk to Miss Maloney about her desires. But she couldn't. Isis didn't want just any woman; she wanted Miss Maloney. And she could tell from the way Miss Maloney sometimes looked at her that the attraction was mutual.

The next morning, Jo dressed quickly for school and then looked carefully around the apartment. She was still trying to retrieve six months of missing memories and felt even now that she was floating precariously in consciousness. Current reality seemed a jumble, but it was less frightening to wonder what had happened to last summer than to worry about what had happened to last night. She scolded herself. "I've been daydreaming again," she said, "and this has got to stop." Jo noted the changes in the apartment. Plants were taller; some furniture had been moved. She shook her head in disgust and frustration.

At least her bad habit of daydreaming had taught her to be observant and cagey at catching up on lost time. She had learned how to ask leading questions that would yield clues.

Jo stood at the window and marveled at how the seasons had changed in her absence. She was glad that she hadn't daydreamed her way through fall.

Nancy appeared behind her. "Oh, Joan Frances, what are you doing in jeans? You've been dressing so nicely since you started high school."

Jo ignored the remark. She didn't care how she looked. She had more important things to figure out. First, her parents. "Do you think Dad's going to come by for a visit soon?" she asked in a forcedly casual tone.

Her mother jumped at the suggestion. "Do you need to talk to your father? Why don't you call him at work and ask him to come see you?"

"N-no," Jo said nervously. Obviously her mother was still pursuing her father. "It's nothing important," Jo said. "I just wondered."

Nancy grabbed the phone. "You seem upset," she said as she dialed. "If you are upset, we better call your father."

Jo waited. She was glad for the chance to talk to her father but wished that she could call him sometime when her mother wasn't around.

"Your kid needs to talk to you," Nancy said, and handed Jo the phone.

"Hello, Dad?" Jo said.

"Yes, pixie, what is it?" Her father sounded concerned. She could hear factory machinery in the background.

"It's nothing. . . . I . . . Well, how are you?"

"Come on, hurry up, I'm at work," Ray said.

Jo wished she could sink through the floor. He was mad and wouldn't want to see her now. She lost her grip on consciousness.

At once, Rusty, the adolescent male personality, took over. "Hey, Dad," he said in a cheerful tone, "when am I gonna see you? Can we go to Norfolk this weekend?"

"Now, that's more like it," Ray said, pleased at the change in his daughter's demeanor.

"Tell him you're having trouble at school," Nancy coached, and Rusty, who hated having this woman breathing down his back, slipped inside.

Joan Frances looked up with a conspiratorial smile. She didn't understand what her mother saw in that jerk, but it was clear that Nancy wanted Ray talked into coming over to the apartment.

"Maybe you could come over tonight and help me with my math," Joan Frances said into the phone. "I'm having lots of trouble, and Mom says that she'll cook dinner."

Nancy nodded approvingly. The kid had it in her after all. Nancy was ready for a reconciliation with Ray. Two years ago, she had had a lover and a new group of friends. But her affair was long over. Nancy was lonely and tired of shouldering all the responsibility for their younger daughter.

In the months that followed Jo's sudden awakening in high school, various personalities were active, often splitting up single days among them. Joan Frances concocted schemes with her mother to help win Ray back; Rusty enjoyed the time he was allowed to spend with Ray and was hurt when his father said, "You can't live with me because you belong with your mother." Rusty refused to acknowledge that he had a mother, and he hated living with Nancy. Isis's crush on Miss Maloney continued and Jo found a rare and trusted friend in Mr. Dunlap.

Soon Jo was keeping the consciousness enough each school day so that she had had continuous memory of five of her high-school classes. Mrs. Adams, Jo's journalism teacher, encouraged her to write for the high-school newspaper. She even made a friend: Brian O'Neil, a year ahead of her in school, was very bright, and liked that the other students thought he was strange. Jo teamed up with him and found herself part of the school's "hippie" crowd.

She had trouble with geometry, but she sat in the back of the room, next to Sam, a friend of Brian's. Miss Hernandez, the geometry teacher, was nice to Jo even though she didn't make very good grades.

Jo hated Spanish. There was no way that she could handle Spanish II after forgetting Spanish I. Mr. Walker made no secret of his dislike for Jo, and ridiculed her. The other students seemed to enjoy having a scapegoat.

Jo had no memory of what happened in gym, and for that she was grateful. She was sure that she made a worse fool of herself in gym than she did in Spanish class.

Despite her fear of Spanish and gym class, she found a sense of stability in school. Mr. Dunlap's office turned out to be a quiet and comfortable place for her. She went there as soon as she arrived at school each day.

Occasionally there were other students in the office, and often Mr. Dunlap didn't have time to talk, but that didn't bother Jo. She would study, or read, or work on a homework assignment. Just being near Mr. Dunlap made her feel a little less lonely.

Jo remained upset that her father wouldn't give her his home phone number—"I know that your mother will get it out of you," he said, "and I don't want her bothering me"—but she had Mr. Dunlap's number for consolation.

Even if Jo couldn't reach her father when she wanted, she could call Mr. Dunlap in the evenings or on the weekends. He trusted her to keep his phone number a secret. Mr. Dunlap offered advice and made her feel better just by listening. Although Jo didn't talk openly with him about how she lost time, his long explanations and careful reiteration of events at school made her think that he somehow knew when she was lacking important memories.

Isis got private gymnastics coaching from Miss Maloney a few afternoons each week and stopped by her apartment when she could find an excuse. Often she knocked on Miss Maloney's door to offer her a sample of the goodies that Nancy baked when Ray came for a visit.

One day in December, Miss Maloney told Isis to start taking the bus and to stop coming to her apartment. She had a roommate now, who didn't like having Isis around. Isis knew she was jealous but felt that she could handle Miss Maloney's relationship if given the chance. She sometimes watched from her apartment window and saw the two of them link arms in the parking lot or touch intimately with a subtle sleight of hand.

Isis kept a frustrated and lonely silence and waited to find the words that would reassure the teacher. Then she wouldn't be excluded. But for now she'd give Miss Maloney some room and stay stoned to escape from her feelings of rejection. Brian, Sam, drugs, and music provided good distractions.

One night late in January, Isis sat on the rug in a candlelit room at Sam's house, smoking hash. She passed the pipe to Brian, who was sitting next to her, and ignored the other people in the room. The company hardly mattered: the music was too loud for any conversation.

The hard rock beat enveloped her and folded her into her favorite fantasy of Miss Maloney touching and kissing her. She lay back on the rug, feeling aroused. Suddenly she realized that this wasn't pure fantasy. Brian was lying on top of her, kissing her and holding her down.

"No!" she yelled, pushing Brian aside and lurching out of the room. "Bad trip," someone said as she passed.

She jerked out into the night, wanting to run from this body, this dirty body. She swore no man would do that to her again. She had to be free of it.

Isis got home and used a razor blade to etch a symbol of death into her left breast. She lit candles and incense. She chanted softly, willing total and final separation from this body. Hoping that her magic would work quickly, Isis drifted off to sleep.

The next morning, before classes, Isis worked out in the gym. She was furious to find that she hadn't died during the night. "This is Miss Maloney's fault," she decided. She'd show her.

Isis worked feverishly on the bars with the bare wooden floor beneath her. She knew that it was against the rules to use the equipment without mats, but she didn't care. When Miss Maloney appeared around the corner, Isis swung in preparation for her dismount, more frenzied than before. The teacher had to pay attention to her now.

Miss Maloney turned and walked into her office. Her rejection was too much. Isis threw herself in a swan dive from the top bar to the floor.

Josie found herself, as she had at other moments in her life, being hurled through the air. She accepted the panic as her own and enjoyed the anticipation of the black relief of impact.

Jo sat up, dizzily aware that her gym teacher was calling her name. "I'm OK," she said automatically.

Jo looked around her at the gym and then down at the leotard and tights she wore. What was she doing? Jo staggered slightly as she wandered into the locker room to find her clothes.

"Yes, I'm sure I'm OK," she said to Miss Maloney, who had followed her. Jo sat silently on the bench until the teacher finally left.

Jo felt odd that day—a little disoriented and uncoordinated. Walking, standing, even moving her arms seemed like an effort that required great concentration. She had a horrible headache.

DIARY *July 1, 1982*

I have begun to arrive at a more complete picture of Jo Casey's adolescence. It is clear that she was struggling with a number of handicaps, not the least of which was her well-established multiplicity. It is obvious that the malady was, by then, a two-edged sword, both preserving capabilities and providing a survival mechanism. But it created additional problems as well. The pathological home situation became worse as each parent demanded that the child serve as confidante.

Nancy would tell her daughter, "Your father just comes around when he wants to get laid," and Joan Frances wondered why her mother would bother with such a man.

Ray told his daughter, "Every time I look at your mother, I think of her screwing that pig last year," and Jo couldn't understand why, then, he spent the night.

Finally, the group looked elsewhere for attention and love. They turned to the gym and psychology teachers, or stopped their aching need with drugs.

So far, Renee is enjoying the detective work without thinking of implications for herself. Since she has no sense of having rights of her own, Renee doesn't yet conceive of her own birth as evidence of abuse. I have a hunch that she is in for some difficult times when she does begin to value herself. At present, the approaching vacation helps her postpone the inevitable.

This is actually a good time for a break. The work has been taxing for me, and I don't want Renee to get in much deeper just yet. The weeks apart will help us both to gather some strength. Since Renee will spend part of this vacation in Richmond, she is hoping to find evidence from the school and hospital to corroborate what reportedly happened during the time we are piecing together.

. . .

17

August 10, 1982

Jo, the other personalities, and I have resumed our sessions after a vacation that stretched into five weeks. After an initial "re-entry syndrome," the personalities are as comfortable with me as they were before the break. They seem calm. Aside from a few minutes spent cuddling Missy every session, everyone seems willing to let Renee and me continue piecing together the period of adolescence. Renee and I are looking closely at the months that preceded her evolution into a separate personality.

Renee did find time during her trip to Richmond to do some research. It was predictably difficult for her to pry records loose from the school, hospitals, and doctors, but she is smug that her tenacity paid off. She produced evidence that corroborated an emergency-room visit for head injuries that fit with Missy's story that, as a preschooler, "That girl Josie got hit against the wall," and has retrieved records concerning a hospitalization in adolescence.

Renee triumphantly displayed her "proof" of the early-childhood incident. I think that Renee needed this evidence far more than I, but since I literally chortled over the records from her adolescent experience, I empathize with her feeling of validation.

I've generally ignored clinicians who deny the existence of MPD or who suggest that the manifestations appear to meet some pathological need on the part of the clinician. But, like Renee with the early hospital records, I feel that I now have proof that I can show anybody who would dare to doubt. Renee brought separate reports from a neurologist and a psychologist that confirm to me that Jo would have been readily diagnosable as a multiple when she was in high school if only her physicians had had an understanding of MPD and thus asked the right questions.

I would be tempted at this point to overcongratulate myself for my perspicacity if I were not so well aware that I came to my information by a different route. Jo trusted me as she had no other clinician. When I met her, she was free of her parents, and she was ready for diagnosis and treatment. I have also become painfully aware that MPD is pretty much dismissed by many in the medical community.

. . .

"Let's pick up after Isis threw herself from the bars," Lynn said.

About a week after Jo's fall, Nancy noticed that there was something peculiar about her daughter. She couldn't quite put her finger on the problem, but there appeared to be a new tension in the teenager's movement. When Jo walked, she worked to keep herself from staggering. Nancy, watching her daughter butter a piece of bread, noticed that the girl held the knife as if it were heavy and hard to control.

"Joan Frances, what's wrong with you?" Nancy asked. Certain that her mother would be angry if she was sick, Joan Frances answered, "Nothing. I'm fine."

"Well, then," Nancy pursued, "why are you having so much trouble with that knife?"

Joan Frances glanced down at her hands. They looked strange to her, like hands that belonged to a puppet on a string; she felt as though she were controlling them from a great distance. "I don't know," Joan Frances finally said.

"I want you to stand up," Nancy said, "and put your feet together."

Joan Frances rose and struggled to get her balance. She found that she had to hold on to the wall or the counter for support.

"Are you feeling OK?" Nancy asked. This time, Joan Frances considered the question. "I do have a headache." The constant pounding behind her right temple had become so much a part of her that she hadn't thought to mention it before. "I think you should stay home from school today," Nancy said. "I want you to come to the office this afternoon and see Dr. Roger."

Joan Frances agreed, as usual, to do as her mother asked, but it was Jo who was pleased to have the day off. She was happy alone in the apartment. She could read, or simply sit and think, without Nancy's demanding that she *do* something. At the end of the day, Jo walked unsteadily to the clinic where her mother worked.

Roger Schuler, Jo's doctor and Nancy's boss, asked Jo to do a number of simple things that Jo found surprisingly difficult.

"Follow this light with your eyes," the internist said. Jo discovered that the pain in her head prevented her eyes from moving from side to side.

"Walk a straight line."

Jo stood up and fell against the wall. "I'm not drunk," she joked, but she was upset that she couldn't keep her balance.

Back in the examining room, Dr. Roger tested Jo's reflexes. Her right leg jumped at his little hammer; the left leg barely moved. "Wait here," he said. "I'm going to talk with your mother."

Jo sat on the table and leaned back against the wall. Her head now pounded in rhythm with her heart. Jo's concern about her lack of coordination and equilibrium was nothing compared with her certainty that her mother would be furious with her. Jo figured that Dr. Schuler was at this very moment telling her mother that she was pretending to be sick. There would be hell to pay when she got home. "I'll tell her I'm sorry and promise never to do it again," Jo decided.

The doctor stated the facts but tried to hide from Nancy his own anxiety over how serious Jo's problem might be. "I want to admit her," he said. "Something's going on here, but I'm not sure what. I think she needs a complete neurological checkup."

Jo had her first of three week-long hospitalizations. After neurologists, neurosurgeons, ear, nose, and throat specialists, and her internist puzzled over the symptoms and the test results and reached no conclusion, she was sent home with instructions to her parents to "watch and wait."

Jo's gait quickly became more unsteady. Soon she could barely walk without support. She fell too often to return to school, but the Board of Education provided her with a tutor who came to the hospital or the apartment. This tutor gave Jo enough background in math so that she became able for the first time to appreciate the beauty and logic of geometry and algebra.

Jo eventually grew less troubled by her loss of equilibrium. The hospitalizations protected her from having to deal with the aspects of her parents' separation that she least liked. When home, Jo would sometimes lie awake for hours thinking of her mother in the next bedroom. She wasn't comfortable knowing that Nancy lay there bitter and alone, but she also wasn't comfortable when her father spent the night. If Ray wouldn't forgive Nancy for having an affair, what was he doing sleeping with her? When Jo was in the hospital, she didn't have to know whether her mother was alone, or sharing her bed with Ray or with someone else. Jo relished being far away from it all.

The doctors remained puzzled by Jo's illness. The first neurologist consulted on the case wrote that he was suspicious of her symptoms. Her skull X-rays, EEG, and spinal tap were all negative. The sudden changes in personality and periods of blankness that Nancy described, combined with Jo's indifference to her physical problems, led him to write that there might be a factor of hysteria in the illness.

The psychologist who examined Jo on the neurologist's referral found her to be a "hysterical, depressed, repressed child" who felt the burden of her parents' problems. Although the psychologist reported that he could not definitely rule out a neurological problem, he recommended that Jo enter psychotherapy to provide support for her and to help her resolve her feelings about her parents. This suggestion was ignored.

A consulting neurosurgeon suspected that Jo might have a brain tumor or allergic encephalitis. Jo was readmitted to the hospital, and came close to undergoing brain surgery in April, after she tried to return to school and was found "wandering through the halls in a confused and aimless way." Nancy and Ray refused to consent to surgery. The neurosurgeon could produce no physical evidence that Jo had an operable brain lesion.

In late May, the ataxia and headaches lessened and then stopped. Jo regretted that she had to return to school for the final two weeks of the semester, but was comforted by the thought that she'd be able to see Mr. Dunlap without having her mother around.

While Jo was ill, Larry Dunlap had visited her at the hospital and at home, but he seemed to be visiting Nancy as well. Jo was worried about the relationship that might develop between her mother and Larry.

Was he telling Nancy everything that Jo had told him? Was her mother sleeping with Larry? Would Nancy try to dominate the time Jo had with Larry the way she did the time she had with her father? Back at school, Jo knew she wouldn't have to compete with her mother for Larry's attention. She resumed her early-morning visits to Larry's office.

Jo also began to spend some time outside of class with Carla Hernandez, her geometry teacher. Miss Hernandez had taken a special interest in Jo while she was sick and had occasionally stopped by the apartment or the hospital after school. Now Jo went to Miss Hernandez's room at the end of each day. Sometimes she helped the teacher; other times she simply sat and talked with this woman who seemed to enjoy her company.

Miss Hernandez was young, no more than five or six years older than Jo, and she treated her the way Jo wished her big sister would. On weekends, Miss Hernandez sometimes invited Jo to accompany her on errands around town. Unlike Jo's big sister, Carol, Carla Hernandez never ridiculed the way Jo looked or spoke.

On the last day of school, Jo helped Miss Hernandez record the final grades for the term. She was fairly sure that Miss Hernandez would say something about making plans to get together over the summer.

"I've really enjoyed our time together," Miss Hernandez said, and Jo waited happily for her to start talking about how they would arrange to get together over the summer. Then the teacher broke the news to Jo that she wouldn't be returning to Kennedy High School the following year. Miss Hernandez was getting married in a few weeks and moving to Mexico with her new husband.

Jo was too hurt even to ask if she could stay in touch.

Nancy and Ray also had an announcement at the end of the school year. They had decided to resume their marriage.

Jo felt more guilty than pleased when her father took her aside and said, "Honey, I want you to be happy. I guess you just can't make it without your old man around." Jo had long been confused about her mysterious illness that no one would discuss. Now she understood that it was forcing her father to do the one thing he'd sworn he'd never do. Affair or no affair, Ray was taking Nancy back. Jo was certain that the reconciliation was being staged in her behalf.

Jo wondered what would happen to her relationship with Larry Dunlap after her parents got back together. Even though she would have access to her father again, Jo still cared for the man who had supported her when Ray hadn't been around. She didn't want to lose Larry just because her father was back.

A few weeks before Father's Day, Jo wrote Larry a long letter telling him how like a father he had become to her. Jo was terrified of expressing her feelings so openly, but she also didn't want Larry to walk out of her life the way Miss Hernandez had. She had to let him know how strongly she felt, even if her expression of caring prompted rejection.

Jo didn't dare call Larry after she sent the letter. She calculated when he would receive it and considered the various responses he might have to it.

Days and then a week passed with no call from Larry. The day before Father's Day, Jo received a telegram—her first ever. She opened it with trembling hands under her mother's glare and read, "Fear not that I will ever abandon you. Love, Larry."

"Do you know how hurt your father would be if he heard about this?" Nancy shouted.

Jo was so touched by Larry's message that she matched her mother's anger with uncharacteristic fury of her own. "So don't tell him about it," she shot back.

She hid the telegram so that her mother couldn't find and destroy it.

Two days later, Nancy walked in the door from work, poured herself a drink, and called to her daughter. Jo could tell from the carefully controlled tone of her mother's voice that she was in big trouble.

"I went to visit somebody in the hospital today," Nancy started, and Jo listened impassively as her mother talked sarcastically about seeing Jo's "special friend and father figure, Larry," on the psychiatric ward.

"Larry pleaded with me not to tell you," Nancy continued, "but he wanted me to find a way to keep you from feeling abandoned if he didn't answer your phone calls or letters right away."

She snickered. "It turns out that this isn't the first time he's had to be locked up for a while. I thought you should know what kind of father figures you choose for yourself. I always knew that man was a little strange." Nancy laughed, conveniently forgetting that he had been a friend of hers too. "You are never to see or talk to him again."

At that, Jo reacted. "I won't be able to avoid seeing him next year at school," she said.

"Nope, he won't be returning to school," Nancy said. "I talked to the principal today. It turns out that there were a lot of things about Larry the school didn't know when they hired him. They've decided that it's not such a great idea for him to be around young girls."

Jo began to call Larry's home phone number every day. Her mother had lied to her before, and surely she was lying this time too. The phone rang unanswered for two weeks. Then one day a woman answered.

"I'm one of Mr. Dunlap's students," Jo said. "May I speak to him, please?" There was a pause, and the woman said with a strong accent, "I'm Larry's sister. He's sleeping now and can't be disturbed."

Jo hung up. The next afternoon, she called again and Larry answered. "Larry! Mr. Dunlap, it's me," Jo said. She was so relieved to hear his voice that she began to cry.

"Jo?" Larry's voice sounded groggy, distant.

"Larry, are you OK?" Jo asked.

"Yes, I'm fine," Larry said, "I took a little vacation, a little vacation, that's all." Larry was beginning to sound more like himself. "Did you miss me?" he asked.

"Oh, Larry," Jo said, "I was so worried about you."

Now Jo felt more certain that her mother had lied about seeing Larry on the psychiatric ward. He didn't sound crazy.

"Larry, I've got to see you," Jo said.

He said nothing. Jo clutched the phone tightly, wondering if perhaps her mother had gotten to him first. Maybe Nancy had told Larry that Jo was forbidden to see him.

"Do you think you can get over here, over to my apartment, without your mother knowing about it?" he asked. Jo relaxed and felt a conspiratorial companionship. She and her father had deceived her mother lots of times. Larry's suggestion only made him seem more fatherly to her.

"Yes," Jo said. She listened carefully as he gave her directions. "I'll be there as soon as I can."

Larry lived in an apartment complex at the edge of a shopping mall. Before Jo left the house, she called her mother at work to say that she was going shopping with some friends. Nancy was delighted that Jo was finally getting out with some girls her own age and arranged to pick Jo up at the mall after work.

Jo stepped out into the July heat and began walking the five miles to Larry's apartment. "This is going to take forever," Jo muttered as she watched the cars whiz by her. She turned and stuck out her thumb and muttered, "Oh, why not?" Hitchhiking might be risky, but she didn't care. The only thing that mattered was getting to Larry.

The second car stopped. "A businessman," Jo guessed, and hopped in the car. The shopping center turned out to be on his way, and as the man drove, he lectured Jo on the dangers of hitchhiking. Jo stared out the window, grunted politely at the man's warnings, and rejoiced that the idea had occurred to her.

Jo arrived at Larry's apartment and wiped her sweaty palms on her jeans before she knocked on the door. It was quiet for a moment; then the door opened and Larry peered out at her.

He looked different, sleepy and pale, wearing jeans and a tee shirt. Jo had only seen him dressed in his school outfit of chinos, sports jacket, and tie. But it was Larry's expression that was most disturbing. He looked at her quizzically, as though he couldn't quite place her.

"Larry, it's me," Jo said. Larry began to smile broadly as though at some private joke. He motioned her in. "My mother thinks I'm shopping," Jo said as she entered the apartment. "She's picking me up at the shopping center at six."

"How about a drink?" Larry said. "Scotch? How about Scotch?"

Jo shrugged. She really didn't care much for alcohol, but she sometimes had a glass of beer or wine with her parents, so she guessed it was OK to have a drink with Larry.

"How are you?" Larry asked. "You're out of the hospital, right? And you're well now?"

Jo was puzzled. Of course Larry knew she was out of the hospital. He had seen her every day at school during the last two weeks of the term. She hadn't even written her Father's Day letter to him until after the school year had ended. But she was tolerant of Larry's lapse of memory. He had, after all, been tolerant of hers.

Jo sat on the couch and took a sip of the drink. She shuddered at the bitter taste. Larry sat in a chair across the room, watching her expectantly.

"Oh, Larry, I've missed you. I was so worried. My mother said . . . I thought you had gone away forever." Jo's voice broke. "Things are so bad at home, and I couldn't find you. . . ." Larry was beside her in an instant.

"Oh, my poor baby," Larry said, holding her against him and rocking her as she sobbed. "I'm so sorry you were worried. I'll never do that again, I promise." He offered her the glass. "Here, drink more of this," he urged.

Jo sipped more of the drink and then told him about her confusion over her parents' reconciliation.

She drank until the glass was empty.

"Feel better now?" Larry asked gently.

"No," Jo said, "I feel awful." Maybe it was the drink, maybe the heat, maybe it was the weeping and the release of pent-up anxiety, but Jo felt dizzy and queasy.

"Come with me," Larry said, taking her hand. "You need to lie down for a while." Jo allowed Larry to lead her into his bedroom and let him stretch her out on the rumpled sheets. He sat down on the bed next to her. "Listen to my voice," Larry said gently, "and you'll feel better."

Jo closed her eyes. She felt comfortable with Larry, and particularly peaceful when he talked to her in quiet, rhythmic tones. "Relax, relax, you need to relax," he said. "Think of the sea. You've told me how much you love the sea. Think of being at the sea."

Larry was right. As he described a gorgeous summer's day at the beach, she felt calmer.

He paused and then talked soothingly again, in time with her breathing. "Think of the ocean, the seagulls, the sand."

Jo imagined that she was really there. She was at the ocean, smelling the salt spray; she felt it in her hair.

She was vaguely aware that someone was taking off her shirt. That was OK. You don't need a lot of clothes at the ocean. You have to take off your jeans to go swimming. Jo was all naked now. It was nice. Swimming in the ocean nude would be good.

"You feel safe," Larry said.

"Safe," Jo repeated, and felt secure in a way that she had never been. Jo loved being at the seaside like this with Larry. She felt good, so indescribably good.

Suddenly Jo was back in Larry's bedroom. Larry! He was naked and on top of her. "No!" she screamed, drowning in the spray of her own shattered self.

Minutes later, I opened my eyes for the first time. The man lying next to me was sated now, but he watched me anxiously.

"Hi," I said softly, smiling at him so that he'd know everything was OK.

"You're such a sweet thing," he murmured, and nestled me to his chest.

"So this is Jo's Larry," I thought. "He seems so gentle and kind. No wonder she loves him."

I lay there, enjoying the calm tenderness but feeling a wonderful tingling in every nerve. I felt vibrant and so very alive.

I was new. My lack of a past gave me a sense of anticipation. I had nothing to fear. I'd do just fine. I already knew the most important thing—how to make a man happy—and felt lovable in every inch of me.

"Jo?"

I looked up at Larry. His smile was sweet and innocent. He looked more like a mischievous little boy than like a grown man. "You better get dressed now," he said. "Your mother is picking you up at the mall."

I got out of bed and stretched up tall, pulling each muscle taut. I spun a quick pirouette in sheer joy; it felt so good to be me.

"My God, you are beautiful," Larry said in wonder.

"Am I?" I asked, and reached for my jeans.

I walked from Larry's apartment across the wide parking lot toward the stores. I felt the humidity, enjoyed the heat shimmering off the asphalt. I took long strides and thought, "I'm tall and thin. I like that. I couldn't stand it if I were short and fat."

I stepped inside a cool department store and looked out at the parking lot. I knew Jo's mother would be picking me up soon and that I had to watch for her car. I couldn't visualize it, but trusted that I would recognize it when it arrived.

While I waited, I exchanged glances with the people going in and out of the store. A lot of them looked back at me appreciatively, especially the men. "Larry was right," I thought. "I am beautiful."

I loosened the braid that Jo wore and shook my hair free around my shoulders. I admired my reflection in the store's window. I wanted to hug my new self and the whole world. This was going to be fun. Soon Nancy arrived, and I raced out to meet her. Nancy mistakenly thought that I was her daughter. But she liked me better than the daughter she had known before. I could make people happy.

From that day on, I was determined to block out all the other personalities, but quickly learned I didn't have the power. So I worked to keep track of what the others did when they were out, and I enjoyed myself when I had control. I was never tired, sad, or depressed. I was happy and made other people happy as well.

Jo called Larry a week after my birth. She had no memory of what had happened that afternoon after she had lain down on the bed. Jo worried about the time she had forgotten. She hoped that she hadn't done something to make Larry angry. She dialed his number and got a recording. The phone had been disconnected. She called the operator and was told that there was no new listing for Larry Dunlap.

Larry had walked out of her life.

*

After piecing together the puzzle, I was impressed by all that Lynn and I had learned, but she still had more questions.

"Renee, how did you come equipped with total knowledge about the current life and no knowledge about what had happened before your birth?"

"I guess I can't explain *how* I had the information I needed, but I think I can tell you *why* I had it and why I lacked information about what happened before my birth."

Lynn nodded. I had never actually analyzed this phenomenon, and now I struggled for the words.

"The way I see it, I was created to make the group successful in dealing with other people. I wouldn't have done a very good job at that if I'd known that people had hurt the group in the past. I was even better than the others were at dealing with Nancy and Ray, because they weren't *my* parents. My ancestors were Jo and the other personalities. I didn't feel a stake in a relationship with Nancy and Ray, so I didn't get bogged down in their problems. I didn't expect anything from them. I couldn't be disappointed."

Lynn considered all of this and then said, "But, Renee, after your birth, the group found that it needed more than an ability to please people."

"That's right," I answered, delighted that Lynn and I were figuring things out together. "That's why there were personalities created after me. Kendra was created for self-protection after I found out that my black boyfriend, Eugene, didn't really care about me. He won a hundred-dollar bet from his brother by having a white girlfriend to take to his fraternity dance and family picnic. Cassandra and Doug were created when I worked at the state legislature and got scared because I couldn't make everyone happy. Charlene and Honey were created because I could never figure out how to be a good wife to Keith."

I stopped my litany and looked at Lynn in surprise. "All of that's changed now," I said excitedly. "I'm much more than a people-pleaser personality. I'm doing a great job teaching high school. I'm getting along well with Steve. And it doesn't seem to matter that my decisions and actions don't always make everyone happy."

"That's right," Lynn affirmed. "All of the major existing personalities—you and Jo in particular—are growing and changing and becoming better able to handle your problems. Not only is there no reason to create new personalities, but there is less need for the minor or 'special-purpose' personalities to come out."

I cut her off. "Lynn, if you're about to conclude that Jo and I will end up being one happy person together, forget it. Even if Jo is getting better, she's still a twit. I'm not going to integrate with her."

"Oh, Renee, you know that I think integration is secondary to having all the personalities inside feel better about themselves," Lynn said.

I nodded. This had been Lynn's response to my fears about integration for some time. I just needed to hear that she hadn't changed her mind.

Lynn looked thoughtful. "Renee, what would you do if you found out that one of your colleagues took a student to bed?"

"I'd kill him," I said reflexively. I loved the kids I taught. I loved them like a mother tiger, protectively and ferociously.

"Why would you react so violently?" Lynn asked.

"Kids are special people," I explained with irritation. "No adult should take advantage of their vulnerability."

"So what does that tell you about Jo and Larry?" she asked.

"Oh."

I was struck by the significance of what Lynn was implying. "Even if Larry's actions did result in my birth," I said slowly, "what he did to Jo was horrible. Even if he was crazy, he shouldn't have violated her trust in him. What you're trying to show me is that it's because of experiences like this that Jo is so screwed up and afraid of people."

Lynn beamed and gave me a quick hug as I left her office. I made my way home, mulling over what I had only just discovered about myself.

My new perspective changed the way I felt about the other personalities. I began to think of them as analogous to my more difficult or disturbed students. I didn't demand proof of abuse from the troubled teenagers I saw at school, nor did I tell them to shape up. I loved them for who they were and trusted that they would grow when they felt safe in doing so. Like these scared, impressionable kids who often weren't easy to love, my internal others were acting out their pain and despair. For the first time, I felt tolerance and compassion for them.

18

I am continually struck by the essential contradiction in Jo Casey. She is both terribly fragmented and tremendously functional. When I first heard the Kendra personality (who rescues Renee when she gets in over her head) say, "We can do anything!," I considered it bravado and exaggeration. Now I see that, in comparison with most people, Kendra is right. The system of personalities can, by most criteria, do anything they attempt to do, as long as no one personality is expected to carry on for an extended period.

Each of the personalities seems to have unique talents or capacities. One personality does well in math, another in languages, another in sciences, yet another in humanities. One personality writes perceptive prose, another loves the rigid structure of logic, another is respected by colleagues for her leadership skills. The personalities seem to think uniquely and independently as well. When I present an idea to the Jo personality, she is either ten steps ahead of me in analyzing the implications or busily attacking my faulty assumptions. Jo objectifies any issue presented. Renee, on the other hand, seems bored by any topic except relationships among people and is unable to make the kinds of connections that Jo makes effortlessly. Neither style seems unduly pathological. In fact, each presents a valid method of dealing with life, and each has the potential for benefiting the system as a whole.

The system's response of creating new personalities when needed is pathological. When Renee married Keith, for example, she couldn't cope with what she felt was expected of her. None of the major personalities at the time—quiet, analytic Jo; anxious Joan Frances; or promiscuous, people-pleasing Renee—knew how to translate their essential strengths into the role of "Keith's wife."

Joan Frances, the most likely to fulfill that role, was paralyzed by the mixed messages her mother had provided about marriage. Nancy claimed to despise Ray but seemed unable to function without him. Charlene, a caricature personality of Nancy's most domestic qualities, was created. Charlene cooked, cleaned, and made her home lovely in a feverish effort to "be a good wife." The Honey personality, also modeled after Nancy, was depressed and despondent. Honey felt certain that, no matter what she did, her husband would not be pleased.

Soon after, Renee's interview abilities landed her a coveted student internship with the state legislature and later a paid position in press relations. Once on the job, however, Renee was overwhelmed. She couldn't find a way to please everybody.

Cassandra was created, modeled on a female legislative aide. Cassandra was productive and professional, cordial and competent, without Renee's anxious need to please. Doug, a male personality modeled on a male campaign coordinator, was created along with Cassandra. Doug tells me that Cassandra did OK on her own, but that he was needed because "this is a man's world." Aside from learning how to play golf, it's not clear what Doug did to "help those girls out."

Capable as the personalities might be, each of them was, until recently, stuck within rigid boundaries. Before beginning therapy with me, they seemed unable to profit from past experiences. I've seen much growth in this regard—in the Renee personality in particular. However, Renee's motivation to excel, like the motivations of the other personalities, seems compulsive rather than fulfilling.

Jo still emphasizes intellect and rationality in a valiant attempt to protect her raw, tender, and infantile emotions. She avoids people in order to avoid feeling, yet she suffers constantly.

Renee's relationships, so easily initiated and full of promise, are shallow and essentially unsatisfying. She often runs at the first sign of trouble, and therefore manages long-term involvements only with those people who are, for one reason or another, incapable of intimacy.

. . .

September 1982 marked the start of my second year teaching high school and my second year of living with Steve.

When I'd moved in with Steve, I'd done so partly because no more attractive option had presented itself. Steve assumed we'd marry someday, but I still doubted it. Even though Steve wouldn't admit it, I knew he had emotional problems as serious as my own. His wife, Sara, had been dead for years, but he still actively grieved. The townhouse I shared with Steve—the townhouse where he and Sara had spent so many happy years—was still filled with his wife's personal possessions. My bottle of shampoo sat in the shower next to hers.

Steve denied that either he or I was experiencing any problems.

More than one of the personalities tried to persuade Steve that the diagnosis of Multiple Personality Disorder was accurate, but he remained skeptical.

When the Jo personality first told him of the diagnosis, he called MPD "clinical bullshit." Then, seeing Jo's stricken look, he softened and showed her how the possibility of many personalities in a single body was philosophically untenable. MPD did not fit into Steve's system of beliefs, and therefore it did not exist.

Later, after Dr. Wilbur confirmed the diagnosis, I tried to convince him. Steve said that Dr. Wilbur spent her whole life trying to find people she could call multiple. I couldn't argue with that. But when Steve implied that Lynn had arrived at the diagnosis for the same reason, I knew it was time that Steve met Lynn.

Steve listened politely as Lynn talked about the various personalities. He agreed that I was "moody," but he flatly refused when Lynn suggested that he read *Sybil.* He continued to ignore manifestations of the disorder that compromised his view of reality.

Despite his denial, Steve lived with many personalities. If he was angry with me, I lost time. He would find himself face to face with Jo in the middle of an argument he had started with me. Jo would blink in confusion and abjectly apologize for whatever she had done wrong this time. Steve came to recognize the sudden blankness and reaction. His anger would subside and he would look at Jo and say, "You don't even know what I'm angry about, do you?"

Most of Steve's arguments with me ended this way. He would sigh, then take Jo on his lap. Since Jo couldn't abide physical closeness, the five-year-old Missy personality would crawl up on Steve's lap and listen while this man told her that he loved her and that everything was OK. Resting her head comfortably on Steve's shoulder, Missy decided to believe him.

None of us forced Steve to acknowledge the discrepancies. He called us all Jo and supplied his own explanations for periodic memory losses. The group's feelings toward Steve were ambivalent. Missy loved him as a father; Jo hoped that one day he would love her as he had loved Sara; I considered him a convenient companion and good friend; and Joan Frances waited for her mother's assessment of the relationship.

But we all loved the house he bought in November 1982. Steve surprised me when he announced that he wanted to move from the townhouse. He said we needed our own home, a place that didn't hold reminders of the past.

I didn't know how or why he had come to this decision, but I rejoiced at the prospect of once again having a place that felt like mine.

When Keith and I separated and we sold the house we had shared, all of my things had been put in storage. There had been no room in Steve's townhouse for my books and furniture. Now we were moving into a large airy Tudor-style house that had room enough for everything.

No one in the group understood that Steve might find the move stressful.

One evening a few days after the furniture was delivered, Steve lost his patience while installing a large wall unit in the spare bedroom. I was frightened. The Jo personality found herself alone at the base of the stairs leading up to the second floor. She could hear Steve swearing from an upstairs room. She clutched the railing. Had she done something wrong?

"Would you like me to come up?" Jo asked.

"Not if you're going to put your soul on the line," Steve thundered.

This was too much for Jo. She grabbed her jacket and ran out into the night. She raced blindly through the strange neighborhood, confused about where she was and where she was going. She was amnestic for the time that I and other personalities had spent scouting the area.

Jo's most recent memory was of being in session with Lynn. "Lynn knows more about my life than I do," Jo thought, slowing down her panicky run. "Maybe she knows why Steve's mad at me."

Jo came to a main street, where she spied an all-night diner. She hurried in from the November chill and called Lynn.

Lynn didn't know what the problem with Steve was about, but she was concerned that Jo felt unable to go home. "Where are you?" Lynn asked. Jo identified the diner, and Lynn said she'd be right there.

Jo sat in a booth, sipping coffee and waiting for Lynn. She felt overwhelmed, drained by her emotions—terrified by Steve's anger and confused by Lynn's response. Jo certainly hadn't intended to disrupt Lynn's evening this way.

Lynn appeared dressed in jeans, boots, a flannel shirt, and a down vest. Jo always thought Lynn looked wonderful, but her beauty was breathtaking as she strode into the diner, her long ponytail flowing behind her shoulders. "She looks more like thirty than fifty," Jo thought appreciatively as Lynn sat down opposite her in the booth.

Lynn ordered coffee and said, "Somehow I'm not surprised that you found this place, Jo. Back when I had a houseful of kids and not an inch of privacy, I used to come here to hide. A cup of coffee and a few minutes of peace helped when I felt too stressed out to be a good mom. I haven't been in here for years, but it holds fond memories for me."

"What happened, Jo?" Lynn asked, after brushing aside Jo's apologies for disturbing her evening.

Jo sketched out the situation as best she could. "He yelled at me and then yelled again when I offered to help," Jo said. She didn't know what Steve had been doing upstairs; she had been too frightened to go up and find out.

Lynn sipped her coffee, then said, "You know, Jo, moving is a stressful time for any person, and Steve's burying a good deal of the past with this move. He was probably just upset about some task that was going badly and overreacted because of stress."

Jo, fingering her coffee cup, smiled ruefully. "You're saying that it's possible that Steve's anger was not my fault."

Lynn nodded. "You're not the only one in your group who finds anger difficult. Renee can't handle it either."

Jo let Lynn drive her back home. "I guess Renee and I aren't so different in some respects," she said. "We both have to learn to let other people be themselves."

Jo arrived home to find Steve anxious about her absence and apologetic for his outburst. Jo hugged him. "It's OK, Steve. I overreacted too." She felt an uncharacteristic connection; she felt empathy.

The group settled into the house and a comfortable routine with Steve.

Missy's rocking chair had its place in the bright sunroom. She could rock undisturbed and watch birds play in the trees and bushes outside the windows. It comforted her to know that her friend Lynn lived in the same community, only three miles away.

Jo loved the basement library with its four walls of floor-to-ceiling shelves and its musty smell. Her books, together with Steve's large science library, filled the room.

Rusty had silently helped Steve build and paint the shelves to hold the books. Rusty, who knew better than to identify himself to Steve, took pleasure and pride in working alongside a man.

Charlene spent hours preparing meals in the large modern kitchen she and Steve designed.

Joan Frances walked smugly through the elegant turn-of-the-century house, sure that her mother, if she ever came to visit, would be impressed by the etched glass.

I loved the space. Steve could work in his upstairs study, and I could putter about in another part of the house, feeling the security of his presence and the freedom of being able to work undisturbed.

Steve maintained a mild-mannered demeanor. His demands were few. He wanted me to be caring and involved in his life. That was easy. I was an expert at being what other people wanted. I had no central core of self to protect. As easily and quickly as a chameleon, I changed to meet the needs of anyone important to me.

Steve often flattered me by claiming to see capabilities in me that I didn't recognize. I thought I had found my niche in life as a high-school teacher and felt content. But Steve thought I had potential that went beyond my job.

"You have to do your Ph.D.," Steve said. "You have important things to say and to write."

When the Jo personality heard this, she swelled with pride. Jo wanted more than anything to spend her life as a scholar. Steve was serious when he told her that she should go to Harvard, where he and Sara had completed their doctoral work. "Maybe if I prove I'm smart enough to go to Harvard Steve will love me as he did Sara," Jo thought.

Jo fantasized about submitting her application to Harvard, but was slow to act. Eventually I applied for her. I began to see benefits in going off to school. My low seniority and the school's declining enrollments meant that I had little hope that my teaching job would continue. Scholarly work was by no means my first love, but I figured that I could rely on the Jo, Joan Frances, and Kendra personalities. And leaving to go to graduate school would also provide a natural conclusion for Lynn's work with the personalities.

Lynn had devoted an enormous amount of time to Jo and the others for almost two years. I knew she couldn't keep that up indefinitely, but it was going to be devastating for some of the others when Lynn said she had had enough. Though it didn't matter as much to me, I couldn't help worrying about what would happen to the others when Lynn cut us loose. If Lynn knew the group would leave in the fall, she would surely not terminate treatment. This way, I would be responsible for taking the group away, and no personality would feel abandoned by Lynn.

Steve insisted that our relationship was solid enough to endure my being away for a while. I assumed that he was urging me to go so that he could ease out of the relationship, but I wasn't worried about his rejection. None of the personalities was as dependent on Steve as they were on Lynn.

But first Steve himself was going away for a time—to serve as a visiting professor at Cornell beginning in January 1983. I had urged him to accept the appointment, hoping that it might help reinvolve him in the academic work he had neglected since Sara's death. And I relished having a semester alone in our wonderful house.

Steve and I were generally content with one another in those last months of 1982. Our occasional disagreements were always over therapy. He admitted that he didn't understand mental illness, but he refused to concede that I was sick. He resented my phone calls to Lynn and the long hours I spent in therapy.

"Aren't I good to you?" he asked when one of the group called Lynn. "Why can't you call me if you're going to be late?" he demanded when my sessions stretched longer than an hour.

One night when Steve asked this question, I reflected back on the therapy session. Throughout most of it, Lynn had been cuddling Little Joe. I turned to Steve wearily and said, "The personality who was out didn't know the phone number, much less that *he* should have called." Steve backed off. He didn't really want to know.

Then, suddenly, therapy became painful. With a start, Jo saw how dependent she had become on Lynn. Lynn's freely offered affection was a first. Jo had chalked up her parents' love to duty; they learned to love her because they were stuck with her. Lynn wasn't forced to love her but said that she did anyway. Jo began to believe.

Each moment with Lynn made Jo desperate for more. The deep longing brought terror. Since Jo didn't understand why Lynn felt the way she did, there was no way to trust that it would continue, no way to figure out what might make it stop.

Jo wanted Lynn to continue liking her, "Yet," Jo thought, "all I do is fight her." She could cite the many ways in which she resisted Lynn, even if the therapist rarely called her to account for it: Jo refused to listen to tapes of the other personalities; she refused to believe that her parents had abused her; she wasn't even able to handle the hypnosis.

Jo could imagine how her stubbornness might hasten Lynn's rejection of her, but she couldn't stop herself. If only Lynn would tell her how to behave. If only Lynn would explain her love, Jo could move this all back to an intellectual plane.

"What do you want me to *do?*" she asked Lynn. When Lynn offered a suggestion, Jo was often too fearful to do her bidding, and furious with Lynn for her suggestion.

When Lynn responded, "You're doing fine, just be yourself," Jo became incensed, sure that Lynn was manipulating her. Jo grew increasingly frustrated, and her frustration frightened us all.

I mentioned to Lynn our concern about Jo, and she tried to reassure me. "Renee, it's going to take Jo a while to understand that she's just fine the way she is. That's part of Jo's problem. She's sure that no person could like or accept her for her own self."

Lynn seemed not to understand the seriousness of the matter. "I want Jo to feel better about herself," I agreed, "but you know how this kind of frustration has sometimes created new personalities in the past."

"Now, Renee," Lynn chided, "you don't need to create new personalities to please me. I care about all of you and am really happy with the progress you are making in therapy."

I still felt uneasy. That we didn't *have* to create a new personality to please her didn't guarantee it wouldn't happen. And I was worried that Lynn wasn't prepared for that possibility.

Jo warned Lynn in her own way. "If I suddenly changed and became the person you wanted me to be, you wouldn't even notice that I was really trapped inside," she accused bitterly.

Jo II, the personality created to be what Lynn wanted, appeared a few days later during a session; to the group's amazement, Lynn recognized her immediately.

"I know you think you're doing what you can to keep me happy with you," Lynn said gently to this personality who insisted she was Jo, "but I need the real Jo to spend time with me and work out her problems."

DIARY *December 2, 1982*

Therapy has become intense. In some respects, I'm pleased about what has happened since Jo's frantic phone call a few weeks ago. I know I'm walking a fine line when I answer Jo's pleas for help. I don't want to encourage overdependency, but have found that, when I give her more attention than she's aware of wanting, I cut through her defenses quickly and cleanly.

Breaking through defenses, however, then increases dependency. It's good in that this young woman must recognize her emotional infancy before she can grow to be a strong and healthy adult. When some aspect of therapy has particularly frightened one personality or more, I'm grateful for the maternal transference that delivers her to the office every afternoon. No matter how much therapy hurts, she has to see how long it will be before this mother rejects her.

Renee has indicated her awareness of the group's need for me by applying to Harvard for graduate school. I have little doubt that she'll be accepted, and equally little belief that she'll follow through. I don't think that she is healthy enough to be away from me and from Steve, her only supports. I expect that some dysfunction, expressed through Jo or one of the younger personalities, will block Renee's plan.

The personalities have given me strong evidence that they want me to help them change their old patterns of defense. I didn't really expect the group to create a new personality, despite Renee's and Jo's warnings. When Jo II emerged, I was surprised at how well she intuited ultimate therapeutic goals. Jo II told me today that her problems stemmed from early abuse. She laid out all the messages I've been trying to give the others: "I created the other personalities because I couldn't cope with the abuse. The other personalities are my internal friends and protectors. They made my psychic survival possible, and I'm trying to appreciate their importance in my life. Once I work out my fears and love all of these different parts of me, I'll accept them into my own being, and then I'll no longer be multiple."

If it were really the Jo personality recognizing all of that, I'd say that my patient was very near recovery. Even so, it is important that recognition of this sort resides in the group belief system at all.

I've read literature that has suggested that MPD can be caused by therapists manipulating highly suggestible patients. I've thought since the beginning of my work with Jo that this was unlikely, and I'm even more convinced now that I see what a personality created for my benefit is like. While I am encouraged that my messages are getting through on some level, I feel it unwise to offer nurturing or support to the Jo II personality.

I have to reject this new personality firmly to keep more from forming. The formation of a "therapist-pleasing" personality is a danger not only to Jo but to our therapeutic relationship as well. If I were to accept Jo II, as I have the others, they could avoid our work by using an old defense. I've got to respond to the needs of the personalities who existed before therapy and simultaneously let the group know that I won't accept any created for my benefit.

. . .

19

Christmas and the weeks that followed brought a small but significant breakthrough. The Jo personality and I finally agreed on something she could do that would help treatment progress. I suggested that she read the summary I prepared for Dr. Wilbur a year and a half ago. I thought that reading it might help Jo understand my perceptions of our therapeutic relationship. She seemed excited by the idea.

The resistance that Jo might normally have offered was overridden by her ongoing suspicion that I had shared some "professional secrets" with Dr. Wilbur. She was relieved and seemed deeply touched by what I had written.

Jo called me the day after Christmas, her voice brimming with uncharacteristic joy, to tell me that she had read the full twenty-five-page summary and that she loved me, and I spontaneously decided to reinforce the new level of trust and understanding. At my invitation—unexpected and definitely unmanipulated—Jo came to my home that afternoon and spent a comfortable couple of hours perched on a stool in the kitchen chatting with me while I cooked. Gordon was at the airport, and my kids, home for the holidays, were off visiting their friends. With no new people around to intimidate her, Jo was almost vivacious.

I wasn't really surprised when Renee asked me a few weeks later if my husband and I would like to attend the housewarming party that she and Steve were throwing. I had suspected for some time that Renee might issue this invitation, and I had considered how I should respond.

I know that many of my colleagues would never understand that going to a party at my patient's house was as therapeutically useful as my other outside-the-office time with her. But, then again, some of my colleagues have trouble accepting that any time outside of the office is therapeutic.

I could tell that my going to the party was important to Renee. And I decided that my attending might help break through the superficial relationship that Renee and I have. If Renee could see that I sincerely appreciate who she is, she might be willing to share some of her weaknesses and fears openly with me.

.   .   .

Lynn and Gordon came to the party, and I made sure that I impressed them as the gracious hostess without a trace of pathology. This was, after all, my natural setting.

Gordon was not what I expected. I had assumed that he would be suspicious of me—this patient who took up so much of his wife's time—but instead he seemed interested in getting to know me. He was deliberate and thoughtful in his speech and actions, preferring to pet the dogs and talk with me in a quiet corner, rather than to mingle with the crowd.

Lynn quickly found some old friends and was engaged in conversation, but whenever I came by, she caught my eye and smiled. I circled frequently among the guests, but I returned each time to Gordon and resumed the conversation, which grew in fits and starts throughout the evening. I learned that night that Gordon was also a high-school teacher and as devoted to his students as I was. When Gordon told me about his "outside" involvement with students who needed special attention, I understood why he didn't resent the extra time Lynn spent with my group of personalities. Like Lynn, Gordon refused to separate his work from the rest of his life. Personal and career responsibilities merged in his desire to do what he could for the people he cared about.

"Have you ever sailed?" Gordon asked. He told me of the limitless freedom he felt out on the lake.

I decided that Gordon honestly liked me. "It would be fun to get together with Gordon and Lynn after all of this multiplicity stuff is over," I thought. "I'd really like to know them as friends."

Steve and I agreed that our housewarming had been a huge success. He was pleased that more than sixty guests had come to welcome us to our new house. And he had really had fun at this, the first party he had thrown since Sara's death. I was touched that Lynn and Gordon had come and that Gordon had gotten to know the real me.

A week later, Steve left for Cornell. I watched him drive off with more relief than regret. Now all of the personalities would have the opportunity to function on an internal clock without worrying about meeting external demands. When I got home from work, I could really be off duty. I was determined to spend the months while Steve was away getting to know the others better and beginning to relax the constant surveillance that I had practiced for more than a decade. Jo spent uninterrupted hours reading her political-science texts and reflecting on her own peculiar existence. She decided to keep a journal and began to trust that she'd have time to write in it regularly.

Missy constructed pictures with paper cutouts and curled up contentedly in her rocking chair with a children's storybook. Rusty puttered in the basement workshop far into the night, making things out of scraps of wood and nails.

Most important, we all had time to think, to reflect, to grow. We began to know our individual selves and the internal others. Since I was in the unique position of being able to monitor what each personality thought and did during its "outside" time, I watched with interest as each personality forged its own self-concept.

Missy, for example, learned to see herself the way Lynn did and decided that she was no longer an unwanted and ugly little girl. If her friend Lynn loved her, she must not be all bad.

Jo as well developed a better self-image. Now that she understood that she shared her body with others, she concentrated on using the time she had without berating herself for "forgetting" or "daydreaming."

Jo thought of the other personalities as alien forces, which didn't help endear her to us. However, she did take a certain glee in giving over to us various disliked tasks. She decided that, if the house got dirty or money got spent at times when she wasn't in control, she'd be damned if she'd clean the house or pay the bills during *her* precious hours.

Jo's increased comfort with herself allowed her to ask Lynn some frank questions.

"How does it feel to be a woman?" she asked Lynn one day late in January.

Lynn seemed perplexed by the question. "I know that the male personalities believe they are boys," Lynn said cautiously, "but, Jo, I thought you knew you were female."

"I know I'm not male," Jo responded, "but I don't really feel female."

"Well, how do you feel?" Lynn asked.

Jo thought for a moment. "I feel not-male. I feel lacking, not good enough. I thought maybe you could tell me if that's what it means to feel female."

"No, my feeling female does not mean feeling that I lack anything," Lynn said confidently, and then stopped. "I've never thought about how to express this," she confided. Jo smiled at Lynn's hesitation, and the therapist smiled back.

Lynn tried again. "Being female is more than biological apparatus, certainly," she said, "but I'm not sure that I can explain how it *feels* to be a woman. Let me think about that." She paused, lost in thought, and then brightened. "Let's start with your perception of physical self," Lynn said. "What do you notice when you look in the mirror?"

Now it was Jo's turn to be perplexed. "I can't see myself," she said.

"You what?" Lynn asked, incredulous.

"I can't see myself in a mirror," Jo explained patiently. She thought Lynn already knew this. "The last time I remember seeing my reflection was when I was a very little girl. My mother made me stand in front of a mirror and told me I looked retarded. I'm sure I haven't seen myself in at least fifteen years."

Jo saw disbelief in Lynn's face.

"What happens when you look in a mirror?" Lynn asked again.

"I lose time," Jo said. Then she tried to explain further. "The same thing happens when I look at photographs of myself. I can only guess at how I look." Her thoughts wandered for a moment. "There are so many things I haven't done for so long." She sighed. "Do you remember that afternoon when you took Missy to the park?"

Lynn nodded.

"I floated to the surface for a minute or two while you and Missy were watching the ship. It wasn't long, but I cherish that memory. I'm sure that it has been a dozen years since I had time outside on a spring day."

Lynn began to understand how much she had taken for granted. She and Jo worked together to locate the faulty assumptions and to puzzle over questions raised by Jo's special life: Is it possible to develop gender identification without social cues? If Jo could be knowledgeable with so little experience, didn't that prove that thinking was more important than living?

Jo worked to open herself up to Lynn, but realized paradoxically that, the more she did, the more dependent she felt. This frightened her.

"The time I spend with Lynn," Jo wrote in her journal, "is even better than the time I spend alone. I know it's not right to depend on another person this way. When I count on Lynn to make me feel good, I'm using her as an object. It's better to avoid people than to use them."

Jo couldn't help being so rational and so rigid. She regretted that the guilt brought on by her intellectual understanding made her push Lynn away as surely as she was drawing Lynn near. With a logician's distaste for inconsistency, Jo tried to make sense of her ambivalent feelings and behavior.

"I know Lynn cares," Jo wrote.

I know that she helps me. But I'm not ready to be cared for, to be helped. Lynn undermines the comforting distrust of people I've built up over the years.

Lynn makes my life fuller by being someone I can depend on, but she also makes my life more complicated. I don't know how to deal with a person who really knows me and who treats me consistently based on *my* actions alone. I don't know how to deal with a person who understands that the other personalities are not me.

Whether I lose five minutes or two weeks of time, Lynn knows me when I return and accepts that I am unaware of what has happened. I resist Lynn's acceptance and understanding. I deny the reality of Lynn's caring and pull into myself. I don't want to do that to the one person who has known and loved me for myself, but it's like trying to tell a turtle not to retreat into his shell. It's the only way I know how to live.

DIARY *February 10, 1983*

Jo and the rest of the group have done well, so far, with being alone in the house. I've seen a real change in therapy.

Renee shows continually increasing interest in the others and willing-ness to help with "their" treatment. She now displays an exasperated parental attitude and protectiveness toward them that is very different from her previous disdain and embarrassment. Renee would still deny that she has any vested interest in therapy, and I have no need to challenge her. I am content to see that her tolerance of the others is growing and that, more than ever before, she feels comfortable using time at sessions to discuss concerns of her own.

Missy is thoroughly enjoying the hours she spends with me. She openly soaks up my admiration and appreciation for her many delightful traits and her special ways of seeing the world, which only annoyed and disconcerted her parents.

Joan Frances continues to avoid the whole situation as much as possible and rarely appears in my office. But it is probably a step forward that she pops out occasionally to plead with me to make her worthy of her mother's love. She disappears the minute I suggest that Nancy's view of her may not be the most valid, but she comes back at a later date to hear the same message.

It is with Jo, again, that the storm is brewing. She has strong primeval feelings and absolutely no tools to cope with them aside from intellectual denial and amnesia. For brief periods, she trusts me enough to engage in theoretical discussions, and she seems at these times truly delighted. But then she feels guilty for her joy.

Until quite recently, the relationship I had with Jo held no meaning for her. It was merely a task that she carried out. But now she cannot deny my caring and, worse, she now cannot deny her love for me. Since Christmas, Jo has seemed increasingly distraught about her inability to acknowledge that she might have been abused. Treatment itself has become a trap, in the sense that she knows a time is coming soon when she won't be able both to continue therapy and to continue to deny the abuse. But she admits neither to feeling trapped nor to her steadily growing anger.

The anger is uncomfortable for both of us, but I see it as my ally. It is creating pressure. Memories of abuse are beginning to "bleed through" to Jo from other personalities.

I continue to push her, even as I offer constant support. And I am prepared for Jo to misunderstand my allowing her pain to persist. Inevitably, she will blame either herself or me and lash out at one of us. This is a dangerous period in therapy, but if I can be prepared for any crisis that might come, our work should reach a new level.

· · ·

Within a few weeks, the time of comfortable, theoretical talk for Lynn and Jo was only a memory. Therapy had become what Jo called an adversary relationship.

"Jo," Lynn said, "you have to hear about how you were abused. You have to think about it rather than dismiss it."

Jo claimed the other personalities were lying. Her father loved her, even if she wasn't the boy he wanted. Her mother may not have really loved her as she wanted to be loved, but Jo didn't think that absence of love amounted to abuse. "I was a difficult child," she explained to Lynn. "I hated being small and ignorant, and I'm sure that I made life difficult for everyone around me."

Lynn tried to enlist my help. "Renee, how are we going to help Jo face the truth about her childhood?" she asked.

I felt irritated that Lynn was trying to involve me in this. It was Jo's problem, not mine, and I thought I had done more than anyone could have asked for. I gave Jo time to be with Lynn, I gave her time in the evenings to write in her journal. What more did Lynn expect from me?

"Maybe Jo's right," I snapped at Lynn when she pushed me for suggestions. "Nancy and Ray didn't seem like child abusers to me."

The mounting pain, pressure, and panic in the group was a greater threat to me than to any of the other personalities. I was the one who was trying to keep a functional life going, and I felt that Lynn was pushing for a psychic explosion. I only hoped that I would be in some deep recess of our collective mind when things really blew.

Jo found that she was being assaulted from the inside as well. Fears from somewhere deep inside her surfaced as a strange mental image of blood on a wall.

"I can't make sense of the fear or the vision," she said, "but I'm so afraid to let go. I feel all this stuff rising and have to constantly fight against it."

"What are you afraid of?" Lynn asked. "What would happen if you stopped fighting the internal pressure?"

"I'm afraid I'll lose time," Jo said. "Maybe I'm afraid that I won't lose time. Maybe I'm afraid of remembering something I don't want to remember."

"Jo, you are safe in my office," Lynn said. "It's OK if you lose time in here, and it's OK if you remember something frightening. It's all in the past and can't hurt you now. I'll help you deal with it, whatever it is."

Jo couldn't let herself relax. Within a week, Jo had gone from comfortably exploring gender identity to shaking with anxiety and panic from unknown origins. Her whole body quaked.

No memories surfaced, and every afternoon overwhelming blackness answered Jo's anxiety. When Jo's fear ran wild, Josie, the personality who knew only panic, took control. Sometimes Lynn recognized the shift from Jo to Josie. She saw the quivering muscles tense, the eyes open wide and fill with terror. Lynn would talk calmly, soothingly as she slowly moved to block Josie from the wall.

Sometimes Lynn managed to restrain Josie for a few seconds, and she used that time to try to reach her. "Josie, Josie," Lynn said with a note of desperation, "you're safe here." But for Josie there was no safety. There was no *here*.

"No," Josie cried, "please don't!" and she struggled out of Lynn's arms until she was free to block out memories and her own awareness with the self-inflicted pain.

When Jo, in her words, felt "the fear scratching and crawling all over in an attempt to escape," sometimes Sissy, the four-year-old past-keeper who held rage as well as fear, appeared, searching for a window. She pounded her fists on the pane of Lynn's fifth-floor window, crying, "Out, please, out. Please, people!"

I was weary and bruised after three of these panic-filled sessions and decided that despite my own anxiety, I had better help Lynn get to the root of this anxiety.

"Josie feels overwhelming panic," I said. "In her memory, it is dark and she is terrified. She wants only the blessed peace of knocking herself against the wall. But I think that maybe she doesn't have the full memory yet. That's part of what's driving her to the wall now. She wants to knock herself out before she remembers the awful thing that caused her terror."

"When Josie finds herself here, it's as though she can't hear or see me," Lynn said. "Is she blind? Deaf?"

"No, that's not quite right," I said, and groped for the words to explain. "For both Josie and Sissy, there's really no past. It's not as if they have memories that they can tell you about. When they do remember something, they're reliving it right here and now. The memory has sight, sound, texture. It's as real as, and then more real than, any reality that you and this time and place have to offer."

"So, if we could transfer the memories to Jo, then she could remember them as being in the past, where those events belong," Lynn speculated. "Jo has no problem distinguishing past from present. She wouldn't be overwhelmed by the memories the way that Sissy and Josie are."

"Yes," I agreed with little optimism, "but it was Sissy and Josie who experienced these things, not Jo." The Jo personality had no memories to correspond with Sissy's and Josie's reliving of past torment.

Jo was frustrated by her inability to name or control the fear she was experiencing, and was further frustrated by Lynn's apparent calm.

"Why aren't you frustrated too?" Jo asked. "Why don't you help me?"

"I'm helping you the best way I know how," Lynn responded, "and I can wait out the bad periods."

Eventually the pressure built to such a pitch that Jo imploded in despair. She grew depressed, more deeply despondent than she had been since starting therapy. She couldn't work, couldn't think, couldn't even enjoy reading.

"Lynn, with her professional distance, might be able to wait this out," Jo thought bitterly, "but I can't wait anymore." Jo was consumed by her depression. "Please help me!" she begged Lynn.

"I'm doing what I can," Lynn said.

By now I empathized with Lynn and searched along with her for some way to help Jo. I knew Lynn wasn't sure what to do. "I guess I've got to push Jo even harder," Lynn said.

I agreed. "Anything is better than this."

Late in February, Lynn forced Jo to listen to a tape of the blood-curdling scream Sissy let out as she dived, furious and frightened, for the window. "You're angry," Lynn shouted at Jo, "you're terribly angry! You're angry at your parents for what they did to you. You're angry at your parents for the feelings you have about yourself. If you can begin to own your anger, you won't feel that blocked rage and pain."

Rather than being shocked into acknowledgment that something terrible had happened to her in childhood, Jo withdrew. She didn't lose time, but sat immobile throughout the tape and Lynn's onslaught. Jo silently reasoned that she had hit on the truth at last.

She was insane, she decided, and getting progressively worse. The horrible, haunting scream on the tape proved it. Soon she'd be locked up in a psychiatric ward. Silently Jo resolved that death was her only alternative to a debilitating chronic mental illness.

Jo left the office calmly, shrugging off Lynn's attempts to get her to talk. Now that she understood, there was nothing more to say. She had to kill herself before they locked her up.

Jo drove home slowly. By the time she unlocked the door to the house, her movements were mechanical. She felt no fear, no sorrow, no pain. She felt nothing.

Jo searched the cabinets for prescription medications and gathered them all on the kitchen counter. She put the kettle on for tea, figuring that the hot liquid would hasten her overdose. She considered the various drugs and piled together what she calculated to be a lethal mixture and dose.

Blocked by Jo's depression and determination, I paced inside and watched the scene with horror. I sought for a break in Jo's concentration that would allow me out before she took the pills. I hoped that if she acted I'd be able to take control and force the pills back up.

Jo placed an afghan on her rocking chair in the sunroom. She found a classical-music station on the radio. Now she would fetch the pills and tea, and cuddle under the cover. She would watch the snow blowing hard in the twilight and wait to fall asleep. Jo was grateful that she had retained enough sanity to carry through her plan.

Returning to the kitchen to pour her pot of tea, Jo was distracted by a sound at the kitchen door. She looked up to see Lynn's face at the window. Jo stared incredulously. Then she opened the door to let Lynn in.

"What were you doing?" Lynn asked gently.

Jo gestured toward the tea and pills. "I can't take any more. I can't let this get worse."

Lynn didn't seem surprised.

"I was concerned when you left the office," Lynn said. "You changed when you heard the tape. You stopped pleading for help. You wouldn't talk to me and you were far too calm. When no other personality resumed control, I was afraid that you were close to suicide."

Jo's defenses dropped and she began to cry. She suddenly understood that Lynn had not given up and would not give up on her.

"You're going to get better, Jo," Lynn said. "You and I are making you well together. Sometimes it means working, but sometimes it means waiting out the bad times."

Lynn and Jo spent a few hours that evening waiting together. They sat on the sofa with a fire crackling in the fireplace, Lynn's arm protectively encircling Jo. Jo rested her head on Lynn's shoulder as only Missy had done in the past. Lynn's rescue did not dissolve the overwhelming fear, but it made waiting to understand it a little easier. Jo finally knew that she was not alone.

BOOK III

20

Then waiting became impossible. Josie dived for the wall a few days later, her feet flailing, and cracked two of Lynn's ribs. Lynn was no longer able to keep Josie and Sissy from hurting themselves. "I'm certain that these memories being unleashed in such a violent way are important," Lynn said. "We've got to control damage to both our bodies, but these memories have to be allowed to surface.

"What about hospitalization, Renee?" Lynn asked.

I was embarrassed and upset that the group had hurt Lynn, but hospitalization was out of the question. Despite the toll of daily therapy sessions, Jo was taking courses toward her master's degree, and I was teaching. The group was undeniably functional. Besides, we were all terrified of psychiatric hospitalization.

"I think that we would, all of us, become suicidal if we were ever locked up," I told Lynn. "There'd be no hope, no reason to go on. Anything that said 'You're really not functional' to the group would be disastrous. It's our functionality that makes it possible to put up with the craziness. You can't take that away from us." Lynn agreed that hospitalization was not a viable alternative.

"Renee, what if I had someone here who was strong enough to hold Josie away from the wall?" I wasn't overjoyed at the prospect, but it certainly was better than hospitalization. And something had to be done. I agreed.

I walked into Lynn's office March 3 anxious about the involvement of another person but relieved that Lynn would be protected. Long before I knew I was multiple, I had figured out that one person's pain didn't justify someone else's being hurt. I had seen Ray come home, upset about something that happened at the factory. Within an hour, Nancy would be sobbing in the bedroom, feeling beaten and bewildered by his demands and sarcasm. "If he can't leave his problems at work, he shouldn't come home," I muttered then, and proceeded to take this on as a general rule. No one had a right to take out his pain on another person.

Now I was doing that to Lynn. My problem was causing Lynn physical pain. I was mortified and would have agreed to don a straitjacket while in Lynn's office if that had been the only way to keep her from harm.

It didn't matter that neither I nor the other personalities wanted to hurt Lynn. Being functional enough to be out on the streets meant, to me, not causing other people pain. I was closer to the edge of what I called dysfunctional than I had ever been. My need to stay away from that edge, even if only by a hair, made me willing to allow someone else to see me "acting crazy."

I reasoned that this "protector" would have only temporary involvement. He would be around just long enough to weather the storm so that the actual memories could surface. Once those memories were uncovered, the panic, with its threat of physical harm, would certainly cease.

Lynn had told me that she would arrange for someone to sit outside her office in the receptionist's area. She wouldn't call for him unless or until Josie or Sissy surfaced.

At the start of the session, I said, "This person knows about the others, right? I mean, he won't think it's me, Renee, acting like that?"

"I'm surprised that you haven't guessed who's out there." Lynn smiled.

I had no idea and nodded for her to continue.

"It's Gordon," she said, with pleasure.

"Gordon?" I echoed, horrified. Not Gordon. I had tried so hard at my party in January to make Gordon see me as a competent, functional person. What would happen if he saw Josie or Sissy? I didn't want him exposed to them. Even if it was true, as Lynn assured me, that Gordon had as much empathy and respect for me as she had, he'd be appalled if he saw what really went on. Angry and embarrassed, I fled inside. Let some other personality deal with this!

Jo emerged. Since she was unaware of the exchange Lynn and I had just had, Lynn again explained that Gordon was the person outside the door, waiting to offer assistance. Jo knew that the Renee personality had met Gordon, and she had looked forward to meeting him herself. She wanted at least to thank Gordon for being so understanding of the enormous amount of time she spent with Lynn. Now he was going to meet not her but Josie and Sissy!

Jo protested and, when Lynn tried to persuade her at least to give it a chance, she too fled from the outside awareness.

DIARY *March 3, 1983*

I was shocked by Renee's and Jo's reactions to my enlistment of Gordon. Renee had so obviously liked him (and I believed Jo too would quickly be comfortable with him) that I expected his presence—rather than that of a security guard or one of my colleagues—would be reassuring.

I thought it would be harder explaining Gordon's presence to my colleagues than to Jo and Renee. But since my sessions with the group don't start until 5:00 p.m., when the workday is over, I anticipated that few people would be aware of Gordon's involvement.

I did tell Harry about it yesterday. It sure helps to have a boss who has known me for two decades. Over the years, he has watched me shelter battered wives in my home and take inner-city kids for rides in our sailboat, and has approved my expense reports for such therapeutic costs without blinking an eye. Even so, I was surprised at how easy it was to convince Harry of this new unorthodox step in the treatment of my first multiple.

Harry said that he thought I had come up with the best solution. He doubted that voluntary admission to the psychiatric ward would work even if Jo and Renee were willing. He reminded me how fascinated yet disbelieving the house staff had been when I had presented Jo's case at Psychiatric Grand Rounds. It was clear that they knew nothing about MPD. "If she were hospitalized, you'd lose control of her treatment, because you're a social worker, not an M.D., and I wouldn't trust the house staff to respond appropriately to her," Harry said. "Any mistreatment at a time of such crisis might leave her in far worse shape than she is right now, particularly if you were the intervening force."

Harry also approved of my choice of Gordon for physical protection, although I suspect that agreement had an economic as well as a clinical base—it wouldn't cost the unit anything to have Gordon involved. "I've known Gordon as long as I've known you," Harry said, "and his presence is not likely to cause the anxiety to you or Jo that introducing a new clinician might."

He told me not to worry about how the rest of the staff might view my unusual treatment methods. They had grown accustomed to the idea of a multiple's being treated on their very service. He said that the only real concerns expressed lately were from clinicians who were afraid that he might want them to put in the inordinate amount of time I was spending with Jo. He reassured them and reminded them that having a colleague treating such an unusual disorder was a rare opportunity for them. "I have complete trust in your therapeutic instincts," he said.

His concern was that I may have a difficult time letting go of Gordon once the crisis is over. I told him that I hoped that wouldn't be an issue. It depended on Jo and the others, of course, but Gordon and I had already discussed the possibility of his having a continuing presence in Jo's treatment.

I know that I could use an adjunct therapist, and Gordon would be my first choice. Treating a multiple is the most intensive and exhausting therapy I have ever done. I don't regret what I have done, or the commitments I have made to the group to see their treatment through, but I am afraid of getting burned out.

This wouldn't be the first time that Gordon and I had combined our talents to help someone in need. Some of the abused and neglected inner-city kids who formed my caseload were students in the school where Gordon taught. We often worked after hours with these teenagers, helping them find alternatives to the drugs, destruction, and despair they knew at home. And he and I spent many productive hours brainstorming together about how to recognize and respond to a particular child's need.

I was relieved and grateful when Gordon volunteered to help with Jo. He and I had become excited when we thought how we might be able to work as cotherapists with the various personalities.

Now this.

Jo apparently wants Gordon to see her and understand her as a person, not as "just a freak to be controlled." That's easy. I'm delighted that Jo wants Gordon here, interacting with her the way I do.

Renee is a bigger concern. She left today, swearing she would "never be back to be humiliated" by me again. Somehow she feels that I have let her down, that I have exposed her to Gordon in a way she didn't want to be exposed. An "anonymous" helper whom she had no desire to include in her "real life" would have been easier for her. She seems to think that if Gordon encounters the other personalities he will lose respect for her.

I am struck, once again, by how separately the personalities view themselves. Renee obviously thinks that, since Gordon saw her acting appropriately at a party, he thinks of her only in that way. But what about all of the late-night phone calls to my house from confused, hesitant Jo and from plaintive Missy? Doesn't Renee realize that Gordon knows they are the same physical entity?

I have a hard time believing the strength of Renee's denial. She must know that my colleagues, my receptionist—even the cleaning lady and security officers—are aware that something strange takes place in my office every afternoon. More than once, after hearing screams from the Sissy or Josie personality resounding through the almost empty wing, the cleaning lady has stopped me to ask "how that poor girl is doing." It's not many buildings where the guards have an order to "ignore sounds of distress between 5:00 and 6:00 p.m. on 5 West."

No, I guess Renee doesn't know. She walks in competent and self-possessed, chats with the receptionist, and assumes that people judge her only on the basis of what she, the Renee personality, displays.

She so badly wants people to perceive her as separate from the other personalities, and she is terribly worried that she will be judged by the actions of the others. On some level, at least, she knows she's not her own self without the others, and she hates this.

I'm concerned, as I always am when I commit some unforgivable "faux pas," that she will not return. But I think I understand, better than ever now, that all of the personalities, Renee included, are sick, very frightened little girls in grown-up clothes. Their need is greater than their competence and even greater than Renee's humiliation. I offer the promise of true health and true growth rather than a temporary mask. I think she'll return for that.

And also in my favor is the fact that Jo has been accepted for graduate study at Harvard. I don't think they'll really go, but Renee's knowledge that she has an escape hatch may keep her coming despite her pain and humiliation.

Even with the trauma, there was humor and some progress made in today's session. After Renee had fled inward in humiliation and Jo had fled inward in anger, Josie was there, scrabbling quickly, as always, for the wall. Gordon said he heard the commotion in my office as I tried to restrain Josie, but he returned to his reading at the receptionist's desk, remembering that I'd said I'd call him if I needed him.

A social-work student who stood nearby, going through her mail, looked at him quizzically as the banging and thrashing resounded through the walls. "Lynn said she'll let me know if she needs help," he told her.

Finally, I maneuvered close enough to fling open the door. The student gasped to see me literally lying on top of my patient. "Shouldn't we do something?" the student asked Gordon.

"No," I heard him reply, "Lynn knows what she's doing."

"Gordon!" I yelled with exasperation. I couldn't imagine why he was calmly sitting there when the need was so obvious.

"I guess Lynn wants me now," Gordon said to the student as he set aside his reading glasses and book.

He walked in, closed the door on the student's astonished face, and wrestled Josie away from the wall. Josie struggled against him, then seemed to realize that she couldn't get past his gentle but firm hold; in a minute, Missy was there. "You want your friend," she whimpered. Gordon looked up at me. I nodded and he quietly left the office and returned to his reading.

He's eager to work as cotherapist, but told me that I'm going to have to be very clear about what I want him to do or not do. No kidding.

I can't help thinking that that social-work student is probably at this very moment considering changing her field of study.

. . .

Two days later, therapy-with-Lynn made a smooth transition into therapy-with-Lynn-and-Gordon. Gordon returned for a session, but this time he knocked on the door and joined Lynn and me in her office. He took off his jean jacket and shoes and settled on the rug. With no discussion, Lynn and I both slid off our chairs. Josie, Missy, Little Joe, or Sissy inevitably moved the session to floor level. What seemed to me at first a welcoming gesture to Gordon relieved some of the anxiety that rushed through the system. It felt safe to be sitting on the rug.

Gordon and I picked up the conversation about teaching we had begun at the party back in January. He and I both had war stories to tell about our attempts to manipulate administrators and the system in order to help students in trouble. Gordon treated me just the way he had at the party, and I responded in kind. "Maybe Gordon is able to understand me the way Lynn does," I thought, and then retreated inward in peace.

Jo liked Gordon instantly. When she surfaced, Lynn gave her usual greeting, "Hi, Jo, it's good to see you," and Gordon smiled as she glanced in his direction. "I've been waiting a long time to meet you in person," he said.

"Umm, you know, do you know, umm, who I am?" she asked cautiously.

"I know you're Jo," Gordon said, "and Lynn's told me that you enjoy thinking about people and reality. Me too. I'm really interested in how people live their lives and how any of us end up being here in the first place."

Jo started to ask him what he meant, but her question was stopped by an icy finger of suspicion.

She glanced at Gordon briefly before turning her eyes to the wall.

"Do you believe me? I mean, do you believe I'm a multiple personality?" Jo asked.

"I think such a phenomenon is possible," Gordon replied.

Jo blushed, now frightened and defensive. If this man thought she was a fraud, she wanted to know it now. "What do you mean, it's possible?" She tried to sound nonchalant.

Gordon smiled warmly at Jo, as though sensing her confusion, and said, "You have a lot to learn about me. I don't accept things the way they are. I do a lot of questioning about what society says is so. I'm open to many possibilities—reincarnation, telepathy, the sorts of things that many other people just laugh at and push aside.

"Now, to answer your question, Jo, I think multiple personality is possible, because I know there are group minds."

Jo remained silent, puzzled. Gordon's calm, deep voice was soothing, but she was still on guard for rejection.

"When I'm sailing, sometimes I'll spend hours watching flocks of birds. They have something special going on there," Gordon continued. "They are all separate entities, those birds, but they share a single thought. Watch them fly in formation and suddenly veer around some invisible obstacle. Watch them flutter in swirling confusion and then, abruptly, move together in perfect formation again, each knowing its part in the whole. That's what I mean by group minds."

Gordon seemed to weigh his remarks, as though each word had significance. And his metaphor appealed to Jo. She relaxed again.

"A flock," she said, testing the term. "I guess my group of personalities is like a flock." She smiled ruefully. "I only wish I could be lead bird sometime."

The personalities monitoring the exchange between Jo and Gordon latched on to the term quickly.

"A flock is what we're like," I thought, "even if we're more 'swirling confusion' than 'formation.'"

"Group mind," Isis considered. "Yes, I share in Jo's group mind, but I'm also separate. I guess it's accurate to say that I am part of the Flock. This Gordon's pretty perceptive, even if he is a man."

Lynn had once said that calling the personalities "the others" was hostile. I had always thought that "the group" sounded too cold and abstract. At last we all had a term we liked for referring to the personalities. We were the Flock.

Jo suddenly realized that she had gone way over her appointment hour and was afraid of intruding on Lynn and Gordon together in a way that she no longer feared intruding on Lynn alone. Flustered, she got up to leave.

"Don't go," Gordon said. "You're not ready to leave yet, and Lynn and I have no place we need to be." Was it possible that Gordon was enjoying their talk as much as she?

During that session, Gordon met Rusty, Theresa, Joan Frances, and Missy, as well as Jo and me, and responded to us all as our individual selves.

During Gordon's first few weeks as cotherapist, Josie fought hard against him in her attempts to reach the wall. But she eventually understood that she couldn't get past his gentle restraint. Gordon held Josie as she struggled against him and against her panic. The memories caught up with her in his arms.

As Josie spat "Don't touch me!" and "Please don't!" in terrified whimpers, I watched the film of past horrors play out before me on an internal screen. I fought to keep my distance as memories slipped through Josie's attempts at repression, bit by bit.

"I can't tell you everything that happened the night that Josie is reliving," I explained to Gordon and Lynn, "because Josie is still fighting the actual memory. I know she was asleep and she awoke to some man fondling her. Each time the memory flows over Josie, she has more details. I think she'll have it all soon."

Josie felt terrorized and attacked because she believed her memories were happening *now*. At the same time, Gordon's gentle hold made her feel safe and protected. As she became able to put more trust in the safety of Gordon's nonsexual touch, she was able to allow more memory into consciousness.

Jo also began to find fragments that added pieces to the puzzle of Josie's terror. Jo was not consciously aware of the substance of Josie's memories, but the release of Josie's old terror triggered the recollection of associated experiences in the other personalities.

"You know, I've been thinking about something that happened the summer when I was twelve," Jo said to Lynn and Gordon.

"My mother was spending most of her evenings out with her new friends, and my father stayed home, alternating between being furious with her and despairing because he couldn't do anything to keep her home.

"One night, I was sitting in the family room reading a book. It was a story about a foster child who was finally adopted and got a family of her own. When I finished the story, I remember feeling empty and aching. I knew I'd never have the sense of belonging that the character had gotten by the end of the book.

"I was sort of weepy and wandered upstairs to find my father in bed, watching TV. He asked me what was wrong. I told him that I had read a book that had made me feel sad. 'Come on in here and crawl in with your old man,' he said. I did. I didn't care what was on TV. It felt good and safe to be cuddling with my father. I must have fallen asleep, and I guess my mother didn't come home that night, because I remember the fuzziness on the TV screen after all of the programs had ended."

That was all Jo remembered, and though her memory was shrouded in melancholy, it held no fear. But her offhanded retelling snapped into place for me with Josie's snatches of memory.

An entire event projected itself on my internal screen. I found myself unable to look away from the scene. Finally, shaken, I turned to Gordon and Lynn. "Josie was raped by her father," I said with certainty.

Josie awoke that night lying on her side, facing the wall, now flickering in the fuzzy light of the TV set. Ray's hand was between her legs. He rubbed himself against her back. Josie couldn't quite conceptualize what was happening, but she sensed that it was dangerous to be awake and aware.

She must go back to sleep. If she were asleep, this wouldn't be real. "Sleep, sleep," she instructed herself, and stared at the wall, losing herself in its blankness, distancing herself from wakefulness by fantasizing throwing herself against the wall. Again and again, until the pain of the wall would bring the pleasure of darkness.

Then she was distracted by his voice, hushed and throaty, so different from Daddy's. "Are you my woman?" he asked. "Doesn't that feel nice?

"You're cold, shivering," he said. "Let me cover you up." He folded her on her stomach and eased himself between her thighs.

In her mind, Josie threw herself against the wall in time with her father's strokes. The pain between her legs she relocated as her fantasy of the deliciously releasing pain of her head hitting the wall. The wall, the wall, nothing mattered but the wall. She imagined the blood she would see on the wall when she hit her head hard enough against it.

An eternity later, he stopped. "You'll tell your mother you were asleep. You just fell asleep. That's all."

Though she had no memory of the event itself, Jo supplied the epilogue to Josie's rape. "The day after I fell asleep in my father's room, I found him crying in the basement," Jo told Lynn and Gordon. "I felt so bad. This was the first time I had ever seen my father cry. I tried to give him a hug, but he ordered me away. I knew I wasn't the cause of his pain," Jo said with confidence, "but it hurt me that he wouldn't let me comfort him. He felt so bad that he and my mother were splitting up."

Jo's amnesia continued to protect her from the memories of abuse. Josie, less panicked now that the memory had surfaced, began to heal. And I felt as if I was the only one horrified by this piece of reality from the Flock's past.

I could no longer divorce myself from the Flock's childhood. Watching the memories unfold and sharing them with Lynn and Gordon made me an accomplice. I knew that my days of saying "That's *their* problem, not mine" were past, but I couldn't figure out just where I fit in.

21

Josie's memory of being raped by her father opened the gate to a stampede of other memories of abusive incidents, relayed now by Rusty, Sissy, Missy, and Little Joe as well as Josie. I became increasingly irritated by Jo's stubborn unwillingness even to consider the possibility of abuse.

"I don't know what she's trying to prove," I remarked impatiently to Gordon and Lynn. "Even the memories Jo does have of her childhood are not worth hanging on to."

"That may be so, Renee," said Lynn, "but Jo is afraid of what will happen if she gives up the perception that she has of Ray. Remember, for that personality, it was Ray's love that sustained her through childhood."

Lynn and Gordon tolerated Jo's stories about her loving father far better than I did. They listened without comment when Jo apologized for "all the lies those other personalities tell." After letting Jo have her say, Lynn would repeat the experiences described by the other personalities. "It's getting through on some level," Lynn assured me.

Jo admitted that her own memories of childhood were not very comfortable. She grew up feeling that her mother thought she was a failure. According to Mother, she was too ugly, too clumsy, too introspective, too everything to be a "good" child. And if Jo was overly endowed with undesirable characteristics in her mother's view, in her father's view she was seriously lacking.

For Ray, Jo was just not good enough—not smart enough, not quick enough, and especially not male enough. "I know you call this emotional abuse," Jo told Lynn, "but from my point of view these were just the facts. Maybe my parents weren't tactful, but you can't call them abusive for telling me the truth about myself."

Jo had learned from her reading of *Sybil* that it's not unusual for a multiple's primary personality to be amnestic for periods of childhood abuse, but her intellectual understanding of this didn't quell her emotional frustration when Lynn detailed yet another abusive childhood episode.

"My father wouldn't have done that to me," Jo told Lynn firmly. "How am I supposed to accept as memory things that I just don't remember? How am I to incorporate these events into my belief system when I'm sure they never could have happened?" In this way, Jo moved the question from emotional reality to philosophical debate that she could handle.

Long before Jo had had a label for her problem, she knew she had no coherent sense of past. Jo's memory was like a small photo album. She sometimes opened up that album and mentally fingered the photos to reassure herself that she had existed before this moment. The snapshot memories did that, but they rarely brought comfort. They depicted scenes she wouldn't have minded forgetting.

One series of mental images showed Jo at various ages, in various places, but always with the same intense expression. Eyes shining, lips puckered in thought. The Jo in those pictures was engaged in MEANINGFUL discussion. A glance at the other people in the photographs reminded Jo that this one was when she had argued that an ideological skeptic was not the same as a political nihilist, and that one was when she had tried to explain why epistemology was more usually relevant than the metaphysical fact of truth.

In this mental scrapbook of the past, she saw the puzzled faces in the snapshots, reread the captions, and heard again what was said to her at those times: "Practicing all of your big words tonight?" "Do you think anyone really cares?" Or, worse, "Jo, why are you acting so different all of a sudden?"

Another series of mental pictures was more painful. In these memories, she stood mute, the accusatory faces of her friends, parents, and teachers frozen for all time. The captions read, "Why did you do this?" "Why did you say this?" "Why are you lying?" Jo had never had an answer when those people questioned her about her behavior. She had rarely known what they were talking about.

When she was about twenty years old, Jo had forced herself to peruse again these mental pictures, looking for a key to lock away future pain. Confusion formed a central theme, but she also noticed another constant in the photos. In none of those horrid memories was Jo alone. Now she understood. If she stayed away from other people, she would be able to live her life in peace. And that was her goal before meeting Lynn.

Only recently had Jo begun to think that maybe there was a way for her to become a social being. She couldn't quite fathom what it would mean for her as her own self to be comfortable with people. But Lynn told her that other personalities managed to have friends. So, although Jo didn't like hearing what the other personalities said about childhood, she listened with critical interest when Lynn talked about their current activities.

As she listened to how Renee handled a troubled student or how Kendra managed to get the phone company finally to issue a deserved refund, Jo fantasized about what it might be like if she could do those things. But, although she had enjoyed these exchanges with Lynn for some time, she knew they weren't "treatment." She wasn't in therapy to dream or to enjoy herself, but to work and to make sure that Lynn believed that she was trying to do *something.*

Now Gordon distracted Jo from her focus on the "therapeutic purpose." He had questions about Jo's reality, and she decided that it would be rude of her not to answer him as carefully as he questioned her. And Lynn didn't seem to mind whenever Jo and Gordon veered into intellectual abstraction. In fact, Lynn would sit benignly at one side as Gordon and Jo hammered at some idea together. And sometimes she joined in.

Spurred on by Gordon's penetrating questions, Jo searched for images and analogies that would help him understand. At night, after the sessions had ended, she wrote in her journal, exploring further the ideas that had surfaced in her talks with him.

"How can I explain what it's like to feel so out of control?" Jo wrote one night.

It's like I'm nothing more than a heavy weight dragging at the bottom of a sea. I am too submerged to feel the pounding waves of my other personalities. I'm too deep within my own mind to be really conscious of the beach of real life. I'm dragged by the backwash, the undertow of what the other personalities decide and do. So I scrape the watery sand, neither tossed onto shore to be

me alone, nor light enough to become part of the lulling rhythms
of life that I sense but do not experience.

"It's like you think of yourself as an object," Gordon said after reading
Jo's journal entry.

"That's because I have no control. I feel like I'm not really a person,"
Jo replied. Gordon shook his head in confusion.

"I don't get it," he said. "What can't you control?"

"Anything. The only times I become aware outside of Lynn's office,
I find myself sitting in a classroom or at my desk at home with books and
papers spread out before me. So I write or study or do what it seems that
I'm supposed to do. I don't really have any choice in the matter."

"What happens if you get up for something to drink or decide to go
to bed?" Gordon asked.

Jo wasn't sure. "I never try to do those things," she said, "because I
know I'd lose time."

Gordon was unsympathetic. "It seems to me that the only way to have
control is to take control."

Jo was embarrassed that she hadn't thought of that herself, but she
suspected that the situation was a little more complex. What she didn't
know was that the rest of us were developing a greater empathy for her
as well. As she explained her unique self to Gordon, she was explaining
to her internal entourage as well.

Jo's complaints made me think about how I could make life better for
her. I didn't have to control who got time when. And even if I wanted
to shepherd the Flock in that way, I now knew that I wasn't powerful
enough. If I were, Josie and some of the more difficult personalities would
never have appeared.

I began listing the variables that determined who had time when. My
desire was only one factor.

External need was another: if there was a class to be taught, I did the
teaching; if a paper needed to be written, Jo did the writing; if the house
needed to be cleaned or dinner needed to be cooked, Charlene took
control. Over the years, we had divided up the tasks of living. Most of
us were a little flexible—I could respond adequately in a graduate seminar
and Jo could cook dinner—but in general the personalities performed the
tasks that they liked.

Each personality also had internal limitations that helped determine who had time. Jo was afraid of large groups of people, so she didn't come out in crowds. Rusty refused to come to the surface unless the body was dressed in jeans or something else that would pass as "boy clothes." I couldn't deal with people being angry with me, so, like it or not, I lost time when I thought I had made somebody angry.

Once I realized that control was such a big issue for Jo, I began to hold back. I stopped stepping in to handle things for her.

Now, if the phone rang while she was studying, I didn't push her out of consciousness to answer it. Instead, I waited to see what she would do. More than once, the caller hung up while Jo and I waited each other out, but she learned that she really did have a choice and could answer the telephone if she wished.

As Jo experienced more of her life, she felt overwhelmed less often. She didn't have significantly more time, but the time she experienced was more comfortable for her. She felt confident. Jo's growth pleased me as the growth of a troubled student might. I found I had no reason to feel threatened by her progress.

Lynn and Gordon also applauded Jo's new control. They delighted in her success and reaffirmed her developing sense of self. Jo still could not see her physical reflection, but she wrote: "How can I think of myself as less than a person when I see myself reflected in the mirror of Lynn's and Gordon's pride?"

Jo no longer worried that Lynn would think her lazy or resistant. She decided that her discussions with Gordon were worthwhile and acknowledged this. "Our talks root and grow for the sake of themselves," Jo said. "Even if that growing seems to be aimless, it brings about further sharing and further learning. That continual becoming is what being a person is all about."

Lynn said, "I love you, Jo." And, for the first time, the words meant something.

Lynn's feelings may have been genuine for a long time, but only now was Jo ready to accept them. Gordon shared responsibility for this change, and Jo acknowledged that to him.

"Thank *you,*" he responded. "For the last two years, I've really felt left out. Now I feel part of the family."

"Family," Jo thought. "So that's the special feeling I share with Lynn and Gordon." She shivered with anxiety that she might actually belong to people in the continuing and vulnerable sort of way that the term "family" suggested, but she shivered in excitement as well. The concept fit. Family. Together Gordon and Lynn were teaching her, through their love, how to love herself. Wasn't that what a family was supposed to be? She had to make sure.

"How do you love me, Lynn? In what context?"

Lynn sighed and hugged her close. "You're a grown woman, Jo," Lynn said, "but you're my little girl."

Jo hesitated, breathing in the safety of Lynn's embrace. She risked her question quietly, tentatively: "Are you saying you love me like a daughter?"

"Yes, I love you like a daughter."

"Daughter." That word was even more emotionally laden than "family" for Jo. She tested the word in her journal:

"Daughter" flutters about, so unfamiliar on my tongue. The word had no place in my childhood vocabulary.

When I was with my mother, I sometimes thought of myself as a trophy—something to be flaunted before friends. When out of public view, I sat on the shelf, ignored and forgotten. Other times, I felt like my mother's intellectual superior. I toyed with her, tying her in semantic knots, as my father did, subtly scornful.

When I was with my father, at the worst of times, I felt "not-a-son," trying desperately to be something I could never be. At the best of times, I was my father's "kid." "Kid." The word is casual, too casual to describe any real bonding.

Why didn't I feel that I belonged to my parents? How early could I have known that I was not right? I think it has always been part of me. Can a newborn sense her parents' disappointment and feelings of frustration at not being able to change the unchangeable?

My mother once told me that she had picked out the name Robin for a girl child. A boy would be called Joseph. Had I been named Joan as a reminder that I was neither the boy she wanted nor a girl she could love? Were they too disheartened to give me a name that would have started my life out right?

Are any of these anxieties or beliefs about my past real? Maybe I'm just making them up—re-creating the past.

I have to smile as I look at what I just wrote. I can tell when my solitary exploration becomes too threatening, or when I'm treading close to a memory too frightening to be remembered. Rather than push through unfamiliar brush, I stomp the well-worn path of "Maybe I'm making all of this up." But retreating there no longer makes sense to me.

The accuracy of my memories, whether things happened exactly the way that the personalities remember, doesn't really matter. If my memory, combined with the memories of the other personalities, provides some coherent past, then that is far better than the blankness I have. Whatever inaccuracies may occur because of the passage of time or because of the colored intensity of "emotional truth" harm no one. All that matters is that I gain a firm grasp on what is real. The memories of the total entity, accurate or not, are providing me a handle. I must have some background to adequately explain where I am now. I must have a base from which to build an unfragmented future.

Jo was at last ready to accept that the other personalities were not lying even if she herself had no memories of Ray's abuse. She now had real relationships with Lynn and Gordon to replace the fantasy of Ray as a perfect father.

"I know that you do love me," Jo told Lynn, "and that makes it possible for me to grow, just as love makes it possible for an infant to grow. But you know that I don't like my dependency on you. I'm willing to accept it for a time, because I believe you when you tell me that my acceptance of dependency on you heals a very old need. But I really hate it. I hate being an emotional infant. I want to grow free of you.

"If I didn't feel that your love accelerated my growth," Jo added firmly, "I'd fight against it."

DIARY *April 3, 1983*

I'm exhilarated and moved by all of the growth that has taken place in the Flock. In February, the therapeutic relationship was stalled. The Jo personality was in agony, and Josie and Sissy spent time almost every session diving for the wall or the window. Now, with the active involvement of Gordon, we—Gordon, the Flock, and I—are a family. I would never have predicted that therapy would take this sort of turn, and would feel very reluctant to counsel someone else to treat in this way. Yet I feel sure that what is happening is right.

Gordon's and my success so far is beyond my wildest dreams. We are not only providing what the various personalities need at various times; we are also modeling good parenting and a healthy marriage for all of them. Jo and Missy both watch me carefully to see how I'll respond to their enjoyment of Gordon. Unlike her mother, I'm not envious of the relationship they have. In some respects, the mother role is not a new transition, just one newly recognized. I've known for two years of cuddling Missy and the other very young personalities that I was providing healthy maternal love. Although Renee would never accept hearing this, I mother her as well, using what I learned when my own daughters were teenagers. Like any wise mother of a teenager, I allow Renee to depend on my counsel without ever drawing attention to the fact of her dependency. Mothering Jo is a joy, if for no other reason than her beginning to realize that, even within her own limited personality, she is a lovely young woman whom I am proud to call my daughter.

Gordon provides his share of parenting as well. Not only does he protect Josie from self-inflicted harm; he provides her with experience of a healthy male, counterbalancing her memory of paternal abuse. The Rusty personality, so threatened by women, is eagerly opening up to Gordon, sharing memories and growing stronger in the process.

I don't think that the personalities manipulated me into this surrogate parenting. It's been clear for two years that none of them ever expected to have their aching need filled. My love grew in spite of all of my early hesitancy and restraint. I need to continue to be very careful to make only promises I can fulfill, build trust, and keep in mind that the personalities need treatment as well as mothering.

I can't deny to myself or to Jo the bonding the three of us are experiencing. I'm a little uneasy about the focal shift in our relationship and know there will be many rocky times ahead as I try to manage both a family relationship and a therapeutic relationship, but I will not abuse Jo by denying its reality.

Jo has recently pushed through to realizations that were simply not possible before. A week or so ago, she asked me, "Why do you want to be around me?" I told her it was because I liked looking at her, liked hearing what she had to say, found her to be an interesting and likable person. "I never felt that way with my parents," she said. "They told me I was ugly, stupid, and clumsy, and I believed them."

"That's all wrong," I said. "You're not stupid. You're very bright. You're not ugly. You're very pretty."

"You mean people aren't repulsed by me?" she asked. "I don't look worse than most people?" Jo suddenly realized that she wasn't the grotesque monster she had imagined her physical self to be.

She stood suddenly and walked to the mirror that hung on the back of my office door. Gordon and I held our breath while she gazed at her reflection. We watched as she stroked her hair and cheek, much in the way that Little Jo touched me. She seemed entranced. "I see myself," she said, "I see me."

Then she turned back to us, eyes flashing with anger. "How could they do that to me? How could anyone do that to any child?"

She flew into my arms, just like Missy, and sobbed. "I can see the me that you see," Jo whispered.

But then, a day later, I had to reassure Jo again after she found a clinical article that described the therapeutic coparenting that Gordon and I are doing with the Flock as "messianic counter-transference."

It's hard knowing that I'd be scorned by most mental-health professionals. I haven't gone out of my way to talk about Flock treatment with my colleagues, but neither have I worked to hide what's happening. Based on my occasional exchanges with Harry, I've assumed that they are all adopting a wait-and-see attitude. Now I see that I've been naïve and must get used to the idea that at least some people might think I am as sick as my patient.

I do feel that this is right for the Flock. I can't deny the progress I am seeing. I can only hope that my "gut" is based on my professional savvy as well as the undeniable personal attraction I feel for them.

I can't help worrying about what's going to happen next. I'm as prepared for the personalities to grow out of their dependency on me as I was with my biological children. But what if I'm wrong? What if the Flock decides that it is comfortable being my "baby"? How will I force growth then? Can I stay objective enough to see that this needs to be done?

.   .   .

22

My understanding of the prime dictum, "Meet the patient where she is," deepens. I am applying it more literally with the Flock than I have ever before in my work. I've responded to the separate personalities as individuals from the beginning and have been able to perceive them the way they see themselves. But that doesn't mean that I have always responded to them in a way that each has needed. My fear of some of them has occasionally made for lousy therapy.

I know, I know, I know that you can't force growth. My past experience with children and adolescents has shown me that growth in those periods has little to do with adults' telling the youngsters that they have to grow up. With some of the personalities, it's been easy for me to keep this in mind. I've been able to allow Missy and Renee to grow in their own ways. I've let Little Joe be the little boy he knows himself to be. I've given each of these personalities the freedom to grow. Jo has been so focused on the goal of therapy that my task has been to get her to relax and let me worry about the therapeutic nature of our relationship.

Yet I lacked faith that therapy would progress with some of the others unless I reminded them of my more objective reality. Whenever Joan Frances, who seems to despise me, appeared, I reminded her that she was multiple and had been abused. I constantly supplied psychotic Josie with our current date and location. When I first met Rusty, clearly male and scornful of women, I felt compelled to challenge his identity by reminding him that he lived in a female body.

As a result, I saw little of Joan Frances and Rusty and simply couldn't reach Josie. I think now that my rigid adherence to what "needed" to be done was dictated by my discomfort with their lack of acceptance of my reality! I didn't really miss Joan Frances or Rusty when they didn't appear. I was content to spend the hours of therapy with those personalities who seemed to appreciate me more.

I actually acted in ways to discourage Josie's appearance. I can't deny that I was afraid of her. I wasn't sure what part she played in the system or how much of a threat she was to the Flock. What if they all got psychotic like Josie instead of her getting better? My time with Josie was spent trying to keep her from hurting herself and trying to shock some reality into her. I had no energy left for creative therapeutic intervention.

Gordon has reminded me that the acceptance I spouted applies equally to all of the personalities. Gordon saw instantly beyond Josie's bizarre and frightening behavior and gave her love without expectations. Relaxed, fatherly, and warm, Gordon has given Rusty permission to grow and develop in ways he was never allowed before.

The simple but elusive concept that people must first of all feel accepted for who they are before they can risk change has once again been confirmed for me. It's so easy to forget when we're threatened. Nowhere is the result of remembering this concept so clearly seen as with Rusty in his relationship with Gordon.

. . .

Rusty had always been a mystery to me, as well as to others in the Flock. When I first accepted the others enough to talk openly with Lynn, I completely forgot about him.

I was surprised when Isis told Lynn that Rusty was another personality and not an external playmate of Missy's, but I still didn't think he'd ever much matter to any of us. I didn't want to think about an adolescent boy living in *my* body.

But then, in January 1983, Rusty popped out during a session, defiant and suspicious, and looking for his dad. He hadn't returned since Lynn said he was a girl. He didn't know much, but he had no doubt that he was a boy. He wouldn't be a girl in a million years.

But Rusty languished in the recesses of the Flock's mind, longing for male companionship, and once Gordon started attending the sessions, it was only natural that Rusty would eagerly come forward. He ignored "that lady Lynn," but responded to Gordon, who seemed to him both safe and smart.

Maybe Gordon could tell him how things were. Rusty knew he forgot a lot of stuff.

Rusty visualized his mind as being like a fishing net. The only things he could remember were the little drops that clung to his mental netting.

When Gordon said, "Tell me about yourself," Rusty remarked glumly, "I can tell you that in five seconds!"

Rusty said that he came from Saint Michaels, a small fishing village on the Chesapeake Bay. He remembered having spent a lot of time with his dad; he had also served as an unidentified helper to Keith and Steve. "I didn't tell those other men my name," Rusty said, " 'cause my dad said I shouldn't say nothin' to nobody."

Rusty wished his dad would hurry up and come get him. As far as Rusty knew, his dad had simply disappeared a long time ago. "Maybe he's gone back to sea. When that lady Nancy bugged him, that's what he said he was gonna do. I seen them freighters in the lake here sometimes," Rusty said, "and I wave in case my dad's there lookin' for me.

"I can read animal tracks," Rusty concluded, "but I can't read no words."

Rusty didn't tell Gordon that when he stared at printed words long and hard, waiting for them to speak to him as they seemed to do to other people, he got real scared. He feared that the lines would notice him watching, sharpen into daggers, and kill him. He didn't tell Gordon how he looked away quick when he saw words glaring up at him.

"Do you have any friends?" Gordon asked. "Yup, one," Rusty said, and told him about Gary, a mongoloid boy who cleaned out the nets on a dock in Norfolk. Gary couldn't read none and he forgot things too.

"I'm a retard. I ain't like other boys," Gary confided, and showed Rusty his bright-green rabbit's foot, which helped him remember the little he could. Rusty showed Gary his own special columbine shell, which he stroked when he realized he had forgotten something important.

Rusty was aware that he was unlike other boys; there was some difference that he couldn't quite name. He figured that he must be retarded too.

Like Gary, Rusty knew the sea and its creatures intimately. Gordon admitted to Rusty that he knew nothing about the seasonal changes of the bay or about the stages in the life of the Chesapeake blue crab, and professed an interest in learning. So Rusty told Gordon, in a pronounced Eastern Shore accent, about "arstering" and how the oyster boats were forced by law to work under sail during certain months of the year.

"It's hard for them arsters to have a fighting chance when they're stuck in those shells and can't move none," Rusty said.

Gordon knew lots of things that Rusty's dad had never known, and shared that in return. Gordon said he didn't know about commercial shellfishing like Rusty, but he also loved the water. Gordon sailed boats and he spent his days teaching young boys how to build things in carpentry class.

Time after time, Rusty was delighted to find Gordon in Lynn's office. When Gordon didn't come for the Flock's appointment, Rusty demanded that Lynn tell him what she had done to "get rid of that man Gordon." "He'll be back, Rusty," Lynn said, and he was delighted to discover that she wasn't lying.

But after weeks of conversations, Rusty stopped talking. Though he still liked Gordon, he was tired of words. Rusty liked doing things. He got fidgety if he sat and listened for very long.

The solution seemed simple to Gordon. He had none of Lynn's professional conventions to overcome. If Rusty wanted to spend time with him working with his hands, they'd do it. Gordon had provided this sort of work therapy in the past, and decided that a healthy male relationship might help Rusty tell his story.

By this point, the Flock had developed our unique relationship with Lynn and Gordon to the extent that, when things were calm, they could often call for any personality they wished. So, when plans were made for Lynn and Gordon to come to the house so that Rusty could work with Gordon, it was Rusty who eagerly met them at the door one mild April Sunday afternoon.

Gordon had a radio and an antenna to install in his car and wanted Rusty to help. Lynn sat off to the side, out of earshot, reading a book and enjoying the sunshine. "That lady knows how to keep her mouth shut," Rusty observed. "That's sometimes so," Gordon said with a chuckle.

While Rusty and Gordon worked on the car, and later, while they built bookshelves at Gordon and Lynn's home, Rusty shared his memories with Gordon and with others in the Flock, who listened intently.

Rusty had the vivid but spotty recall that Gordon and Lynn had come to expect from past-keeper personalities. Rusty had watched while his dad spliced and knotted ropes with fisherman friends. Never allowed to touch the ropes himself, Rusty nevertheless committed all the intricate steps to memory. Now, many years later, Rusty demonstrated for Gordon all of the knots he had seen Ray create. Gordon was appropriately impressed and taught Rusty how to tie a few more.

Rusty also remembered drives to the shore with Ray. He talked with his dad about the things they both loved most—animals, the woods, the sea. When they neared other people, Ray cautioned, "You can come with me, but keep your mouth shut. If you say one word, I'll send you back to the car."

Silent but content, not wanting to embarrass his dad, Rusty watched while Ray shared a beer with the fishermen.

When Rusty could sit still no longer, he wandered out to the docks. During the spring and summer, Rusty watched floaters—molting crabs in their netted pens. He admired their willingness to work hard enough to cast off old shells, and he felt glad that they didn't know they were about to be eaten. Rusty listened while the boats, snug in their slips, talked to him in their special language of creaks and groans and told tales of their travels with decaying fish and seaweed.

As Rusty worked alongside Gordon, he was able to push through to his earliest memory of how he came to be. "I was in the woods, I saw my dad, and there I was," he said.

But with memories supplied by Missy, Josie, and some of the other personalities, Gordon and Lynn learned over time that this boy personality was created not in response to a single event, but in response to many years of provocation.

Ray began taking his daughter with him on weekend jaunts to Norfolk and other parts of the Virginia shore where he visited with commercial fishermen or explored pine-forest properties for real-estate speculation. The Missy personality loved being with Daddy. He taught her about different kinds of boats and knots. He helped her recognize birds by their songs. She learned to sit quietly on fallen logs so as to watch deer and fox moving through the foliage.

She was often entranced by the magic world of the forest, until Ray broke the spell by announcing that he "had to take a pee." He stayed just close enough to be in sight of his young daughter. She didn't look his way very often, but she noticed that he sometimes took a very long time.

On one trip, when the Flock was seven, Ray indulged a growing desire to involve his daughter actively. It was early spring, just after the violets began sparking the pine carpet. Missy leaned against a tree deep in the forest, smelled fresh pine sap, and tried not to watch her father. She saw his penis swell and quickly glanced away. "I wish he'd hurry up," she muttered to herself.

Missy glanced over again and her father caught her eye. "Betcha wish you had one of these," he said.

Missy was made uncomfortable by her father's throaty tone of voice, and she felt so very sad. Yes, she did wish she had one of those, because then her dad would like her better. Every night, before Missy fell asleep, she prayed to God to please make her a boy. She thought that, if she remembered to repeat the prayer for a long time, maybe a whole month, God would know she was serious and grant her wish.

"Hey," Ray said sharply, and Missy looked over. He was several feet away from her, but still exposed. "Come on over here," he said. Missy looked away, and Ray said again, more forcefully, "Come on over and see what I've written in the dirt here. Don'tcha love your old man?"

Missy suddenly felt cold. Conversation and coming close were something new in the "woods game." The rules were that he moved away from her and took his penis out. She'd look but pretend not to notice. After a while, he'd come back and they'd continue their hike.

But this time there was something new in her father's voice. He sounded almost angry. When his temper flared, someone always got hurt. She better move back.

"No, sir," she said, standing up and edging back behind a tree, "I'll stay here and wait for you to finish." Ray did not like to be disobeyed. Rage building, he zipped his pants back up and walked slowly toward her. Terrified and trapped, afraid to run and afraid to stay, Missy disappeared into herself.

None of the already existing personalities surfaced. They also felt terror at their father's infrequent but devastating rage.

Rusty was born. Brand-new, but ready to handle the situation, he stepped boldly from behind the tree to face his father. All Rusty knew was that he was fourteen years old and that this was the father who cherished him.

"Hey, Dad!" Rusty said, his voice and face reflecting all of the love the Flock had for Daddy with none of the complicating fear.

Noting the sudden change in his daughter's voice, gait, and manner, Ray stopped and said nothing. Rusty smiled disarmingly at his dad and looked pointedly at Ray's crotch. "I got one too, Dad," Rusty said proudly.

"Come over here," Ray said. "Let me see."

"Nope, Dad, I ain't gonna come over there," Rusty said with an assuredness that none of the girl personalities possessed. "I ain't gonna let you cut it off," he added in a cheery voice.

"Well, come over here and see what I've written in the dirt," Ray said, trying his ploy again.

"Nope, Dad," Rusty said again, smiling and confident.

"Why not?" asked Ray. "You scared of your old man?"

"Heck, no, Dad, I ain't scared of you," Rusty said.

"Well, why not?" Ray asked again.

Rusty stopped and searched his virtually blank mind for a moment, knowing that there must be an answer in there somewhere. When he found it, he smiled broadly again. "I ain't comin' over there to see 'cause I can't read."

Ray was apparently so perplexed by this turn of events that he forgot his sexual urge. His daughter had been able to read for years. What did she mean, she couldn't read? And if she didn't stop acting funny, there would be hell to pay when they got home to Nancy.

"Why are you talking like that?" Ray asked as they left the woods together, Rusty staying at least an arm's length away. Rusty didn't rightly know.

"Jist 'cause it's the way I talk, I guess," he finally answered.

"Well, don't talk like that around your mother," Ray cautioned.

"Oh, I don't got no mother," Rusty replied, "jist you, Dad." Ray let the matter drop.

From then until Ray's death, Rusty occasionally surfaced when the Flock was alone with him. Ray learned that his daughter liked to be called Rusty sometimes, and he himself rather liked it when they could both pretend that Joan was his son. He taught this "son" many things, including the inadequacies of women, of Nancy in particular.

Ray said that women were the most worthless creatures God had ever put on earth—"Jesus's one mistake." Rusty guessed that Gordon's woman, Lynn, was no exception.

Rusty was puzzled by Gordon's attitude toward women. No matter how many times Rusty gave Gordon the chance to vent his hatred of women, Gordon never did. Once Rusty overheard Lynn say something to

Gordon about her sailing lessons. Later, as they worked on the car, he questioned Gordon in private.

"Do you really let that lady sail your boats?"

"Yes," Gordon said.

"Does she sail as good as you?"

"No, she doesn't," Gordon responded calmly.

Rusty looked smug and satisfied.

But Gordon wasn't through. He finished tightening a bolt and surveyed Rusty's expression. "Lynn hasn't had as much practice sailing as I have. That's why she's not as good. But Lynn is much better than many of the male racers I know."

As he helped Rusty work through his hatred of women, Gordon stubbornly resisted supplanting one stereotype with another. He didn't tell Rusty that men and women were just alike. As usual, Gordon didn't see the world in line with the social convention and rejected my urgings to offer Rusty the expected "healthy" alternative.

"I don't see the world that way, Renee," Gordon said. "I just don't believe that everyone is the same. There are gender differences. All persons have important male and female aspects. They differ to the extent of how male or female their mixtures are.

"People who are homophobic or who, like Rusty, refuse to see worth in the other sex are really denying some intrinsic part of self," he said. That acceptance, Gordon explained, would come not from argument but from appreciation. Time and a noncommittal stance would take care of Rusty's problem with women.

"I won't force him to deny his male parts in an effort to accept his female parts. The more Rusty is around Lynn," Gordon decided, "and the more he is with me, the more he will come to see that who he is is his own delightful mix of male and female attributes."

Rusty flourished under Gordon's attention throughout the spring. Time and again, however, he became frustrated with his own limitations. "I know I'm really stupid," Rusty said. "I guess I'm just like that boy Gary."

"No, you are definitely not stupid or retarded," Gordon responded. "You learn quicker than most people I know. You see me do something one time and then you know how to do it. Most people can't learn that quick."

Rusty shrugged off the evidence. "But I can't read nothin', and I always forget, and I can't pound nails good."

Gordon didn't respond to the first two complaints. He hadn't yet determined the extent of Rusty's reading problem, and he knew that suggesting to Rusty that the "forgetting" was because he lived in a female frame with a lot of girl personalities would cause that personality to dive deep inside.

Gordon did address Rusty's third concern. "You're not really good at pounding nails with a hammer because that takes lots of practice."

Rusty listened quietly.

"Do you want to know how I help my boys at school learn how to hammer?"

Rusty nodded eagerly. He was sure that he wouldn't have forgotten so much if he had ever had a teacher like Gordon.

"I give them a board and a hammer and a hundred nails," Gordon said. "They learn how to hammer by pounding those hundred nails into that piece of board."

Rusty resolved that that was exactly what he would do, but he'd do it in a special way, to make Gordon proud. He found a piece of oak stump with beautiful swirling grain and bark around the edges. He bought some brass nails at the hardware store. For several nights, Rusty worked alone in the basement workshop at Steve's house.

"A flying horse," Rusty decided. That's what Gordon reminded him of. Rusty remembered having seen a picture of Pegasus many years before, and he was so entranced by the idea of a horse that could fly that he remembered the picture in vivid detail.

A few weeks later, Rusty had grown competent with a hammer. And Gordon had a brass-nail Pegasus that shimmered against an oiled wood background, the flow of the grain used to simulate coat and movement.

DIARY *May 1, 1983*

Gordon has bonded with the personalities so easily that I can't help being a little envious. I can rationalize how and why it happened: the personalities were ready to relate to another person whom I trusted; they craved a male model and parent as much as they craved a female; the various personalities in the Flock were eager to love him because of their identification with me.

I can trace their readiness for involvement with him back to the progress

I *had made with the Flock, but it's still sometimes frustrating. The relation-ships that it took me two long years of hard work to develop, Gordon established with ease in two months.*

And it's even more frustrating that I can't talk to my favorite confidant about this. Even now, even with the clear bonding and love he has with Jo, Rusty, Josie, and Renee, he seems ready to back out at the slightest criticism.

For example, Gordon is dealing with the Flock and their gender issues much differently from the way I deal with them. Jo and I, and Renee and I as well, have had long talks about maleness and femaleness. For Jo I try, from time to time, to describe the feelings that go along with being a woman. Renee and I talk about sex, but from a different perspective. Renee has trouble reconciling the fact that Ray sexually abused his daughter with his derision of women in his conversations with Rusty. I've pointed out that Ray's sexual behavior is more rightly labeled "pathology" than "expression of gender." Through our talks, Renee is beginning to understand that "female" is not synonymous with "victim," although she's still not sure that men are governed by anything other than sexual impulse.

But Gordon honestly believes it doesn't matter much that he was born male. When he thinks of who he knows himself to be, physical gender is just not significant.

He responds to Rusty's refusal to accept any femaleness by saying, "Who cares if you're a boy or a girl?" He responds to Jo's lack of gender identity by saying, "Why don't you work on feeling you rather than worry-ing about feeling female?" When I commented that his approach, so unlike mine, might muddy the waters a bit, he said, "I don't want to do anything wrong. I'll stop anytime you want me to."

He knows as well as I do that we're all too deeply into this now for anyone to back out, but I guess this is Gordon's reminder to me that he has his own way of doing things. He probably also would like to maintain a position from which he can disclaim responsibility for anything the Flock might do and distance himself from Flock overreactions. I wouldn't mind being able to do that myself sometimes.

Last week, Gordon talked on the phone with Steve in one of our now regular attempts to prepare Steve for how intensely involved with us he is likely to find "Jo" upon his return to Chicago next month. For once, Renee's anxiety doesn't seem out of proportion with reality. She's begged us to help Steve understand.

Gordon said that Steve sounded far less wary when he learned that Harry approved of the work Gordon and I were doing together; Steve was glad to hear that Gordon and I met with my supervisor periodically to talk about the Flock's progress and brainstorm next steps.

"I think I convinced him that we're not doing anything 'kinky,' " Gordon said after the phone call. If Steve understood that our "consults" with Harry were actually happy-hour meetings at the campus bar where the staff congregates on Friday afternoons, he might feel differently.

Unfortunately, Steve told Renee a day later that he thought he could handle the inordinate amount of time she spent with us now that he understood that the only interest we had in her was clinical. Despite two years of evidence to the contrary, Renee called me enraged.

"I know we don't mean anything to you. That 'family' crap was all a sham. You just want us to get better and leave you alone."

It took four days to help Renee regain her trust in us. This was a good object lesson in how shaky things are for the Flock. We make many steps forward, but one false move, one misstatement, can send them all scuttling back to their former wariness. I need to keep their vulnerability in mind as treatment progresses.

But that's the therapist talking. As a "mom" in her early fifties who ends the workday to start raising an unplanned "flock," I sometimes feel underappreciated and unable to share my needs with Gordon. I knew months ago that the therapist-versus-parent role would be difficult, but I was prepared for the problems to be the Flock's, not mine.

.   .   .

23

Jo, Josie, Rusty, and Missy all felt secure in their relationships with Gordon and Lynn. I felt envious.

I knew it was my own fault. I had carefully distanced myself from "therapy" for the two years and two months that Lynn had worked with the Flock. I called myself the "message-and-delivery" person: I made sure that Lynn knew what was happening in the Flock's life and that we got to the appointments with her on time, but I was delivering those other personalities, not myself. *I* didn't need therapy. My only real problem had been that the other personalities fought me for *my* time and *my* body.

But now things had changed. Being a family with Gordon and Lynn was different from being in therapy. I desperately wanted to feel connected to people, but was afraid to take relationships too seriously. Everything remained on the surface. I told myself to expect nothing so that I wouldn't be hurt when relationships ended. My husband, Keith, had been the only person who I thought would stay forever. In the end, he left.

I watched with detached amazement through March and April as Lynn and Gordon demonstrated their acceptance of the various personalities. I monitored carefully, but never heard Lynn say, "We'll have to get rid of this one." Gordon never said, "I hate it when this personality is out."

Gordon even defended Josie. If ever there were a personality I would have gleefully turned from the fold, it was that deeply troubled, inarticulate, panic-filled personality.

Gordon saw a different Josie. He helped her communicate, helped her grow stronger, encircled her with love as she fought the approach of her memories, held her quietly as, exhausted from panic spent, she trustingly fell asleep on his shoulder. "Josie has strength. She has something important to give to the Flock," he said to me. "You'll see."

I could tell that Gordon genuinely loved Josie. I could tell that Gordon and Lynn loved them all. Since I didn't throw fits which needed their attention, I decided that they must not care for me as they did the others. On some level, I figured that that was probably OK; at least *I* wouldn't get hurt if they decided to give up on the Flock. But I still felt left out.

Then the others began to take more of my time outside Lynn's office. Kendra and Isis often popped out during shopping trips. Rusty pushed me aside at home to take time to work in the shop. Even Missy whined when she didn't have time to play, and she threatened to "tell her friend" that I was mistreating her. These were annoyances, but there was other interference that felt more dangerous.

Josie was now fully awake and filled with memories—her as-real-as-today memories of abuse. She still had little understanding of current reality, aside from a new desire to call for Gordon when she groggily reached consciousness. I lived in fear of her coming out at some inappropriate time.

Once I fled a faculty meeting when I found myself fixated on a painted white concrete wall. Josie, I realized, was fantasizing throwing herself against that wall. I left because I was a little unsure as to whether Josie had made her presence apparent.

One morning early in May, I called Lynn from my school phone. "Hi," I said. "My first class starts in ten minutes and I had to make some contact. Josie is really close to the surface, and I'm feeling a little desperate. I'm so afraid of losing control in front of my students."

Lynn responded sympathetically, but I suspected that she didn't really appreciate the depth of my anxiety. "Damn it," I said, "there are only six more weeks left in the school year. I have to get through the year without the Flock ruining everything for me. Can't you tell them that that's only fair?"

"I know, sweetie, I hear you," Lynn said.

But eventually I had to return to my classroom alone. I took a deep breath and faced the kids, worried that Josie might suddenly appear, anxiety-ridden and confused. What would it do to them if they saw a favorite teacher "go crazy" in front of them?

An hour later, I congratulated myself on having made it through the class without incident. Only four more classes left to teach today. "I can do it," I said to myself, "I've got to." I turned to watch the next group of kids pile in and noticed Gordon standing in the doorway. "Gordon," I said with embarrassment and relief, "what are you doing here?"

"Lynn called and said you were having some trouble," he explained. "I got a substitute for my classes and thought I'd drop by."

I smiled at Gordon's understatement. It was not easy to get substitute teachers at his inner-city high school, and he had driven more than thirty miles to "drop by." I smiled at him gratefully and shook my head in amazement.

"I've got a class to teach," I said.

"I know," he replied. "I'll do whatever is good for you. If you want, I'll hang out in the back of the classroom so that the whole Flock knows I'm here. Or, if you prefer, I'll run some errands and come back to see you this afternoon, after you finish with your teaching."

"Go!" I said, "I think we'll be OK now."

I got through the rest of the day without worrying about losing control. Gordon had left, but he'd be back at the end of the day. "Why would he do that for me?" I wondered.

After my last class, Gordon and I sat under a tree in the schoolyard. I marveled aloud at how wonderful he was to have gotten so involved with the Flock, how special a person he was to have "adopted" us.

"I adopted Lynn's children," Gordon said. "Why not one more?" I was silent. "Oh, you didn't know that?" he said. Gordon had married Lynn some twenty years before, when she was a divorcée, alone with all those children.

Later that week, Lynn left a session early to pick up her granddaughter, Hilary, from the day-care center. Gordon was in no hurry, so he and I sat on a grassy knoll outside Lynn's office, enjoying the sunshine.

"Lynn says that this is all going to end with the Flock integrating and becoming one person, but you know that's not going to happen," I said.

Gordon shrugged noncommittally.

"No matter how much I get to like the rest of the Flock, I'm going to stay me, Renee, forever. I'm going to stay my own person."

Gordon chewed a blade of grass and finally said, "I guess I don't understand why integration is such an issue."

"You don't understand?" I sputtered and quickly filled him in. "I'm not Rusty, Jo, Josie, or any of the rest. I'm me and want to stay me. I don't need them! How would you like it if someone told you that you had to merge your being with another person?"

Unlike Jo, I didn't have the patience to sit still while Gordon worked his way through a thoughtful explanation. He watched me closely as I trailed off. I stopped, but grinned, knowing that he hadn't taken offense at my cutting him off. Lynn, too, often jumped in before he finished speaking.

Gordon waited until he was sure I was done. "I guess I start from a different basis, Renee," he said. "I've never been sure just how separate individuals need to be. I know I'm limited by only having my own thoughts, my own perspective, my own mind. I think that one day humans will evolve to the point where we can all integrate with one another at will. Maybe it will be like putting two heads together for a special project. Maybe it will be a way of bonding with people you feel very close to.

"If that time were now, I'd happily integrate with you. I'm sure I'd learn much more through Renee-Gordon awareness than I can learn on my own."

I didn't respond. I couldn't force this man to argue with me about integration when he didn't even accept "one mind, one body" as a necessary concept. I was disappointed that I couldn't use this time alone with Gordon to persuade him that we shouldn't integrate, but I felt special. "Gordon wants to integrate with me," I thought, assured that he had seen something worthwhile in me, maybe something I hadn't yet seen in myself.

That evening, I mulled over Gordon's words and felt a touch of fear. Was this some sort of subtle seduction? I had been formed, literally, through a sexual act. Every man I had been close to had wanted me sexually. Was Gordon like that?

I hoped not. That would ruin everything. I knew Lynn could not have tolerated it. If it happened and she didn't know, I wouldn't be able to pretend and couldn't stand the probability that some other personality would tell her. As it was, I was scared that some other personality would share my suspicion with Lynn.

"Lynn says that she and Gordon love the Flock in a way we've never been loved before," I remembered. "I hope that's true."

I decided it was time that I let Lynn and Gordon know how my feelings about them and about their relationship with the Flock had changed. I was no longer the message-and-delivery person. I was Renee, as much their surrogate daughter as the rest.

On Mother's Day, I supplemented Missy's inevitable homemade card with a small gold unicorn for Lynn to put on the delicate chain she wore around her neck. The unicorn had become a significant symbol since Isis had early in therapy presented Lynn with a print of a medieval tapestry depicting a unicorn fenced and leashed by a gentle maiden. My gift to Lynn was chosen so that she'd know I was part of the special relationship she shared with the Flock.

She accepted my gift with hugs and smiles while Gordon watched. "Can I be part of the family too?" I asked.

With that, Gordon joined our embrace. Lynn laughed. "Don't you know how important you are?" she asked. "Where would the Flock be, where would our family be without you, Renee?"

I guess I did know. Just like Jo, I finally did belong. Just like Jo, I needed to hear that said.

Any personality who was in crisis had priority in the time with Lynn and Gordon, but I now no longer felt guilty about the time I took. I had as much right to be with them as the others.

"I've been thinking about teaching summer school," I told them one day soon after Mother's Day. "Any extra money I earn will come in handy at Harvard."

"I know you need the money," Gordon said, "but, if you teach, that might interfere with our trips."

"Our trips?" I asked.

"Yes," Lynn said, "we thought we'd spend some weekends up at the cottage this summer. That would give us long, uninterrupted time for Flock-work."

I quickly gave up the idea of teaching summer school. I had seen pictures of Gordon and Lynn's lakeside cottage, nestled on fifteen acres near Kenosha, Wisconsin. I wanted to go with them, wanted days when the Flock could be free, days when we all could soak up our new parents' nurturing.

My anxiety about Steve's return lessened once I knew about the upcoming weekends at the cottage. The Flock had changed significantly in the months Steve had been away. He was going to need to accept our changes and the changes in our relationship with Gordon and Lynn. I might even be able to tolerate Steve's disapproval if I knew that special time with Gordon and Lynn could continue.

DIARY *June 5, 1983*

Isn't it interesting that Renee, who has always perceived herself as the "healthy" one, is the one who has made the clearest strides toward health over the last couple of months? Despite the body's chronological age and despite Renee's claim to be nineteen or twenty years old, she really is a delightful (though sometimes exasperating) young adolescent. She now moves between the role of "mother's helper" in dealing with the rest of the Flock and the role of my daughter, with all of the predictable associated conflicts.

I've known for months that Renee was envious of the closeness that Jo and Missy were developing with Gordon and me, and I wondered how she'd handle it. Female closeness had always been dangerous for this personality; male closeness had always meant sex.

Gordon and I watched during the spring as she grew from a personality who distanced herself from the other personalities to one who sought our approval for her good work. Renee would tell us about some gain that the Jo personality had made and then add, "Isn't it good that I'm giving her time to do that?" We gave Renee continual positive reinforcement, but it was clear to us, if not to her, that this wasn't enough.

Renee needed to know that we'd respond to her, and we waited, knowing that an opportunity would present itself. As with most things in this therapeutic-reparenting relationship, it was pure luck that Renee called me from school frantic and raw on a morning when Gordon could take the day off to respond in ways she hadn't imagined. His surprise visit told her clearly that we heard her need and would respond as surely as we responded to the rest of the Flock. Mother's Day gave her a perfect opportunity to tell me what I represented to her.

The sexual issue has been more difficult, because Renee is still not able to admit her own desires. She responds to men who want her, she says, but denies that she might "go after" someone on her own. So I've watched her flirt with Gordon, a man on whom three adopted daughters have checked to see whether Daddy could assure them that they were attractive without taking them up on their subconscious offers.

The subtlety of her seduction is amazing. She's intense, virtually vibrating with passion, and simultaneously whimsical and needy. Gordon says that she touches every conventional male nerve in her call to "take me."

I like Gordon's approach of refusing to acknowledge Renee's sexuality while seeking to bond with her on every other level. He will be her father, her friend, her cosmic intimate, and she's discovering through experience that he will not be her lover. Best of all, this is happening without Renee's being forced to acknowledge the sexual urges that would now humiliate and frighten her.

I don't mean to imply it's all been easy. Renee is a delightful daughter, going shopping and taking walks with me, giggling with me over shared secrets, modeling herself after me, but she's also volatile and just one part of a very troubled entity. Sometimes, when she rages at me that she "knew all along that I didn't really care," I have to bite my tongue to keep from telling her that she's an ungrateful little bitch. Instead, I remember that this is an expression of an incredibly complex combination of ignored needs. I calmly remind her of the many hours Gordon and I spend with her and with the Flock and tell her that needing some time to myself is not a rejection of her.

This is all a great gamble on Gordon's and my part. The stakes are very high for us and for the Flock. Steve returns this week, and we have three months before the Flock goes away to Harvard (I've now convinced myself that she is actually going off to school). Weekends at the cottage will give us time to work through pathology and make everyone feel secure in my caring. This summer will have to be spent both trying to satisfy their seemingly endless thirst for parenting and helping them let go of us so that they can begin to meet some of those needs internally. I have come to believe that concentrated time, when it's needed—freely given and with a special purpose—can accomplish goals that even years of traditional treatment sometimes cannot.

. . .

24

Harvard and Steve. These are what I worry about when I'm not worrying about whether or not Gordon and I have gotten ourselves in too deep.

I wasn't really surprised when Renee submitted an application to Harvard. Both Renee's need to run from me and Jo's need to prove herself to Steve were very strong last winter, when they applied. I also wasn't surprised that the Flock was accepted. Despite all of their denials, this entity is very bright, very creative, certainly Ivy League material.

I honestly didn't think that Renee intended to go until April, when she made arrangements to quit her job. The Flock spends up to twenty hours a week with Gordon and me. Even with Steve returning, the relationship they share with Gordon and me is clearly what's most important to the Flock. I couldn't then and still can't understand how Renee thinks that they can ever function so far from home.

I called Connie Wilbur, who didn't seem particularly concerned about the situation. She suggested contracting with all of the personalities to attain cooperation with one another at Harvard. I wish I could do that, but cannot imagine how. The only ones who really want to go now are Renee and Joan Frances. Jo tells me she's not ready; others in the Flock would have no idea about the decision and what it means. I can just see myself peeling Josie off Gordon's shoulder and saying, "Ignore your abreactive hallucinations for a minute, dear, and talk with me about going to Harvard."

But, even if I can't imagine how it will work right now, in many ways it's too late to worry about that. It must work. I have a sense that they are going to go, or die trying. But it's also possible that my analysis of the strength of their desire is partly wishful thinking. Gordon and I have committed ourselves to making the Flock our priority for the next several weeks. This is emotionally draining work and possible only because there is a foreseeable end to the intense time and effort.

Steve returns from Cornell tomorrow. I have no idea what will happen. Steve and the Flock (mostly Renee) managed a relationship because they both were willing to deny the disorder most of the time. Now I think that this is impossible for Renee. If she had to choose right now between her relationship with Gordon and me and her relationship with Steve, she'd walk away from him without a backward glance.

I think Renee understands now that the only way to deal with the pathology is to face it squarely. If Steve continues to fight treatment, as he did before his departure in January or, even more subtly, in his phone calls, the Flock will, self-protectively, withdraw from him further. There may be no relationship left by the time the Flock and Steve are willing to deal with one another honestly, but her personal growth is more important now than a relationship based on the pathology of both partners.

.   .   .

I couldn't imagine how Steve would make sense of it all. When he left, Lynn was my therapist, a therapist who saw me far too often for his liking. Now Lynn and Gordon were my Flock's surrogate parents.

I cared about Steve, maybe even loved him, and I knew that others in the Flock cared about him too. Before Steve left, I thought of the multiplicity as a nuisance, something I tolerated out of lack of choice. Now I knew the other personalities as people, struggling for fulfillment. I wouldn't deny their existence or need for time, even if that's what was necessary to make Steve happy. If Steve loved me as much as he claimed, he was going to have to learn to love the other personalities as well.

As I waited those final hours for Steve's return, my resolve weakened. I'd give him a nice homecoming and not get into any discussions about the Flock for a few days. Maybe I'd let him see the others for short periods of time over the next few weeks. And I had better ease off on the long hours the Flock spent with Gordon and Lynn. Steve had to know that he was important too.

All was well until Steve and I went to bed. We hadn't made love in months, and I anticipated that this might be difficult. Josie was distressingly close to the surface. I reminded myself that Josie had never actually appeared outside Lynn's office.

For a while, everything was fine. I relaxed. Steve was tender, protective. I felt loved and safe and honestly responsive. Then, suddenly, without warning, Josie dived for the wall.

Terrified by the bizarre behavior, Steve pulled Josie to him. Tense muscles melted, and, just as suddenly, he had Missy in his arms. She pulled from him and petulantly curled up with her pillow. That was too much for Steve. He reached for the phone on the night table, found and dialed Lynn's number. "What should I do? I can't 'just calm down,' " he yelled into the phone.

Jo slowly gained consciousness and looked around in bewilderment. She was glad to see Steve home, but he seemed terribly upset about something; she didn't want any part of that. She pulled on jeans and shirt and left the room. Steve had witnessed three obvious personality switches—me to Josie to Missy to Jo—in less than five minutes. With a vengeance, Steve was finding out that things had changed.

Steve, no longer able to call the diagnosis "clinical bullshit," told Lynn that he was willing to help. He wanted to be involved.

As impressed as I was with Steve's change of heart, I was uncertain. I was protective of the Flock's relationship with Gordon and Lynn. I didn't want that to change or them to pull away because Steve was back in town. There was a big difference between Steve's saying he wanted to be involved and his getting used to sharing his house with personalities of varying ages, dispositions, and sexual identities.

"Give him a chance," Lynn counseled. "We're not going to desert you. We'll be your parents and therapists, but it won't hurt the Flock to have a loving friend."

I tried. For a few weeks, the personalities cycled out at will, as they had before Steve's return. Jo worked on her master's thesis; Charlene did the cooking; Rusty changed the oil in the car; Missy played in the yard with the dogs. Each, in his or her own way, tried to make friends.

Steve tried, but couldn't believe enough to make it work. And he could make no sense whatsoever of Missy's attempts at conversation.

"You like it here," Missy said, trying to let Steve know that she felt at ease.

"Yes, I like it here," Steve responded gently. "Do you?"

"Yes, you do," Missy said.

"What about *you?*" Steve asked again, a little more sharply.

Now Missy was uncertain. This man was getting angry. She enjoyed living in his house and was trying to tell him that. Lynn never got angry at her because of the way she talked, so Missy slipped inside to the safety of memories of her time with her friend Lynn.

I patted Missy's shoulder reassuringly on my way out to talk to Steve. Poor kid. Maybe I could mediate between them. "Steve, I know you're really trying," I said. "You're compassionate and accepting of the different parts now, but I'm afraid that you're just going to have to translate for Missy. She says 'you' when she means 'I.' She's terrified still of being self-referential. Lynn says she'll grow out of it."

"Well, then, why do you act that way?" Steve asked. "I like you a lot better when you're normal, like now."

I gave up.

I developed an informal schedule that lasted through the summer. On most weekdays, while Lynn was at work, the Flock spent a couple of daytime hours with Gordon. I had dinner with Steve and spent time with him when he got home from work, but left for Lynn's as soon as I had cleaned up the kitchen. I knew Steve was hurt by my absence, but I had no choice. Steve wanted to be with me at the only time Lynn was available to be with the Flock.

Steve and I had gone around often enough about the disorder for me to know that he thought he was doing just fine with the other personalities. I tried other tactics to explain my time away from him.

"Flock-work has to be a priority this summer," I said. "I'm not going to be able to be functional at Harvard unless the Flock works some stuff out pretty quickly."

"You did pretty well before you got into therapy with Lynn," he responded.

I knew that was true, but my new difficulties were not based on some pathological tie with Lynn. I had managed before because all of the memories of abuse and pain had been hidden, festering below the surface. Now they were all coming out. There was no way I could stop the flow, no way I could hide it all again. I had no choice but to see it through.

"Steve, I love you," I said. "But I can't really *be* an adult, I can't be the woman you want me to be, until the Flock works through the past abuse and our emotional dependency on Gordon and Lynn."

"That's another thing that bothers me," Steve said. "Why do you have to spend so much time with Gordon? He's not a therapist."

"Let's be accurate here," I shot back, losing my patience. "*I* don't spend that much time with him. Rusty is the personality who is usually with Gordon, and he's thriving on the healthy fathering that Gordon provides. In that sense, he's as much a therapist as Lynn. Besides, Rusty is learning to sail. Sailing is an important part of therapy right now."

Rusty began to sail the first weekend we spent at Lynn and Gordon's cottage. As soon as we arrived at the cottage, Gordon took Rusty to the dock. For Rusty, it was love at first sight. The eighteen-foot centerboard sailboat was rigged to be sailed by one person or by two. She purred contentedly as the waves rubbed her against the berth's rubber padding.

"Let's try it," Gordon said. He said to Rusty, "Do this. Now grab that." Rusty followed his lead so intently that they were out into the lake with sail furled before Rusty realized that he had done it all alone.

Tentatively, then more forcefully, Rusty moved his strength with the boat's, using rudder and ropes to nose the boat into the wind. His visual memory served him well. As Rusty learned to control the sails, he memorized the horizon, the taut pull of sails and ropes when the boat was well directed, the angle the boat made with the sky and the lake when she slipped along in harmony.

Rusty forgot nothing Gordon taught him. It was undeniable. Rusty could sail a boat. He glowed when Gordon said that he was learning faster than most students he had taught.

Rusty learned to trust as well as to sail.

Gordon offered Rusty the freedom that comes from doing something well. He sat quietly, watching patiently while Rusty sailed. Gordon encouraged Rusty to practice maneuvers over and over until he got them just right. And Rusty's confidence in himself grew. This was not a false confidence that he could do no wrong, but one based on the sureness that he could correct mistakes.

Ray hadn't tolerated mistakes. When something went wrong, he told his kid, "You don't think. You're stupid. You have no common sense." Rusty, as well as the other personalities, felt devastated when they made mistakes. Even a grade of A— indicated that something was lacking.

Gordon, on the other hand, treated mistakes as opportunities for learning. A mistake was something to be fixed. He taught Rusty that fixing things could be even more fun than getting them right the first time.

On the face of it, taking a multiple out in a sailboat seemed dangerous. The little boat sometimes skimmed the water at precarious angles. What if Josie found herself there and panicked? How could Gordon calm her and keep the boat from capsizing?

Gordon and Lynn recognized within the Flock a sense of internal coordination that none of the individual personalities could see. No matter how often I worried about losing control in the classroom, it never happened. Lynn and Gordon were confident that there was some internal harmony and logic as to which personality surfaced when. Lynn used this understanding to help me accept what had happened on Steve's first night home.

"If you had been able to pretend that everything was all right that first night, both you and Steve would have continued to deny the reality of the Flock, just as you did before he left," Lynn said. "Somewhere, down deeper than you know, the entity made it impossible for you to make the Flock's needs secondary."

Lynn said that the same force made it possible for Rusty to have all of the sailing time without pathological intervention from the others. "You'll see more and more evidence of 'entity' understanding as time goes on," she said. "You've got to put some trust in the 'group' mind."

With no thought that it might be otherwise, Rusty had the sailing to himself. Alone with Gordon on the water, Rusty talked in detail about his memories of his father. Rusty had never liked what Ray did in the woods, and he was relieved to hear Gordon say that Ray's behavior was wrong.

One day, the subject of Ray's mysterious disappearance arose. "I know my dad's gonna come back from the sea and get me someday," Rusty confided with an equal mix of hope and dread as they were bringing *Mantra* in from a sail.

"No, Rusty, I don't think that's going to happen," Gordon said, handing him the rope to cast to a piling. "Those girls that you don't want to know about told me that your father got very sick and died."

Rusty smiled at Gordon's oblique reference to the taboo subject of girls. He didn't want to talk about that, and Gordon was apparently willing to wait until he was ready. Rusty focused instead on his father's disappearance.

"I guess you're right, Gordon," Rusty said. "I guess my dad ain't ever comin' back."

Gordon nodded and waited while Rusty looped the rope and patted the boat on her stern as he vaulted ashore. "If my dad ain't ever gonna come back," Rusty fretted, "then I ain't got no dad. A boy needs his dad."

"Oh, I wouldn't worry about that, Rusty," Gordon said, and walked from the dock, his arm around Rusty's shoulders.

Rusty asked hesitantly, "Will you be my new dad?"

"I guess I am, Rusty."

25

The summer continues to be an intense time for all of us. Gordon and I spend an average of four hours a day with the Flock, not much of it in anything that looks like in-office psychotherapy. But it is therapeutic nevertheless.

Individual personalities are working through pathology. More important, they are beginning to emulate Gordon's and my parenting internally. They are taking better care of one another. Although Renee and Jo, in particular, often express frustration about the others, they both seem eager to listen to ideas of how to make life more comfortable for everyone, not just for their individual selves. That, I think, is a significant change.

Now that the personalities (aside from Joan Frances) have accepted the incredible dependency they feel toward Gordon and me, they are both enjoying it and working their way out of it. It's hard being "on call" twenty-four hours a day. Gordon and I need breaks and we take them— a weekend away by ourselves, an evening out for dinner and a movie—but we know that we can't stay unavailable to the Flock for long. It's hard, and perhaps only tolerable because we know the Flock will be leaving for school in September.

Renee is eager to talk with me about the dependency, partly because she wants me to appreciate all the times the Flock deals with crises internally rather than calling Gordon or me, and partly because the dependency is newly recognized. Renee needs to press at her new feeling as though it were a sore tooth. She describes her feeling as a "deep, overwhelming hunger" that never is totally satisfied. "Why don't you say 'enough already' and get it over with?" she asks.

I reassure her that neither Gordon nor I will reject the Flock. I know that they'd almost prefer it if we did. It would be easier for them than having really to feel the dependency and work it through. At the same time, they recognize that they must limit their own desire for us. "You can't make up for a lost childhood," Jo said to me. I told her that she was right—I couldn't—but that Gordon and the Flock and I could do it together.

The Flock's basic need for unconditional love from all three of us must be accepted before they can grow emotionally. It's clear that the personalities' history of abusiveness toward one another reflected the parenting they received from Nancy and Ray. It's up to Gordon and me to fill them with healthy parenting so that they have new messages to take in and use internally.

Some of that parenting is noninvasive. The Flock, Jo and Renee in particular, like being at our house without involvement from Gordon or from me. Renee works on a project or Jo reads, but the time is really spent finding out that it's safe simply to be here. They can observe how Gordon and I are, moving in our own rhythms, without the Flock's being the center of attention. They can know that they are loved without being in crisis or needing attention.

Weekends at the cottage reinforce these learnings in ways we could not otherwise.

. . .

Like any infrequently used weekend cottage, Lynn and Gordon's house always offered chores. Rusty helped Gordon repair screens and plumbing. Jo and I had a hand in running the lawn mowers over the cleared three acres near the house. Missy decided that she loved Gordon as much as Rusty did the day that Gordon called her name and then tossed her two spotted frogs.

Rusty and Gordon sailed the O-Day to the marshy end of the lake and surveyed the progress on a large beaver lodge. Rusty also spent time with Lynn, since Gordon included her in most of their plans.

Josie found beauty that counterbalanced the horror of her memories. She felt the roughness of tree bark, heard ducks quacking and frogs croaking; she lay flat on the grass and watched leaves shimmer silver in the wind against a background of blue sky. She felt peace. No longer simply a keeper of panic and violence, Josie began to awaken to the present.

Jo loved being at the cottage. Her time with Gordon and Lynn was unhurried. She felt no pressure to "do therapy," felt no fear of losing time to another personality. Jo trusted that if she cycled in she would eventually cycle back out to consciousness again. She enjoyed her theoretical conversations with Gordon and felt comfortable with Lynn as they stretched out side by side reading in the sun, close without needing to talk.

I watched Lynn and Gordon in wonder as they related to each other. "So, this is what marriage is supposed to be," I thought, "and this is what it means to be part of a family."

We had fun together—Gordon, Lynn, and the Flock. They were both so accepting of the Flock's reality of many minds in a single body that we all sometimes forgot the limitations of this existence. One Saturday, Lynn said to Gordon, "Maybe Renee and I will run into town while you and Rusty finish patching the screen door." Then Lynn caught herself and went off by herself, chuckling at the absurdity of her suggestion.

Later Lynn said, "You know, Renee, at the beginning I was afraid that I wouldn't be able to remember that the personalities saw themselves as separate. Now I am embarrassed to say that I sometimes have trouble remembering that you are all in the same body."

We all had periods of solitude at the lake as well. Lynn took long walks along the lake. Lynn and Gordon went into town together, leaving the Flock at the cottage feeling simultaneously loved and alone. The Flock explored the woods and meadows surrounding the lake.

At the cottage, Jo often woke earlier than Gordon and Lynn. She quietly pulled on her jeans, sweatshirt, and sneakers and set out to see this special world at dawn. Jo always wrote a note before she left, "I've gone for a walk," so that Gordon and Lynn wouldn't worry about her disappearance. "Don't worry," I added in my own distinctive scrawl, "we'll stay as a group."

26

"Renee, you seem down," Lynn said, taking me in quickly and then returning her attention to the rural lakeshore road. It was late August, our last weekend at the cottage before the Flock left for Harvard. This Saturday evening, Gordon was back in Chicago. Lynn and I were on our way to Manny's North of the Border Taco Bar.

"Worrying about school?" she asked.

"That too." I shrugged and continued my silent review of all the changes that had taken place since I had met Lynn in March 1981. Only two and a half years before, I had felt threatened by internal "compulsions" that had no name; now I knew I was multiple. Once I had wanted to destroy the other personalities; now I wanted everyone to be happy. The only thing that hadn't changed was my feeling that we would never integrate. I couldn't imagine what it would mean to turn all of the personalities into one. The personalities were much too different from one another for me even to consider that possibility.

Integration also seemed a denial of the other personalities. If all of us were unique and good, as Gordon and Lynn preached, what right did I have to destroy us all by integrating?

No. Not integration, but I did want cooperation. I knew we'd have to do a better job of working together if we were to be so far away from Gordon and Lynn. Our surrogate parents protected and comforted the young and more disturbed personalities. They relayed messages to the amnestic personalities and kept everyone calm. How would we manage without them?

I glanced over at Lynn. The potholes in the road were taking a fair share of her attention, but I knew her well enough to know that she was working hard to be silent until I was ready to talk.

"Did you know that I was still trying to run away from you when I sent in my application to Harvard?"

Lynn nodded.

"I was trying to get away from my growing dependency on you and trying to run away from the reality of the other personalities."

"Renee," she said, "I fooled myself about Harvard for a long time. I didn't really believe you were going until you quit your job. You were so close to becoming dysfunctional last spring that I didn't think there was any way you would make it. But now I feel better about it. This is truly an extraordinary flock—"

I cut her off.

"I am going to Harvard, but now I'm not running from you or from the Flock. I know they are as real as I am. I know they have needs as important as mine. And, Lynn, I love you."

I told Lynn of the intensity of my own need for her, of how that need was felt manyfold by Jo, Missy, and others in the Flock. "And their need is as strong as Rusty's and Josie's need for Gordon." I told her I knew that, despite or maybe because of the depth of our need, it was time for us to go away to school.

"We've had our time of being an emotional infant. Now we need to grow on our own. You and I both know that would be impossible if we remained here. You'd have to cut us loose in one way or another so that we could learn to take care of one another. No matter how you did that, it would be perceived as rejection."

Lynn nodded and gave a sigh of relief. "Renee, I'm glad you understand that. But you know that Gordon and I will still be here for you. We're all still family, even when you are gone. We know there is more Flock-work to be done. When you're home on school breaks, we'll spend lots of time together."

Lynn was being sincere, but it was hard for me to trust that our relationship would survive separation. Keith and I had moved around a lot, and I had never managed to continue friendships once we moved on. I wanted to believe that my relationship with Gordon and Lynn was different, and it felt different, but I didn't want to expect too much.

I shook that worry aside. "I am concerned about how the Flock is going to manage school," I said. "This degree is interdisciplinary, and the Flock has always split up academic work. Jo does theoretical work; Kendra is the writer; I'm the one who does negotiation and policy—no surprise. My worry is the amnestic blocks. I can usually know what the other personalities *did*, but I don't have access to their understandings. Even though Kendra and I can talk internally, that's not the same thing as having her skills. Jo and I can't talk at all, no matter how hard I try. Her amnestic wall against the rest of us is still soundproof."

"I know it will be hard—" Lynn murmured sympathetically.

"Then there are the little ones," I said, cutting her off again. "Missy, Rusty, Josie, and some of the others will be terribly upset by leaving you. I don't know how to get them through that trauma *and* handle school *and* handle all of the new relationships I'll be developing with other students and professors. I hereby resign as leader/manager/whatever of the Flock."

"I would feel better about your leaving if there were greater cooperation in the group," Lynn said. "How about some little fusions among the personalities?"

I was gearing up to argue against the absurdity of making one person out of all of the various personalities, and to add that I didn't know how to do it anyway, when Lynn said, "Now, Renee, I'm not saying you have to integrate, but if a few of the personalities got together in some comfortable way, I think you'd all feel a little less vulnerable."

Lynn's suggestion sounded surprisingly reasonable to me, and I grew interested in the idea as Lynn and I discussed the various combinations. Certainly I wouldn't have my academic worries if Jo and I fused and I suddenly had all of Jo's intellectual talent accessible to me, but that combination seemed far from feasible.

"It just won't work," I said. "I can't talk internally to Jo, and, besides, Nancy and Ray were *her* parents. I don't have any parents. We're too different from each other to come together. But I do like the idea," I added quickly, so that Lynn wouldn't think I was being stubborn.

"It sounds good to me too, Renee," Lynn said, "but I'm no more sure than you as to who would combine best, or how to make it happen."

Nevertheless, by the time we reached Manny's, two other personalities were also thinking about a merger. Kendra, with her strong protective feelings, and Isis, with her ability to distance herself from external demands, could provide me, the people-pleaser, with enough strength to handle the complexity of the relationships I'd face at Harvard. But this merger meant compromise, and we weren't sure how much we'd give up for the good of the group.

However, none of the three of us claimed Nancy and Ray as our parents. We were willing to talk.

Three personalities sat down in our single body in the crowded, noisy bar. Suddenly, and for the first time, Kendra, Isis, and I were co-conscious. All there, at the same time, but still separate. Kendra sipped her beer and squinted at Lynn through the smoke. "OK," she said, "Renee, Isis, and I are ready to talk about it."

"Talk about what?" Lynn asked. She seemed confused.

"All three of us are able to listen and talk to one another and to you," Kendra explained with a trace of impatience. "Treat it like a conference call. Let's talk about whether or not we should fuse."

"Kendra, is that you?" Lynn asked.

"Yes, it's me," Kendra said, grinning wickedly at Lynn's surprise. "Remember, you're the one who started this conversation."

"It's me too," Isis said in her breathy, delicate voice.

"And, by the way," I added, "it's me, Renee, too."

Lynn shook her head in wonder and looked around at the strangers sitting at her elbow. She gulped her beer and plunged into the conversation. "OK, I guess nobody around us will be able to make sense of the discussion anyway."

Kendra, Isis, and I were amused at Lynn's concern for discretion. None of us cared. For a change, we were single-minded in our decision to talk out this fusion idea.

"It might be good if Isis, Kendra, and I got together," I began, "but I'm not completely in favor of it. I mean, Kendra is a bitch, and Isis is a lesbian."

"Wait a minute," Lynn said, protective of everyone in the Flock. "Kendra's not a bitch. She steps in to take care of the Flock when you're too involved in pleasing everyone outside to take care of yourself."

"Thanks for the support, Lynn," Kendra said dryly, "but, Renee, my so-called bitchiness really is your fault. You simper around other people so much that when I finally get out I have no choice but to defend us. If I'm a bitch, you're a doormat!"

"I wouldn't put it exactly that way," Lynn demurred, "but it's the essence of what I was trying to say."

Isis smiled serenely at Lynn. "You can see why they both need my broader view of the world," she said.

"I feel like I'm at a tennis match," Lynn observed. "Why don't I just facilitate instead of offering my own opinions? Isis, what do *you* think about all of this?"

"I'm not the sex maniac Renee seems to think I am," she responded.

"Sure, I had some affairs with women years back, but I've had far fewer affairs with women than Renee has had with men. The essential characteristic I bring to this merger is my ability to find peace in myself without depending on other people, like Renee, or fighting them, like Kendra."

Isis continued speaking aloud so as not to be rude to Lynn, but she directed her comments to the two other personalities. "Don't worry, Renee," she said. "I'm not going to attack our roommate when we get to school. I don't desire every woman any more than you desire every man. If it will make you feel better, I promise to refrain from sexual activity at Harvard. If we join together, will you promise to do the same?"

"Ah, OK," I responded a little hesitantly. I wasn't used to the other personalities' talking to me directly about what they wanted.

I turned to Lynn. "Do you know what I've just realized?" I said excitedly. "Kendra can be more subtle in her self-protection if she has a chance to do it earlier. And if Isis joins us both, Kendra and I will be able to feel a little more distanced from other people. We'll be able to understand that each person's perception of us is not a life-and-death matter."

"Exactly!" Kendra and Lynn said together.

The Alliance, the first fusion within the Flock, occurred that night over tacos and beer. Neither Lynn nor I was exactly sure how this fusion would work, how tightly woven the three personalities would become.

Kendra, Isis, and I retained the individual right to pull out if we liked. I didn't feel much change that night, but there were no longer any barriers to communication among the three of us.

The next day, the change was more apparent to me. Suddenly the world was filled with color, form, and design that I had missed through my neurotic focus on people alone. "Isis-and-I-together sees so much that I never saw as Renee-alone," I told Lynn. "And there's something else. I feel more like my own person now. Kendra has given me a protective coating. I don't feel dependent on anyone's acceptance, not even on yours."

Lynn smiled lovingly. "The Flock is growing up."

A few weeks later, Lynn, Gordon, and the Flock stretched out on Lynn and Gordon's living-room rug, reminiscing about cherished times from the summer. Lynn and Gordon cuddled all of us between them.

After midnight, I sat silently in the car while Lynn and Gordon drove me back to Steve's. In the morning, we would begin the long drive to

Cambridge. I hugged Lynn and Gordon, and then the Flock parted from the people who had nurtured us through our emotional infancy. Now, at the end of a summer that had been both demanding and fulfilling, it was time to set aside infantile needs for the demands of graduate school.

DIARY *September 9, 1983*

Summer is over at last. I am physically and emotionally exhausted, but I believe we have achieved what we hoped for. The Flock has gone off to Harvard armed with new strengths. The Alliance has pooled resources from personalities who before got in one another's way or worked at cross-purposes.

I will always marvel at how it came about. I will probably never have another experience like our four-way conversation at Manny's. I couldn't believe what I was seeing and was equally surprised that the other people in the crowded bar were oblivious to the miracle happening before them.

Particularly this summer, when I spent so much time with the Flock, I sometimes forgot that they shared the same body. Renee caught me once, but she didn't know of the many times I planned an activity that I knew would be nurturing for little girl Missy or insecure Jo, completely forgetting that the Flock set its own agenda of who might be present when. I learned to work around the unexpected presence of a personality and (therapeutically) always kept in mind that some of the others might be "watching" while I spent time with another. But I never thought about what it might be like to interact with more than one at a time.

It was astounding. I wish I could have filmed that conversation at Manny's and show the film to every clinician who doubts the reality of MPD. Voice, mannerisms, essence changed, literally from second to second, as Kendra, Isis, and Renee spoke during our conversation. It didn't take me long that night to realize that my role was primarily spectator or cheerleader. The real drama happened internally for them.

They (she?) compared the forming of the Alliance to single strands of rope entwining to make a strong cord. I think this is a nice metaphor, but it doesn't touch my experience of watching it happen. I felt a chill, an excitement unequaled by anything except giving birth. "My God, there's a person becoming here!" I thought. I felt so enthralled to be part of it; I felt so sad that Gordon wasn't with us.

And, to extend my metaphor, I have to admit to some "postpartum" sadness as well. Renee changed drastically overnight. By morning, she walked with the grace of Isis and spoke with the confidence of Kendra. I felt the kind of sudden realization that I had felt when my own little girls became adults.

The Alliance couldn't have been achieved without our summer of nurturance. I think we have greatly improved the chances of Harvard's working out. Even Missy and Rusty have accepted that they are going, secure in the knowledge that Gordon and I love them and that we'll be in contact through letters and phone calls. Josie doesn't really understand, but I think she will stay quiet and save her appearances for school vacations, when we are together.

Jo, still outraged that she didn't have a say in the decision to go to Harvard, is the only really important holdout. I'm counting on her being unable to resist the academic atmosphere she has thrived on in the past.

Gordon and I are slowly beginning to bask in the luxury of having time for ourselves and for each other. It is only now that the Flock has left that we, and especially I, have fully realized what a drain this summer has been. I have used my resources to the last drop. I'm looking forward to a long hiatus (until Christmas), with only occasional phone calls from the Flock, so that I can build up emotional energy again and make plans without considering the Flock every minute. I'm sure that by December I'll be ready, even eager, to invest some concentrated time again.

. . .

BOOK IV

27

"I feel like I'm driving my daughter off to school," Steve reflected at the start of our trip to Cambridge. We had rented a station wagon so that he could fly back to Chicago after the trip, and the car was packed to the roof with books, typewriter, clothes, and enough familiar objects to make a dorm room home for the school year. My relationship with Steve had so deteriorated through the prolonged summer of dependency on Lynn and Gordon that "father-daughter" seemed a not too inappropriate description.

We didn't talk much during the long trip. When Steve did break the silence, he spoke of the wonders of Harvard and his special memories of being a student there.

"You're not making this any easier," I snapped. I didn't want to think about how disappointed Steve would be if I didn't love Harvard the way he had. But that qualm distracted me only briefly. I was too busy withdrawing from Gordon and Lynn.

Steve wouldn't have understood if I had tried to tell him how painful this withdrawal was. There was no way he could appreciate my relationship with Gordon and Lynn.

I experienced equal silence within. None of the other personalities was injecting internal comments or pushing to share the outside awareness. We were all miserable to the core. I had ample time to worry about what would happen next.

I knew that it was ridiculous to blame Lynn for my being a multiple. I had been plagued by it for many years before I met her. Yet the Flock seemed worse, with personalities further apart and acting out more vigorously now than we had been before beginning therapy. Lynn had said that therapy was like separating the strands in a tangled web of yarn. It made sense that things would keep getting more separate for a while so that we eventually came back together in an organized way.

"Maybe the others won't surface so much away from Lynn and Gordon," I considered. "Maybe I'll have all of the time."

This thought, which would once have brought me great comfort, now brought only fear. I had never been the intellectual in the group. How could I do it alone?

I would have been scared even if I hadn't been multiple. I had never been on my own before. I went to school in Charlottesville, which I knew as well as I knew Richmond, and shared my apartment with cousins. I made new friends in the security of familiar surroundings. Every move to a new town had been with my husband. When we separated, I remained in Chicago, a city I already knew, and I quickly eased into a relationship with Steve.

Now I was going to a new place. For the first time in my life, I'd be sharing living space with a stranger. Even if I could manage to hide the fact that I was multiple from my roommate, would she be able to stand me for a year?

I was alone in the suite for two days before my roommate, Bethany, arrived. During that time, as my anxiety built, I decided that, Alliance or no, I would handle things myself and keep the other personalities from surfacing. Maybe I could fake my way through the theory classes.

The minute Bethany walked into the suite, I lost control. Joan Frances took over and fell all over herself in a clumsy attempt to make a good impression. She insisted on helping Bethany move in. As Joan Frances chattered on about the cultural advantages of Boston, Bethany looked up, her clear blue eyes blinking in wonder. "Are you always like this?" she seemed to be asking. Her concerns about the year were palpable.

Without the benefit of knowing my diagnosis, Bethany met several of the personalities. I suspected that if I told her I was multiple she'd be frightened. But even if Bethany was not provided with a label, she learned to respect my "moods." Shy Jo seemed frightened and hid in her bedroom when Bethany returned home to our suite. Joan Frances needed constant reassurance that Bethany liked her. I was nice to Bethany, but careful not to expect too much from our forced relationship.

"Well, the Flock is still very much with me," I reported to Lynn during a phone conversation. "I tried to ignore them, but that didn't make them disappear."

"No kidding," Lynn said, and then offered suggestions on how to help the group manage. I began taking daily walks off campus, during which

I could relax my hold and let other personalities experience the day. Missy shuffled in autumn leaves; Rusty sat by the Charles and watched boats slip through the water.

If I couldn't ignore the Flock, I decided that I had to be ready to contend with any possibility. How could I keep people from seeing and labeling the changes? What would happen if Josie suddenly appeared, panic-stricken and psychotic? The answer was all too obvious—I'd be committed, locked up in a psychiatric hospital.

In Chicago, Lynn provided the guarantee against hospitalization. But she was now too far away. I needed a safety net in Boston, someone who would help me in a crisis and protect the Flock from commitment.

Lynn agreed and, with Dr. Wilbur's help, found the name of a local psychiatrist who had treated a multiple. I met with Dr. Timothy Matthews, and was delighted to find that he was willing to make himself available to me in emergencies.

I told him about the Flock and about the special relationship I had with Gordon and Lynn.

"You know I can't provide that for you," he said.

I was relieved that he wouldn't try. "One set of therapist-parents is enough," I said. "I just need someone to call if things get out of hand while we're here in school."

Dr. Matthews assured me that he understood that some self-destructive gestures went along with the disorder and agreed that commitment was not the appropriate response. But the Flock should feel free to call him in an emergency. Dr. Matthews seemed calmly accepting of my situation. He telephoned Lynn to get a better understanding of the Flock and provided me with his home and office phone numbers so that I could reach him at any time.

Now I could concentrate on academic work. And since the other personalities were not going to disappear, I had better find some way of using them. The Jo personality, with her extensive knowledge and equally extensive amnesia, was a problem. I needed her intellect. I looked over my schedule and worked out a plan. Jo would take the theory courses, and the Alliance of Kendra, Isis, and I would handle everything else.

Unfortunately, Jo didn't appreciate her assumed participation. She found herself sitting in the dormitory room with economic-theory books open before her, or became aware in the lecture hall, pen in hand, at the start of a class. Jo hated feeling so out of control, but she did as expected, perceiving that she'd have no time at all if she balked. "I wouldn't even know how to get from that dorm room to this damn lecture hall," Jo observed one day in self-disgust. She was right. I took the body to class and home again. Jo's only purpose was to absorb knowledge.

I made a trip to Richmond after I had been at Harvard for a few weeks, to attend a friend's wedding; Joan Frances wanted to bask in her mother's pride at having a daughter at Harvard. No one in the family had gone to graduate school; no one had ever attended an Ivy League school. Joan Frances was sure that she finally deserved her mother's love.

The weekend didn't go as planned. Nancy's boyfriend didn't seem impressed. Nor did she. "Harvard is just a rich kids' playground, and anyone can buy a degree there," Nancy told Joan Frances, echoing her friend. Joan Frances returned to Harvard feeling uncertain and betrayed. Again she had failed to please her mother.

After the weekend in Virginia, the Flock began calling Lynn on a regular basis. The experience with Nancy rekindled old fears. "Why don't you write to us?" I asked Lynn. "Why don't you respond to the questions in my letters to you? Why won't you help anymore?"

The harder I pushed, the more I felt Lynn pull back. "I love you," she said, "and you're still family, but I won't do long-distance therapy. If I tried and failed, I'd hurt both of us badly."

"Maybe Lynn's feelings have changed," I thought. "Maybe she's just happy we're gone. Maybe what we shared this summer no longer exists."

"I can't take this anymore," I told her. "I have to come home for a weekend and find out where our relationship stands."

"You're welcome to come home if you wish," Lynn replied. "Gordon and I can spend *some* time with you, but we have other plans as well. You know, Renee, that the Flock was our priority this summer. But it can't be that way forever, and it can't be that way now."

DIARY *October 10, 1983*

The first few weeks of the Flock's stay at Harvard seemed to go well. As I had expected, Renee had to come to terms with the continued presence of the other personalities and had to develop ways to keep them comfortable, allow them expression, and use their strengths. Their letters were entertaining for Gordon and me, and therapeutic for them. Occasional

*phone calls provided gossip from home, reassurances, praise, and commis-
eration from us.*

*I was pleased when Renee decided on a backup therapist and even
more pleased when I talked with Dr. Matthews. He seemed to understand
what Renee is asking for and was open to consultation with me. All
seemed to be going as smoothly as anyone could have hoped, and I
looked forward to more and more freedom in the periods between school
vacations.*

*The weekend visit to Virginia upset the developing equilibrium. Pre-
dictably, Nancy did not react with joy and pride in her daughter's achievement. This was devastating to Joan Frances and sent repercussions through
the whole Flock. Old pain was resurrected, and feelings of rejection were
transferred to me. This produced a clinging dependency for which I was
totally unprepared.*

*Depleted as I was, what little energy I had left went toward raising my
defenses, and I drew back on the support I had been giving, fearful of being
sucked completely dry. When Renee said she was coming home for the
weekend, I reacted with anger and despair. I questioned the good that I
thought the summer had brought. I felt I could not face a four-day weekend
of endless recriminations and dissection of "our relationship." I was afraid
that if I didn't provide some response and support she might not return to
school. I couldn't even think of what I might do with the Flock at that
point.*

*I had enrolled in a yoga class that began the night she arrived, and I
went there rather than meet Renee at the airport. I was determined not to
structure the weekend around her visit, as we had structured everything all
summer, and as I had done to a large extent for the two years before that.
It was both a battle of wills and a test of the Flock's growing health. If they
refused after all this time to see that I cared and would continue to care,
there was nothing more I could do. I had gambled that the summer would
provide that kind of security, and it had looked, for a while, like a success.
If I was wrong, we would both have to live with that failure.*

*I was prepared for Renee's hurt reproaches, but when Steve dropped the
Flock off at the house after I returned from my class, I thought at first that
it was Joan Frances who knocked formally on the front door instead of
letting herself in the side door as usual. Cold and formal, Renee barely
tolerated my hug. There was no smile, no warmth as she sat stiffly, ankles
crossed, and made polite conversation.*

Renee began, legalistically and coldly, as though she had been taking lessons from Jo: "You told me on the telephone that I need to separate what is family from what is treatment from what are Flock issues; I find that I fail to understand the distinctions among the three." She called me into account for every statement I had made, pointing out inconsistencies and apparent contradictions. She innocently pleaded lack of understanding, and I became more and more frustrated and angry, and more and more adamant about what I would not do.

Things were at an impasse when Steve returned an hour later to pick her up. I reassured Renee that she was welcome to come back, but she remained cold and distant. After she left, I felt guilty and uncomfortable, but I reminded myself that what I had done was justified and necessary. I certainly was not pleased with my very untherapeutic emotions and worried that my approach might have been wrong. But, at the same time, I had the sense that the Flock didn't really need from me as much as they now felt they did. Renee had not dissolved or folded in the face of my ultimatums. Something else was going on that had little or nothing to do with what was happening between the two of us.

When Renee appeared the next day, she was much warmer, ready to discuss rather than accuse, and I found it easier to respond to her. We talked about how destructive Nancy's most recent rejection had been.

Renee eventually asked the underlying questions: Do you still love me? Are you rejecting me like Nancy? Can I always come home again? These issues settled (for now), I could begin to assist Renee in dealing with the intricacies of helping the Flock survive at Harvard.

Clearly some support, even if it wasn't ongoing therapy, was needed at school. Renee decided to take the risk of telling her roommate and a few others about being a multiple. Reassured of Gordon's and my continued love and support, and buoyed by her new understanding of her own strength—strength to withstand my anger—the Flock returned to school.

.   .   .

I couldn't figure out how to tell Bethany that I was a multiple, but trusted that the right time would present itself. It did, a few days after I returned from my weekend in Chicago. Bethany rushed into the suite that afternoon and barely mumbled hello as she stormed through our shared study space and slammed her bedroom door behind her. I waited a few minutes, then knocked hesitantly. "Yes," she said, in a distracted voice.

"Sorry to bother you," I said, opening the door, "but are you mad at me about something?"

Bethany looked up from her bed, puzzled. "Mad? No, why should I be mad at you?"

I wasn't sure. I didn't *think* any of the personalities had done anything to upset her, but I couldn't be certain. "Ahh," I started lamely, "you just seem sort of pissed off."

Bethany laughed and sat up. "Come on in," she said. "I am pissed off. I got a B on a paper and it should have been an A. But I'm not mad at you, I'm just in a bad mood."

"A bad mood," I repeated, mulling this over. "I don't think I know what it means to be in a bad mood."

"What are you," she laughed, "a person from another planet?"

"No," I said, "I'm a multiple."

Bethany and I talked through the night, and she took it all with the calm and curiosity of a well-read and well-traveled young woman who had heard and seen stranger things. I found that it helped me understand the disorder better to describe it to someone else.

Within a few weeks, Bethany recognized Jo, Joan Frances, and Missy, and called us all by name. Bethany and I got along better after that, but we continued to live in our own separate graduate-school spheres, friendly yet not overly involved with each other.

In November, Bethany rushed into the suite between classes and called to me, "Hey, Renee, how did Jo do on that poli-sci exam?" I told her, proud of Jo's ability, and then realized that I was equally in awe of my roommate. "You are amazing," I said to Bethany. "How can you deal with my being a multiple so easily?"

Bethany shrugged, but a grin twitched. "I once shared a one-room hut with twelve other people in a small village in New Guinea. Your group is more compact, and our suite doesn't have a dirt floor."

I also told Lillian. Lillian was the one real friend I had made in Cambridge. She was thirty-five and had a husband on the West Coast. They both valued her completing her degree enough to tolerate a commuting marriage. I spent most evenings at Lillian's apartment, sharing dinner and coursework. We had many of the same classes and found that we studied well together. But the night that Lillian wanted to discuss John Locke, I knew she had to be told.

I wasn't taking that class; Jo was. Like Bethany, Lillian seemed to have little problem believing in the disorder. However, after a few study sessions with Jo, Lillian admitted that she was more comfortable with me, though she had to admit that Jo had a knack for the theoretical work.

I wasn't surprised. For her part, Jo never even noticed Lillian's discomfort. She knew that Lillian admired her talent for quoting accurately from memory, and she enjoyed solidifying her own understanding through Lillian's questions and comments.

After getting A's on all of our midterm exams, I realized that the Flock was doing well. We were stimulated by the competitive graduate program. Bethany told me that the other students in the dorm had decided that I was "low-key" about my mental abilities, but "brilliant." I chalked up most of my success to the time that the Flock spent studying. I was too worried about the other students' sensing the switching of personalities to become involved in the student social life. "But there's another possibility," I said to Bethany. "Maybe two or more heads *are* better than one."

The changes in posture and mannerisms that signaled a switch between Jo and me were subtle enough that they didn't attract attention. Only Lillian, who sat next to the Flock in lectures, knew, by glancing at the distinctive handwritings, when she was sitting next to her friend Renee, and when she was sitting next to political theorist Jo.

Sometimes, though, the Flock's academic enthusiasm had to be curbed so that we wouldn't attract attention. The Alliance was loose enough so that Kendra, Isis, and I sometimes functioned autonomously but co-consciously. Kendra and I both loved the law class. Together we researched the cases and did extra reading at the law library so that we'd be prepared for the exciting Socratic method used by our professor. When called on to recite in class, I did the talking, but kept an internal ear cocked to listen for Kendra's suggestions and comments. She often picked up things that I missed in the reading.

As other students recited, or when the professor was lecturing, I scribbled notes on my tablet right-handed, with the casebook opened to my left. Able to use both hands equally well, Kendra often made notations in the casebook with her left hand at the same time that I was taking my notes.

One day, I noticed a classmate nudging another and gesturing toward the Flock's two-handed notetaking. "We've got to be more careful," I warned Kendra. "You can't write with your left hand while I'm writing with my right. It looks too strange."

Finally, I solved the problem by taking only one pen to class. Kendra and I were then forced to take turns. A switching of pen from hand to hand was more acceptable than two pens writing in different scripts simultaneously.

28

The Flock went home for Christmas feeling more self-confident than ever before. Professors held up our work as a model; fellow students asked for advice. The more functional personalities cooperated in making notes on the calendar so that every personality could keep track of the day despite amnesia. The kids were allowed physical and mental space to play.

Lynn and Gordon shared in our joy and pride and told us all to hurry home. We stayed with Steve over vacation, but he and I were included in the Wilsons' family Christmas.

My apprehension that maybe Gordon and Lynn didn't *really* want us around, and my anxiety that their own kids visiting from California would add stress, were inspired by years of tense holidays with Nancy and Ray. Gordon and Lynn were different.

They didn't care any more than they ever had what shape the house was in or when dinner got served. Nancy was always so frantic in her need for everything to look perfect on holidays that no one was allowed to relax enough to enjoy the occasion.

Lisa and Victor visited with their parents, and hung out at the house, but they went out with friends as well. They were friendly with the Flock and didn't seem to be jealous of the hours we spent with Gordon and Lynn. Any way we looked at it, we belonged.

That knowledge, pure and obvious, finally permeated to the deeper levels of the Flock. This was our family. Not just for the summer, but forever.

The last evening before the Flock's return to Cambridge, Rusty appeared, sitting on the rug in Lynn and Gordon's living room. Rather than demanding to know Gordon's whereabouts, as he usually did, Rusty gazed thoughtfully at Lynn. He stared steadily at her long, loose hair and raised his hand as if to touch it.

"When I was a little boy, one time and one time more, I touched the lady's hair," he said slowly.

"Yes, that's right, Rusty," Lynn said, and pulled her hair over one shoulder so that it would be both visible and accessible. He didn't move toward her, but remained in the warmth of his feeling.

"Big boy," Rusty said dreamily, content. As simply as that, Rusty had absorbed Little Joe. For the first time, Rusty had memory prior to finding himself in the woods with Ray. The memory was a little confused, since the Little Joe personality had felt loved and cherished first by Nancy and later by Lynn. Rusty didn't care which mother he remembered through his assumption of Little Joe. What was important was his new feeling— love and tenderness for this woman, for women in general.

Rusty now had a mother as well as a new dad, and he called her Lynn-mom.

Lynn, Gordon, and I barely had time to marvel at the quick and seamless merging of Rusty and Little Joe when the Jo personality pushed me aside with a great deal more force than usual.

Jo looked around the room and smiled at Gordon and Lynn in an easy, relaxed way. Her face showed none of its normal tension.

"I was just thinking that I started off OK," Jo said. "There wasn't anything different or wrong with me when I was born. I wasn't inherently bad or freakish."

"That's right, Jo," Lynn said.

"Other people—my mother and father—did things to me that made me feel all wrong about myself," Jo said, another warm wave of new, sure knowledge washing over her. "Sometimes, early in therapy, I tried so hard to figure out what I was supposed to do that I lost myself in the trying. I won't do that anymore. I know I'm OK. I'm OK just the way I am."

Jo accepted Lynn's hug, but smiled uncertainly at Lynn's tears. "Why are you crying?" she asked. "This is just what you've been telling me all along."

Jo felt that she had reached a new understanding that made her feel at peace with herself. Those outside of Jo's experience—Lynn, Gordon, and I—realized that another fusion had taken place, a merging even more important than Rusty's absorption of Little Joe.

Jo had taken on the personality we called "the Good Infant," the whole child, healthy and inherently good, as she had been before the first personality splits. Jo had also absorbed the "Jo II" personality, the only personality the Flock had created in reaction to treatment. An unneeded defense from the start, Jo II was never to emerge again.

DIARY *January 2, 1984*

Having the Flock and Steve here for Christmas was a huge success. The new security that had been forged in October was strengthened and solidi- fied as the Flock saw the warmth flow among us with our adult children and grandchildren. They realized that these feelings were all part of rela- tionships that had existed since birth and had grown and changed as we all grew. The Flock understood that the feeling Gordon and I had for them was the same as the love we have for our other children. The personalities developed a sense of the continuity and stability of our caring. By now we have had several different kinds of meshings and groupings that are harbin- gers and precursors of what presumably is to come. It's all growing naturally out of our work together.

Robin and Reagan were the first personalities to merge. Their sole function was to preserve information, and they were absorbed within the system once they had shared their stories with me. Their legacy to the other personalities was an increased ability to know and to share.

Renee, Isis, and Kendra banded together in a loose and flowing way to achieve a specific goal—success at Harvard—sometimes sharing only co-consciousness, at other times seeming to become one augmented and fully experiencing personality.

These new integrations are different. As Jo and Rusty experienced the continuity of Gordon's and my love with all our children, they were able to accept their own essential rightness as epitomized by Little Joe and the Good Infant. By absorbing and making these little ones' memories their own, they created their own sense of continuity in our love. In turn, this freed Jo to begin to fulfill the promise of growth through treatment that Jo II had foreshadowed.

My concern now is how this fuller acceptance of a new family will affect the Flock's relationship with Nancy. Renee is showing signs of increasing intolerance and seems less capable of pacifying Nancy than she has been in the past. And Jo is less tolerant of Nancy now than ever before. I fear that they may leave it all to the consistently vulnerable and depressed Joan

Frances. This issue may come to a head later this month, when they go to
Virginia for a visit.

· · ·

The Flock returned to Cambridge for a week of final exams. Stress
from external pressures and from internal growth concentrated in the
Flock's most vulnerable physical spot—the stomach. We did well on the
exams and felt relatively calm, but we all experienced abdominal pain.

This ailment wasn't personality-specific. Sometimes, if I had a headache, another personality could take over the awareness and not feel the
pain I experienced. I tested whether or not our stomach problem was
organic by checking to see if all the personalities experienced the same
symptom as they each came out. They did. I wondered if we had finally
developed an ulcer. I made an appointment at the Harvard Health
Service.

"Your upper GI is perfectly normal," the internist informed me.

"Now what?" I thought. "No matter what the tests show, I hurt and
can't eat." I sighed and stood to leave. "Thanks anyway," I said.

"Sit down, Joan," the doctor said in a firm voice, and Joan Frances
was the personality who obediently placed the body back in the chair.

"I know there's nothing wrong with me," Joan Frances said, "there's
never anything really wrong with me." Her mother's words—"You're
wasting the doctor's time"—echoed through her mind.

"You suddenly seem anxious, upset," the internist now said. "You
might feel better if you talked with a psychiatrist." Seeing Joan Frances's
stricken look, she quickly added, "It's OK. Nobody at Harvard will know.
The doctor I was going to recommend does some work for our service and
takes Harvard Health Insurance, but he's part of a group practice on the
edge of campus."

A psychiatrist. No. Joan Frances certainly couldn't do that. Lynn was
like a psychiatrist, and she had tried to turn her against her mother. Lynn
had said she was a multiple. Joan Frances knew that was wrong; Nancy
said it was ridiculous. A psychiatrist would only try to turn her against her
mother. A psychiatrist might try to lock her up. She had to get out of here.

"I can't see a psychiatrist," Joan Frances told the internist calmly.
"My mother would be very angry."

"Your mother?" the internist said unbelievingly as she shuffled through the medical record. "You're over eighteen. What does your mother have to do with this? Don't tell her!"

Joan Frances flinched at the suggestion that she conceal something from Mother. "You don't understand," she said. She got up and edged toward the door.

"Well, take this," the doctor said, and handed her a slip of paper with a name and phone number. "I really think you should give Dr. Tate a call. He's very nice; you'd like him."

Joan Frances took the slip of paper back to the dorm and placed it in a desk drawer. She didn't need a psychiatrist. She was going home to Mother in a few days. Her mother would take care of everything.

Nancy met her daughter at the airport. "You look like hell," Nancy said. "You need a haircut, and you look skinny and tired. Why did you wear that dress? It hangs on you like an old rag."

Joan Frances had gotten up an hour early to make sure that she was dressed and groomed properly for Mother. But she had failed.

"I . . . I've been having some trouble with my stomach," Joan Frances confessed.

"That anxiety crap again? What do you have to be anxious about?" Nancy said.

She tried again. "Hey, Mom, guess what? I got all A's for my first semester!"

"Have you been so busy studying that you haven't bothered to take care of yourself?" Nancy inquired. "You've got to eat something," she said as they walked in the door.

"Yes, Mother," Joan Frances said meekly. Joan Frances may have been feeling compliant, but I was mad as hell.

"Wait, wait," I said, taking over. "If I'm going to eat something, it will be what I decide I can tolerate."

Nancy backed off, and headed upstairs to her collection of pharmaceutical samples. "Let me see if I can find you something to settle your stomach," she said. As Joan Frances had predicted, Nancy did find some medication that stopped the cramping and pain; indeed, she found enough sample bottles so that we'd be able to medicate ourselves for years.

A few days later, I borrowed Nancy's car and drove to Aunt Christine's house. She was Ray's sister and one of my favorite relatives. When I had visited in the fall, Christine had told me she was proud of me. She had said that she had worried a great deal about me when I was a child. I was intrigued by her remark, by the possibility that someone in the family might have noticed something amiss when the Flock was young. I wanted to talk to somebody in the family about the Flock's memories.

I told Christine that I *had been* a multiple, rather than confusing the issue by telling her that I was currently multiple. I felt uncomfortable about the lie, but didn't want the conversation diverted by interest in my fragmented existence. "And besides," I rationalized, "this is probably good practice. If I ever really do become a past multiple, I'll have to talk about the childhood as though it were something that I experienced."

I told Christine that I wanted to make sure that my therapeutically evoked memories of childhood were accurate. "Do you think I was abused?" I asked.

Christine paused as that simple question helped her make sense of fears she had not been able to name twenty years before. She looked at me through tears of sadness and guilt. "Yes, I think you were abused," she said wearily. "You were so quiet, such a frightened little rabbit, with no energy. Your childhood was beaten out of you. You were humiliated for being a child."

"My parents really wanted a boy, didn't they?" I asked.

"It was your father who wanted a boy," she said. "I never understood why they didn't just adopt a son."

"I wish I had done something to help you," Christine said, "but I was raising my own family. Is there anything I can do for you now?"

"You did more for me than you know," I said. "You gave me a safe place to be when I was little. And now you're helping me believe my own memories."

"Tell me more about multiple personality," Christine urged.

"Well, it always begins with childhood trauma," I said. My conversations with Bethany and Lillian had helped me organize a mini-lecture on the development of MPD.

"Multiples are almost always victims of physical, sexual, and emotional abuse," I said. "Not all abused children become multiples, but all multiples were abused or suffered other overwhelming and sustained trauma. Some of the clinical articles I've read suggest that kids who become multiples are in homes where there's no one to make things better—it's not possible for the child to have a nonconflicted relationship with either parent. Kids become multiples by being good at autohypnotism. They psychically remove themselves when life's too rough on the outside."

Aunt Christine looked pained and puzzled. "I don't understand," she said slowly. "Who abused you sexually?"

I hesitated, now regretting my blithe description. I looked at her and made a calculated decision to be honest about what had happened to the Flock. But I took a deep breath first. It was going to be hard saying this as though it had happened to me.

I looked away from her before I spoke, not wanting to see her angry denial. "Aunt Christine, my father began molesting me when I was very young. He raped me when I was twelve."

Christine began to sob softly.

"Oh, God, I'm sorry," I said, moving close and putting my arm around her. "You've got to understand that I loved my father and love him still. He was sick, but he gave me so very much that I'm thankful for." I realized with a start that I was paraphrasing Gordon's words of reassurance to Rusty.

Christine shook me away. "No," she said, reaching for a tissue, "it's you who don't understand."

Suddenly I did. Christine was crying for her own pain, not mine. I paused, needing to hear, yet terrified of what she might say.

"My father abused me too," she said, "and in thirty-eight years I've told no one."

"Oh, Aunt Christine," I murmured, "what a terrible secret to keep for so long."

"I was twelve too," she continued. "My mother and sisters were out, and a horrible thunderstorm came up. I was afraid all alone in the girls' bedroom, so I went to my father's room and told him I was scared. He invited me into bed, and when I was not quite asleep, he put his fingers inside me. I lay still until I heard him snore. I slipped from his bed and ran to my own, terrified but knowing I could never tell."

I remembered reading that child abuse was a chain, linked through generations, but had never given much thought about how that applied to the Flock. Nancy had said that her stepfather had abused her, and now I had reason to wonder about Ray's childhood as well.

"How about your brothers and sisters?" I asked Christine. "Were they also abused by your father?"

"I don't know," she said. "I've never told anyone about this. I was afraid that they wouldn't believe me."

"I understand," I said, and held the abused child buried deep within her.

"Two more days at Nancy's house," I thought as I drove away from Christine's. "How am I going to stand it?" I was furious with Nancy and longed to confront her.

"How could you have let Ray get away with that?" I wanted to ask Nancy. "How could you not have known what was going on?" But I was afraid that Nancy would only deny it all. So I kept silent. I gave up the time with Nancy to any personality who could tolerate her.

Unfortunately, the only personality interested in being with Nancy was Joan Frances. This personality had blocked out the talk with Aunt Christine, yet she knew vaguely that she had done something very wrong, something sure to compromise her mother's love. She waited anxiously for her mother to discover this huge shadowy sin but heard only the same litany of how she had better start taking care of herself.

29

Joan Frances returned to Cambridge feeling tremendous guilt and wanting to die. She unpacked from her trip, fingering the bottles of pills her mother had provided to help with her nervous stomach. "If I took all hundred and fifty of these pills, I would probably die," she thought. "I'm never going to be what my mother wants."

Then she found the slip of paper given to her before the trip by the internist. She had the name and phone number of Dr. Barry Tate. Joan Frances thought it might be futile to talk to a psychiatrist, but then considered the finality of death. "Maybe I'll give it one more try," she thought. "I'll call this psychiatrist, and I won't lie to him. I won't pretend. I won't let him think I'm a multiple personality. I'll just be honest and tell him that I want to die because I can't please my mother. Maybe this doctor can help me become the daughter my mother wants."

Joan Frances called Dr. Tate and set up an appointment.

I called Lynn. "I'm not sure how I feel about Joan Frances seeing this psychiatrist, but it's better than an overdose," I said. "I'm really worried about her depression."

"Why don't you take the Flock to see Dr. Matthews?" Lynn asked. "He said he'd be available to you in emergencies."

"I don't think that would work," I said. "Joan Frances doesn't trust him, because he knows we're multiple. She still thinks that if she denies the rest of us her mother might love her. I think that if I take her to Dr. Matthews she will just feel more trapped and confused by her lack of control."

I pointed out that, despite Joan Frances's depression, she was moving forward. "This may actually be a breakthrough for Joan Frances. It's the first time that *she*, as a separate personality, has ever decided to seek anyone's help. I think she feels more desperate than ever about not being able to please Nancy. Maybe she's really ready to hear that her survival doesn't depend on Mother. The fact that *she* decided to see this doctor may make her more willing to listen.

"So are the rest of you going to stay in the background while Joan Frances sees the doctor?" Lynn asked. "Are you all going to try to hide your being multiple from Dr. Tate?"

"No," I said, after a pause, "I don't think that will work. Joan Frances has never had enough strength to stay out on her own for very long unless her mother is around. My guess is that the doctor's questions will make her feel so uncomfortable that she'll lose time to another personality."

Then I had an idea. "Lynn, would you call Dr. Tate before we go in to see him and explain the situation? That way you can check him out. If you think Dr. Tate won't be able to help Joan Frances with her mother obsession knowing that we're multiple, I'll just cancel the appointment."

Lynn wasn't sure. "You know, Renee, Dr. Tate may see my call as interference."

"Well, if he does, then we'll know that he's not the kind of doctor Joan Frances should see," I said.

DIARY *January 24, 1984*

I had to be careful in approaching Dr. Tate. I knew nothing about him, but knew that he might well resent the implication that I was telling him what to do, particularly since I was not an M.D. Therefore, I began by telling him that I was approaching him only because Multiple Personality Disorder was relatively rare and I didn't know if he had had experience with it. Knowing the Flock as well as I did, I might be able to help.

Dr. Tate seemed warm and accepting. I was encouraged and described Joan Frances's most recent trauma with her mother. I told him that, although the Flock as a whole was not suicidal, Joan Frances was feeling very depressed. The rest of the Flock would work against any of Joan Frances's suicidal impulses, but that personality's depression needed to be addressed.

I thought that he might be able to get through to Joan Frances in a way that I could not. Dr. Tate was a new person, whom Joan Frances had chosen to see; she interpreted any help taken from me as disloyalty to her mother.

I suggested that Renee and Jo might be very helpful—Renee because of her broad understanding of the group, and Jo because she had by now read everything published on the disorder. I stressed that the group wanted to help Joan Frances through this crisis and that they would all provide what help they could.

. . .

Dr. Tate was not available for another five days, and I worked to keep Joan Frances as comfortable as possible, but a crisis was brewing.

Bethany sat me down one evening. "Renee," she said, "I have to tell you that Joan Frances is driving me crazy. She won't leave me alone."

"Sorry about that," I said to Bethany. "Joan Frances isn't much fun for anyone right now. I'll try to keep her out of your way." I didn't need to alienate my roommate on top of everything else.

Jo learned about Joan Frances's upcoming appointment with a psychiatrist from my notes on the group calendar. At first Jo objected: a strange psychiatrist's office was the last place she wanted to find herself. But she talked to Lynn and wrote in her journal about the differences between her own new feelings of self-worth and Joan Frances's perceived worthlessness. Jo wrote:

I've started thinking about how close I've come to committing suicide. The first time I can remember feeling suicidal, I was ten years old. I sat on my bedroom window ledge, wondering if it would hurt very much if I jumped. With my new sense of well-being, I know that I'll never feel suicidal again. But I think that now I understand how suicides happen.

The possibility of death came closer each time I felt suicidal. The most difficult part of any suicide is the actual decision to die. Once that struggle is completed, once that decision is made, the act that brings about death is anticlimactic.

A lot of people probably misunderstand what it's like to feel suicidal. They think that repeated threats mean that the suicide is less likely to happen. I think that the reverse is true.

If making the decision to die is the most difficult part of suicide, then that decision-making becomes easier with practice. The decision is tremendously hard the first time, a struggle the second and third. But then there comes a time when the thought that death would be better is almost simultaneous with the fixing on a method. Reaching for pills, a razor blade, the window becomes reflexive.

Most suicides are probably the result of years of practice, so that the thought and action become blended into one. I suspect that the final act happens quickly, with little fear.

Now I'm grateful that Lynn always took my suicidal feelings seriously. I wonder how many suicides are successful because the potential helper thinks that the suicidal person is calling "wolf," when in fact every threat pulls the victim closer to the actual event.

I was uneasy about letting a doctor so near to the Harvard community know that I was multiple, but I felt bolstered by the talk Lynn had had with Dr. Tate.

The personalities agreed that this was to be, as much as possible, Joan Frances's appointment. She was the one in crisis.

Joan Frances spent forty-five minutes telling Dr. Tate about her wonderful mother and how much she wanted to please Nancy. She explained that she had come to the doctor because she felt terribly depressed and despaired of ever being what her mother wanted.

When Dr. Tate said that he had had a call from Lynn Wilson, Joan Frances cringed. "Lynn is all wrong," she said. "I'm not a multiple. My mother says so. She should know." Joan Frances told the doctor that, if she couldn't figure out how to be the daughter her mother wanted, she might as well die.

I pushed Joan Frances aside a few minutes before the end of the session. I introduced myself to Dr. Tate and told him that I was available and willing to do what I could to help.

"Joan Frances really needs someone to talk to right now," I said. "She doesn't think life is worth living if she can't please her mother. Everyone inside, Joan Frances included, hopes that talking with you will make her feel less dependent on her mother's approval." Dr. Tate didn't comment on my analysis, but said that he wanted to see me again in two weeks.

The weeks between the appointments were hard on the Flock. Joan Frances's depression was dragging everyone down. I felt continually on guard, watching so that Joan Frances did nothing physically harmful.

I took the time at the beginning of the next appointment with Dr.

Tate, hoping that I could give the doctor enough information so that he could really start helping Joan Frances.

"Joan Frances has got to talk this through," I said to Dr. Tate, and then set out to answer his many questions about the Flock's past. When, after an abbreviated history and explanation of the etiology of the disorder, Dr. Tate focused on how poorly I had handled my relationships with Keith and Steve, I sensed I was wasting precious time. The problem right now was Joan Frances's depression, not how I handled relationships with men. I slipped inside and pushed Joan Frances out.

"What can I do to help you?" Dr. Tate was asking as Joan Frances became aware of her surroundings. She brushed aside the confusion of how she had gotten to Dr. Tate's office and answered, "I want to become a better person; I want to stop feeling that death is the only answer."

Dr. Tate cut her off. "Can you put me in touch with Renee?" he asked. Joan Frances looked at the doctor helplessly, but answered firmly, "I am not a multiple."

"Nevertheless," the psychiatrist persisted, "can you put me in touch with Renee?"

Tears ran down Joan Frances's face. "Please, can't you help me?" she asked, and then felt overwhelmed. How did she make people think she was multiple when she wasn't? Why wouldn't this doctor help her? Why didn't the doctor care how bad she was feeling?

Then Dr. Tate found himself with a personality he hadn't met.

Jo looked around, taking in the doctor's office. She quickly figured out where she must be and smiled hesitantly at the psychiatrist. "Lynn said that I don't have to cover things up for you," Jo said. "You are Dr. Tate, aren't you?"

"Yes," he said, "and who are you?"

Jo identified herself.

"Can you put me in touch with Renee?" the doctor asked.

"No, I can't," Jo explained slowly, ready to help the doctor understand. "I'm largely amnestic and I seem not to have the ability to control which personality is out, but I do have a lot of theoretical knowledge about MPD." Jo told Dr. Tate how grateful she was that Joan Frances finally had someone to talk to.

"Your time is up," Dr. Tate said.

"Am I to see you again?" Jo asked. "Definitely," responded the doctor. "How about March 1?" Jo shifted uneasily; she never knew her schedule without looking to see what the other personalities had penciled in. I took over and agreed on the date and time for our next appointment.

"You know, Renee, talking about your relationships with men made you uncomfortable," Dr. Tate observed.

"Well, yes, I suppose that's true," I replied politely.

"And that's why you lost time!" he ended triumphantly.

"What should I do about Joan Frances's depression?" I asked.

"We'll talk about that next time," the doctor promised.

I left Dr. Tate's office very worried. The doctor didn't seem to understand that Joan Frances was in crisis and getting worse. March 1 was yet another two weeks away, and I was struggling day by day to keep Joan Frances from acting on her self-destructive impulse.

Two days later, I called Dr. Tate. "I'm really worried about Joan Frances," I said. "I don't think she can wait another couple of weeks."

"What do you want me to do?" Dr. Tate asked. I thought that was obvious. "I would like you to see Joan Frances before March 1," I said.

The doctor said that wasn't possible; he was all booked up. "I understand that you're busy," I said, "and I'm open to other suggestions. I've got to find a way to help Joan Frances feel better about herself. I just don't think I can get through two more weeks of monitoring her actions and keeping the rest of us going. When I tell you how serious Joan Frances's need is, I don't feel you are hearing me."

Dr. Tate replied that it was difficult to do an evaluation-intake on a multiple.

Yes, I could appreciate that, but . . . Suddenly I knew there was nothing left to say. I'd have to find a way to struggle through on my own.

That night, I removed a razor blade from Joan Frances's hand and tried to keep busy enough to remain the personality in control. The next day, Saturday, I worked in the library from opening to closing—anything to avoid the dorm room, where Joan Frances might surface. By Sunday night, I was exhausted and Joan Frances had found another razor blade.

She scratched her wrist and watched drops of blood form on the cut and run down her arm. "I'm worthless, an utter waste," she said. "My mother can't stand me no matter what I do." She ran the blade across her skin again. "Even that Dr. Tate didn't care how bad I felt. All he wanted to do was tell me that I had multiple personalities." This time, she stabbed at her wrist with the blade's sharp point. "Why doesn't anyone care how *I* feel?" The blood and tears welled up simultaneously. "I'm not worth it, that's why."

I pushed Joan Frances aside, wiped the blood from my wrist and tried to control my trembling hands. I felt so alone. There was no sense in calling Lynn. She couldn't do anything from such a distance, and Joan Frances wouldn't talk to Lynn anyway. But I knew she needed to talk with someone.

I called Harvard Health Service and told the nurse on call that I had a friend who was feeling suicidal. I hoped they would have a hotline number my friend could call. "Tell your friend to come into the emergency room," the nurse said. "She can talk to a nurse, the internist, or we even have a psychiatrist on call. There are professionals here who can help."

I thanked the nurse and tried to maintain control by doing some reading for a course. At 11:00 p.m., I found Joan Frances again scratching her wrist. I had to get out of the dorm room.

I walked through the night, fighting to stay in control and trying to decide how best to handle the situation. I didn't want to die; Jo didn't want to die; not even Joan Frances really wanted to die. But her depression and need were overwhelming the system.

No other personality could reach Joan Frances to let her know that we were there and caring for her. We could only try to control her actions.

"This is really absurd," I thought. The situation seemed incredibly simple to me—Joan Frances felt bad because she couldn't please her mother and she wanted to talk to somebody about that. Being a multiple had little to do with her immediate crisis.

Even now Joan Frances was reaching out. The scratches on my wrist were far from life-threatening. She was punishing herself, not trying to die. She was asking, as loudly as she could, if there weren't someone willing to pay attention to her and her pain. "I'm trying, sweetie," I murmured.

After I noticed the avidity with which Joan Frances was watching the cars speeding by her, I steered her toward the emergency-room entrance at the health service. Rather than have to explain we were multiple—Joan Frances was the problem, not multiple selves—I allowed Joan Frances fully into consciousness as I pushed the body through the emergency-room door.

Joan Frances blinked uncertainly in the bright lights and at her own disorientation. She hadn't made the decision to come here. Or had she? A nurse looked at her and led her quickly into a back room. "What's wrong with you?" the nurse asked. "Have you been drinking? What drugs have you taken?"

Joan Frances bridled at the questions. She didn't drink except for an occasional glass of wine with her mother, and she would never use illegal drugs. But that all seemed like too much effort to say. The nurse wouldn't understand any more than anyone else had. Finally, Joan Frances told the nurse that she had cut herself and pushed up her sleeve to expose her bleeding wrist.

"I don't really want to die," Joan Frances began. "I just feel so bad and nobody will listen. . . ."

The nurse cut her off. "Do you know Dr. Tate?" she asked.

"Yes," Joan Frances said, startled to hear the doctor's name.

"Dr. Tate is the psychiatrist on call tonight," the nurse said, and left the room.

I was as startled as Joan Frances by this new bit of information, and inwardly mused that coming in may not have been such a great idea. I had no idea that he moonlighted with the service. If Dr. Tate had not heard Joan Frances's need during our office visits, I didn't hold out much hope that he'd understand now. But I reminded myself that Dr. Tate didn't have to get involved in this. The emergency room was filled with nurses. There was an internist on duty. Any of them could spend a little time talking with Joan Frances and helping her feel less depressed.

The internist came into the examining room and handed the phone to Joan Frances. Dr. Tate was on the other end.

Dr. Tate angrily demanded to know why Joan Frances had cut her wrist. "What happened tonight to make you do this? Did you know I was the psychiatrist on call tonight?"

"No," Joan Frances replied. There was no special reason she had acted this way tonight. The depression was just getting worse, and no one was listening.

"I can't decide if you belong upstairs in the infirmary or if I should put you on a psychiatric ward," Dr. Tate said.

Joan Frances hung up the phone, shrugged into her jacket, and walked out of the examining room toward the entrance hall. The doctor and nurse stood in front of her, blocking her way to the exit.

Trapped. The scene bent, twisted. The image of walls, walls everywhere, trapping and releasing, shook me from my own shock. Josie, I realized, was very close to surfacing. "No, Josie, not now," I pleaded silently. "Let us handle it. Stay inside."

Joan Frances calmly told the doctor and nurse that she was fine now and just wanted to go back to the dorm.

I was furious. I knew Lynn had told Dr. Tate how terrified we all were of commitment. All we wanted now, as we had wanted for the past month, was for someone to talk with Joan Frances and help her through her depression. Despite Joan Frances's panic at Dr. Tate's threat, she was acting far less hysterical than many of us were feeling. For now, we let Joan Frances stay in control.

The internist led her back to the examining room and sat down near her. "I've called Dr. Tate," he said, "and he's coming in to talk with you."

"I don't want to talk with anyone," Joan Frances responded shakily. "I want to go back to my dorm."

The internist soothed her: "There's nothing for you to fear. No one can make you remain here against your will," he said. "I wish you would stay, because I know that you'll feel better after you've had a chance to talk with Dr. Tate about what's troubling you. Give him a chance. Why don't you wait here for him to come in?"

The desire to run vibrated throughout the Flock, but I stifled the urge. "Look, gang," I said internally, "what if we tried to leave and someone physically prevented us? You know that would bring Josie, and we'd be sure to get locked up."

And I had a ray of hope that the internist meant what he said. Maybe Dr. Tate finally did understand that Joan Frances needed to talk. I calmed the personalities poised for flight and held back the others so as not to interfere with Joan Frances. I wanted her ready and willing to interact with the psychiatrist.

Dr. Tate arrived, demanding to know specifically what had happened tonight to make Joan Frances feel so bad. Joan Frances had no new answers; she had felt like this since her return from Virginia.

"What do you want me to do?" the doctor asked.

Joan Frances shook her head in bewilderment. She had told this doctor what she wanted so often that it seemed silly to repeat the litany. "I don't want you to do anything," Joan Frances finally said. "I just want to go back to the dorm."

"No," Dr. Tate said firmly, "I'm having you admitted to a locked ward." Joan Frances lost awareness in a rush.

Jo found herself in the small examining room. No windows. No clue as to whether it was day or night. "There's a sliding wall instead of a door in front of me," Jo observed silently, "and Dr. Tate is sitting in front of that exit." Jo looked at her watch, checking for the time, knowing that her gesture was clumsy, obvious, but she didn't care. Her hands were clammy. She felt very frightened, but didn't know why. Maybe if she could figure out where she was and what was going on . . .

"Well, ask," Dr. Tate said.

Jo relaxed instantly. Dr. Tate's reaction was so much like the way Lynn responded when Jo appeared suddenly, feeling anxious and confused.

"Where am I?" Jo asked.

"The emergency room at Harvard Health Service," Dr. Tate said.

"Why?"

"Look at your wrist," the psychiatrist said.

Jo again looked at her watch, confused by the doctor's direction.

"No," Dr. Tate said with a trace of irritation, "look at your other wrist."

Jo looked, inspected the cuts long enough to realize that they were not dangerous, and said, "Oh, this has happened before. Joan Frances's work, I'd guess."

Dr. Tate looked a little startled by Jo's blasé attitude.

"Oh, I know this is a problem," Jo said. "It's something to be taken seriously. But Lynn calls this a gesture, not a suicidal act. She says that these scratches are the way that a really troubled personality broadcasts her need. If Joan Frances had been serious about killing herself, she would have taken an overdose."

"Who are you?" Dr. Tate asked.

Now it was Jo's turn to look startled. She knew she had talked to the psychiatrist during one of the Flock's two visits to his office. Didn't Dr. Tate remember?

"I'm Jo," she finally said, slowly and carefully. "Don't you remember talking to me?" Dr. Tate said nothing, but watched Jo for a time silently. Jo began to shift uneasily in her chair, feeling like a bug pinned to a board. "I want to go back to my dorm room now," she said.

"No," Dr. Tate said matter-of-factly. "As soon as I can find you a bed, you're going into a psychiatric ward."

Jo didn't panic. Lynn had told her that there was no reason for the

Flock to be locked up. "Lynn told me that I'm supposed to call a Boston psychiatrist by the name of Timothy Matthews if someone tries to lock me up," she said. She remained calm. All she had to do was to follow the emergency procedures Lynn and I had worked through.

"Have you ever seen this Dr. Matthews," Dr. Tate asked, "or is he only a name to you?"

Honest to the last, Jo sighed. "That's a really ambiguous question."

"At least you haven't lost your sense of humor," Dr. Tate responded dryly.

"I'm not trying to be funny," Jo said. "I know that some of the other personalities have met with Dr. Matthews, but I've never talked with him personally."

"Well, it's one a.m.," Dr. Tate said, "far too late to call another doctor."

Jo wondered why he wasn't being more helpful, but didn't panic. All of the contingencies had been worked through. For once, she knew the plan.

"Dr. Matthews gave me his home phone number so that I could reach him whenever I needed," she explained.

"Well, where's the number?" Dr. Tate asked, sounding annoyed.

Suddenly Jo realized that this doctor didn't want anyone to rescue her. She began to feel trapped and frightened. She frantically patted her coat pockets and found no number, nothing in her jeans pockets either. The phone numbers, Jo suspected, were back at the dormitory.

"You don't have the number here, and you're not in good enough shape to be out on the streets. I'm having you pink-slipped!" said Dr. Tate.

Jo took a deep breath. That was impossible. "I want to call Lynn," she said.

"Your therapist in Denver can't help you," the psychiatrist said firmly.

"Lynn is in Chicago, not Denver," Jo responded with equal control. "I'm very frightened by what you are suggesting and I want to call Lynn."

Finally, Dr. Tate led Jo to a phone. "Don't stay on the phone all night," he warned. "I'm tired and I want to get home to bed."

Jo glanced curiously at the doctor, not wanting to believe that the psychiatrist was really so unconcerned about the crisis that he was now escalating. Though she felt surges of panic, she had to appear calm and in control.

When Lynn's answering machine picked up at the first ring, Jo quickly hung up and dialed again, knowing that the phone had to ring at least a couple of times before it would wake Lynn or Gordon. "Unless Lynn can help," Jo realized with certainty, "this doctor is going to have me committed."

Lynn answered sleepily, but quickly became more alert as Jo filled her in on the situation and handed the phone to Dr. Tate. "This woman has no impulse control," Dr. Tate shouted long-distance, and Jo gratefully gave up the consciousness.

I took over. I stood quietly, listening to Dr. Tate's side of the conversation, imagining how helpless and concerned Lynn must be feeling. I seethed with anger. I concentrated on that anger, letting it grow to replace some of the terror that triggered the Flock's need for flight.

I was frightened, more frightened than I could ever remember being. Psychiatric hospitalization. There was no way I could convince myself that it might not be so bad. We'd be restrained, drugged. I pushed the fear aside and concentrated on my anger.

"Stupid, stupid, stupid!" I muttered. I was angry at myself for not realizing how this situation might be perceived. Joan Frances's depression was not nearly as life-threatening as commitment.

I was angry at the internist who had lied to Joan Frances. The doctor had said that no one could lock her up against her will, and Dr. Tate was preparing to do just that.

Dr. Tate hung up the phone and turned to me. I smiled broadly and said, "Tell you what. How about if I make an appointment with Dr. Matthews and you let me out of here so that we can both go home and get some sleep?"

"Renee?" Dr. Tate asked. He seemed weary and agreed to let me go, but only on the condition that I reach Dr. Matthews before I leave.

"His phone numbers are back at the dorm," I said, "but I'll call my roommate and have her find them for me."

"No," Dr. Tate said, "I don't want any more people involved in this. I'll reach him through his answering service at the hospital."

While Dr. Tate called the hospital, demanding to be put in touch with Dr. Matthews NOW, I docilely followed the nurse into another room to have my wrist cleaned and bandaged. "Don't worry about hurting me," I said to the nurse cheerfully. "I know the cuts aren't that bad." The nurse said nothing. Her hands shook as she washed the cuts.

The nurse finished bandaging my wrist, and Dr. Tate came in with the internist.

"You've got to see this," Dr. Tate said to the other doctor. "This is Renee, the in-charge personality."

I smiled brightly at the internist and thanked him for being so helpful with Joan Frances. "If they think I'm serious, then I'm a better actress than anyone has ever given me credit for being," I mused silently.

Dr. Matthews didn't return Dr. Tate's call, despite his demands, and the psychiatrist was tired. He offered a compromise. If I stayed overnight in the school's infirmary, he wouldn't have me committed.

I knew that wasn't good enough. The threat of hospitalization had shaken us all. I had to get someplace where everyone felt safe, and I needed to get there fast. "No," I replied breezily, "I'm going home to the dorm."

"But, Renee, I want you to be comfortable with the infirmary so that you'll feel you can use it in a crisis."

I bit my tongue to keep from asking why he hadn't recommended the infirmary days ago, when I had called about Joan Frances's crisis. This was no time for a debate.

"I can have you committed, you know," the doctor said.

I decided that if that were so he would have done it by now. I looked at the doctor calmly, steadily, and told him that I was in full control.

"How do you know that you'll remain in control?" Dr. Tate asked.

"Fear," I lied. "The rest of the Flock is so scared they're not going to surface for a very long time."

"I don't like fear being your method of control," Dr. Tate said.

Silently I countered that that was obviously the method *he* preferred, but I grinned conspiratorially at him. "At this point, I'll take what I can get."

Dr. Tate gave in. I walked out into the night, feeling more protected than frightened by the now empty streets. I got to the dorm and called Lynn. In the hour between phone conversations, she had been figuring out the quickest way to get to Boston.

I was exhausted, unnerved by the experience, but pleased that the Flock had worked together. Lynn and I were both giddy with relief.

"I'd like to strangle him," Lynn said.

"Yet more evidence of your extreme countertransference," I countered.

Just before we hung up, Lynn chuckled. "We'll both probably sleep better than Dr. Tate tonight," she said.

"I hope so," I agreed. "The bastard deserves to worry."

The next evening, Bethany came into my bedroom and sat down. "I saw the cuts on your arm and I called Lynn," she said. "Lynn said that everything is under control, but that I should talk with you about it." I told Bethany the story, just as I had told Lillian earlier in the day. Lillian had known something was wrong when I missed class. Bethany said, as Lillian had, that I should tell her when someone in the Flock was in trouble. Then she paused.

"Could I talk with Joan Frances?" she asked.

"I'm not sure," I said. "Things are a little chaotic, but let me try."

"Hi, Bethany," Joan Frances said. "Did you have a good time at the movies last night?"

"Cut the crap, Joan Frances," Bethany said. "I know you are having a rough time."

"Oh, I'm OK, there's nothing wrong. I just need to try harder."

"Joan Frances, you may not understand this, but I want you to listen," Bethany said. "You are a really neat person. You are smarter than anyone I know. You're cute, you care about other people, and when you are not worried about whether or not I hate you, you are a nice person to have around. Basically, what I'm telling you, kiddo, is that, if your mother can't see that, she's crazy."

Bethany got up and walked out of the room before Joan Frances had a chance to protest.

I kept my March 1 appointment with Dr. Tate. This was my chance, I decided, to make him understand how damaging this experience had been for the Flock.

"There's a difference between a suicidal personality and a suicidal entity," I told Dr. Tate. "Yes, Joan Frances was depressed, but her suicidal gesture was after two weeks in which Joan Frances, Jo, and I all tried to tell you that she was in crisis. She needed a professional ear far more than she needed an 'intake-evaluation,' but you never seemed to hear that."

Dr. Tate shot back that I was manipulative. The Flock had been called that so often by people who didn't understand that the label had no sting. "I can have you withdrawn from school if I decide you can't manage in the Harvard community," he warned. I nodded and left his office. His threat was clear, and I'd keep my distance.

The Flock's experience has made me think long and hard about what is needed to treat a multiple and how to convey this to others. In spite of all of my best efforts to smooth the way for the Flock with Dr. Tate, they landed in greater jeopardy than at any time since I began working with them. Ironically, they've never been healthier or better able to articulate their needs.

I attempted to be clear and straightforward in my approach to Dr. Tate, deferring to his medical expertise and stating my desire merely to be helpful. Renee and Joan Frances, in turn, were clear and straightforward about their needs in a way that was new for them. Yet we were seen as manipulative multiple and puppet therapist. Renee had probably never been less manipulative in her life than when she was trying to reason with Dr. Tate.

I can't help speculating on what happened between this psychiatrist and the Flock. Renee secured and sent me Tate's clinical reports, but they only add to my confusion.

The psychiatrist wrote that he found the dramatic changes hard to believe. He described Renee as attractive, confident, intelligent, dynamic, and reasonable. He described Joan Frances as depressed, schizoid, and childlike.

My guess is that Dr. Tate just couldn't accept Renee's explanation of what was wrong and what needed to be done with Joan Frances. He interpreted Renee's willingness to help and Jo's willingness to teach as no less indicative of pathology than Joan Frances's cries for help.

Perhaps he even saw my warning that the suicidal personality needed urgently to be addressed as some sort of warning that the Flock would attempt to manipulate him. I'll probably never know. I don't think that either the Flock or I could have handled the situation much differently, but it's clear that the doctor felt very threatened.

Somehow this disorder hooks into all kinds of fears and insecurities in many clinicians. The flamboyance of the multiple, her intelligence and ability to conceptualize the disorder, coupled with suicidal impulses of various orders of seriousness, all seem to mask for many therapists the underlying pain, dependency, and need that are very much part of the *process. In many ways, a professional dealing with a multiple in crisis is in the same position as a parent dealing with a two-year-old or with an adolescent's acting-out behavior. It is essential for the parent or the therapist to accept and not be threatened by any manipulation that does occur and to help the child, teenager, or patient understand that there are better ways of communicating and meeting needs.*

The Flock have come a long way in their acceptance of this, and when a professional refused to deal with them in a straightforward manner— and, in fact, manipulated and deceived them in return—they rebelled fiercely but self-protectively.

I made the clear and, I hope, threatening statement that night, all deference put aside, that I knew this patient better than he did and unqualifiedly recommended against hospitalization. I said firmly that I was certain that hospitalization would do them more harm than turning them free. My implied threat, combined with Renee's obvious presentation of competence, secured the Flock's release.

There are some "silver linings" even in this horrible experience. Renee felt and expressed justified anger. She was able to share her experience with Bethany and Lillian and receive support from them in turn. I gather that even Joan Frances listened to what Bethany had to say.

It is clear that the Flock is continually becoming stronger and less dependent on our therapeutic relationship. I suspect that Renee will turn some of her energies toward her relationship with Steve and others she cares for.

. . .

30

Steve met me in Cambridge at the end of the academic year, and we spent a few weeks exploring the New England coastline and rekindling our romantic relationship. I began to believe that Steve and I had a future together after all. I had grown up a good deal in our four years together and felt the difference in our ages becoming less significant. I was beginning to get a sense of what Steve had tolerated over the years of therapy, and felt amazed that he had remained supportive and in love with me.

Steve and I decided that we would marry after I finished my coursework. If all went as planned, I'd finish up at Harvard in one more year. No one could predict the state of the Flock twelve months from now, but the small fusions and the Flock's strength in dealing with Dr. Tate augured an increasingly optimistic future.

And I wanted to have a baby. If Steve and I married during the summer of 1985, I'd move back to Chicago and spend the following year writing my dissertation and, I hoped, growing a baby as well.

DIARY *May 27, 1984*

The Flock has returned home, and Renee is full of her plans to marry Steve. I find it difficult to get seriously involved in discussing the details of the wedding or how well it will fit in with Renee's scheme for finishing her time in Cambridge early by cramming two years of coursework into one. None of the others in the Flock who would be seriously involved—Jo in particular—seem especially enthusiastic about the prospect. I haven't discussed it with Josie, Rusty, or Missy but can't believe that these stunted child personalities could even conceptualize what Renee has in mind. Steve seems agreeable but not eager.

Also, Renee's reasons are spurious and seem to have more to do with proving something than with a genuine wish to share her life with Steve. Steve has certainly provided security for the Flock in many ways. Though this support has been invaluable, I suspect that it has derived partly from Steve's own need to distance himself from the disorder and deny much of the Flock's pathology.

I think that the strong desire for marriage and children is closely tied to Renee's need to grow beyond the dependency she still feels for Gordon and me. She knows that this summer will be different from last. Perhaps she thinks that she can substitute intense commitment to Steve for the intense dependency on Gordon and me that she felt last summer.

I'd be tempted simply to dismiss Renee's talk of marriage, but I have to keep in mind that she succeeded in going to Harvard when I was sure that she couldn't. Impatient or not, I have to analyze rather than ignore her marriage plans. I'm just glad that she's talking about a year from now rather than next month.

. . .

I was happy to be home for the summer. I looked forward to time with Steve, and to dumping the Flock in Gordon's and Lynn's laps. I was eager to have the nurturing the Flock had relished the summer before, and again at Christmas. I knew Gordon and Lynn would be eager for this too.

But a summer-long fight started my first day back. When Steve and I returned home, Lynn was in bed with a bad cold. Even though Lynn couldn't help being sick, I still felt annoyed. The Flock had been gone most of nine months. Why did she have to be sick now? I wanted to give Lynn space to recover in peace and I wanted to see her. I waited anxiously for Lynn to call, for her to say, "Why don't you come over now?" Patience gone, I called and asked whether I could visit. "Sure," Lynn said, and when we got there, she seemed honestly pleased to see us.

But somehow that wasn't enough.

"If you really understood how afraid I am of bothering you, and if you really understood how much we needed to be here, you'd have called me," I lashed out at her.

The fights continued even after Lynn recovered from her cold.

At the end of one of Rusty's sailing lessons, I told Gordon that I felt guilty about not being able to pay him for the instruction. I knew that he was well paid for coaching racers.

"How about paying me for treatment?" Lynn said. "Don't you think the work I've done with the Flock is worth anything?"

I stared at her in disbelief. She and I had talked through all of that a year ago. Lynn was paid a straight salary. Student health insurance had initially paid the clinic for our hours of treatment. But once Flock-work moved to Lynn and Gordon's home in the summer of 1983, the clinic was no longer compensated, and Lynn spent time with the Flock after a full day's work. Lynn said that nobody could pay her for being a mom, but she was also my therapist. I knew I had to pay her, worked out a plan to do that, and had gotten what I thought was agreement from her. Now she apologized for her outburst and said that she was feeling unappreciated at work.

Each incident got resolved with tears and hugs, and there were days of quiet and comfort, but the tension hung between us. Lynn told me that I was angry. I couldn't locate the feeling. I was on edge and out of sorts, but this certainly wasn't the kind of justifiable rage I had experienced with Dr. Tate. "Maybe I'm just learning what it means to be in a bad mood," I joked. "Moods have reasons," Lynn said, failing to see humor in the situation.

I was sensitive to anything Lynn might say, and she couldn't seem to find a level where we could relate. When she offered advice, I told her to stop smothering me. When she suggested I make my own decisions, I felt rejected.

"Why don't you get angry at Nancy?" Lynn said. "That's really what this is about, you know." The Flock had twenty-eight years' worth of reasons to be angry with Nancy, but that anger still seemed unsafe.

"What's the worst that could happen if you told Nancy that you are angry with her?" Lynn asked.

"She'd be more angry in return," I said. "Nancy's anger terrifies Joan Frances."

"But, Renee," Lynn said, exasperated, "why do you continue to put up with it?"

The Flock had its reasons. "She's my mother," Joan Frances said. "It's not right for a daughter to show disrespect to her mother. I want my mother to love me."

"I promised my father when he was dying that I'd look after her the best I could," said Jo.

"And anyway," I reminded Lynn, "I'm mad at you, not Nancy."

Lynn tried to sidestep situations before they erupted, but again and again that summer she and I became embroiled in arguments without even knowing how they came about. Though I felt guilty about what was happening, I couldn't seem to control my impulse to push her past her limits.

"You know, Renee," Lynn said after one fight, "you're testing our relationship, and you are learning that both your anger and my anger are safe. It's hard on both of us, but I promise we'll survive. You don't think that it is safe for you to be angry with Nancy, so you are testing out that anger on me."

"Transference!" I shouted. "That's all you think about. Isn't it possible that I have some legitimate reasons for being annoyed with you?" But I could rarely put my finger on those "reasons"!

In July, I knew my anger had a cause. Lynn and Gordon were deserting the Flock. They were leaving for a three-week trip to the West Coast. Perhaps I couldn't expect them to cancel their vacation two years in a row, and I could understand that they might need rest and time alone, but I didn't want them to leave the Flock. I knew that I was being irrational and refused to discuss my feelings about their trip.

The evening before Lynn and Gordon left started out peacefully enough. I chatted with Lynn while she packed. Gordon wandered in and out of the living room, interjecting a comment or two, and then went off to pack in another part of the house. I was glad that the Flock would have an evening like this to remember during the weeks ahead.

"I'm surprised how much I miss kids," I said, thinking back to my teaching days. "I wonder if I could babysit for Marianne and Neal sometime," I said casually. Lynn's daughter and son-in-law lived nearby with their preschooler and infant.

My remark hadn't been very serious, and I expected an equally offhanded "Sure, why not?" from Lynn. Instead, she paused and said, "Well, I guess you'll have to ask Marianne and Neal."

"Do you think they might not trust me or something?" I was puzzled by Lynn's response. Marianne and Neal were aware that I was a multiple, but the only personality they had met was me.

"Well, I can understand why someone who didn't really know you might not trust you with their children," she said.

Lynn's response cut deeply. "You know no one in the Flock would ever hurt a child!" I shouted angrily. I felt betrayed.

Lynn said soothingly, "Renee, if I had young children, I'd trust you with them. Gordon and I trust you to take care of the house, the plants, and our animals while we're away. What I'm saying is that other people don't know the Flock as well as we do. Marianne and Neal don't have any reason to be sure of you."

Nothing Lynn said now made any difference. I was hurt. I was angry. All I heard was that Lynn's daughter might not trust me with her children and Lynn understood why she might feel that way.

Gordon wandered into the room and found Lynn and me fighting yet again. He listened silently until he had picked up the essence of the quarrel. "I don't know why you'd want to babysit anyway," Gordon said. "You're busy enough as it is.

"So what if they don't understand," he said. "There will always be people who won't take the time to understand," he said.

I felt misunderstood and betrayed. Just as Nancy and Ray had done so many years ago, Lynn and Gordon were now ganging up on me. I couldn't fight them both.

"What if Josie came out and found herself with little kids?" Gordon suggested. "She certainly wouldn't know what to do with a baby."

This upset me even more. "Josie would never appear around children, any more than she or any of the others who couldn't handle it would appear when I'm driving the car or when Rusty is sailing with you," I said. "You know that the Flock has better control than that."

Yet, even as I spat out my rebuttal, which was technically true, I remembered, and knew that Gordon and Lynn were remembering, how close I had occasionally come to losing that control.

I felt trapped between my obvious ability to function well and my equally obvious pathology. I felt trapped by the mixed messages I seemed to be getting from Lynn and Gordon. They knew the competent me, and they knew the Flock's pathological responses. They had dealt with suicidal impulses and shattered child personalities. Still, they agreed with me that I had the strength to do anything. They cherished the Flock as a unique entity. And now they seemed to be saying that I was too sick to babysit for their grandchildren.

So many memories and conflicting feelings. I felt backed into a corner from which there was no escape. I got up from the sofa and started for the door.

"I don't think you're ready to leave," Lynn cautioned firmly.

"No, you shouldn't drive like this," Gordon agreed.

This was too much. "Great," I said. "Now you think I'm too crazy to even take care of myself."

I stopped at the head of the stairway, paralyzed by my own ambivalence. I didn't want to leave like this, didn't want Lynn and Gordon to go away while we were still angry with one another.

Josie found herself mid-step, teeming with panic and rage. Those feelings hurled her through the air, as they had so many times in the past. She threw herself through the glass door.

Lynn and Gordon rushed out to see Josie lying amid broken glass, bleeding and dazed by it all. Gordon led Josie inside, and after taking a look at the deep cuts, Lynn called a friend who was an M.D. Someone had to decide whether the arm needed to be sutured. An emergency room was out of the question. That would cause further trauma.

Josie disappeared, and Jo found herself sitting on the rug, Gordon's arm draped protectively around her. Amnestic as always, Jo knew only that the cuts were deep enough to hurt and that blood was spattered on her jeans and the rug. "Sorry about the blood," she said. "What happened this time?" Jo shook her head in disbelief that Josie had gone through the door because Renee and Lynn had had another fight.

Jo stayed in control while Lynn's internist friend examined and bandaged the cuts. It was well after 3:00 a.m. by the time she wearily drove home to Steve's. Humiliated that I had proved myself to be exactly as sick as I denied, I didn't re-emerge until the next afternoon, when I went back to Gordon and Lynn's to strike an uneasy peace before they left on their trip.

So often now, estranged from Lynn, I found that Jo and Steve were sources of empathy and counsel to me. Jo was a good mediator between Lynn and me. When Jo heard about our arguments, she ventured perceptions that rang true to Lynn and, much to my surprise, to me as well.

I was too caught up in my struggle with Lynn to accept much that *she* had to say. Jo became an inner counsel, a wise older sibling who could point things out to both my mom and me.

In her journal, where Jo so often criticized the Flock—referring to the other personalities only as "they"—she wrote:

Renee, I feel close to you now. I've known about you from the glimpses and shadows I've caught out of the corner of my mental eye. I've seen evidence of your accomplishments, have been shamed by your competence, and have been forced by circumstances to pretend that I am you. Usually I am aware of you only peripherally. It's different now. Now I see deeply into you, within the recesses of myself.

Now we face one another. When I look into you like this, essence to essence, we soften the barriers between us. It scares us. I can see your fear reflected in my own. But isn't it exciting as well? We're on a roller-coaster ride at the very peak and have each other's hands to hold for the breathless ride down.

Jo and I were becoming friends, and I realized that I loved the rest of my Flock as well. Missy was a fun-loving, artistic kid. Rusty had a droll sense of humor. Everyone seemed to be getting healthier, happier, and more productive. When I wasn't putting stress on the Flock by fighting with Lynn, I now felt that I was sharing this body, this physical space, with a whole group of very interesting and worthwhile people.

I was learning to depend on Steve too. He comforted me throughout the summer as I returned home from the latest bout of the ongoing, unresolved conflict with Lynn. He also spent more time than ever before with other personalities. Now, if Steve and I began talking about some serious abstract idea, I willingly moved aside and let Jo finish the conversation. Missy often joined Steve when he walked the dogs, and on a few occasions Rusty helped cut some wood.

Steve said he was glad that I trusted him to develop relationships with the other personalities. He knew that my acceptance of them was a sign of greater health, but he really liked *me* best and wanted to know when I'd be integrated—when the other personalities would be gone.

"Look, Steve," I said, "whether you like it or not, all of the personalities are part of this entity. No personality is ever going to disappear."

"What about Robin and Reagen? Little Joe?" he asked.

"Those personalities were absorbed, not exiled. No one inside will ever disappear. We're all real. We all matter."

DIARY *August 23, 1984*

Contrary to my expectations of a placid summer, we have had a horren-dous time—in some ways more wearing than last summer for me, because of my complete lack of preparation I was proud of Renee's new ability to stick up for herself with Dr. Tate. It was quite different to have her direct her anger toward me, particularly since she could not stand to have it labeled anger.

This summer was the October weekend all over again, without its redeeming features. I was faced with a full-blown adolescent, churning with inner turmoil she was projecting on me. And I wasn't ready for it, didn't understand it, and resented it fiercely.

I found it especially hard to deal with in the Renee personality, with whom I had always had so much fun. Now I could do nothing right. I was used to having long, painful discussions with Jo in which I had to be very careful of what I said and did. Renee and I, on the other hand, had discussed, argued, agreed, and disagreed, easily exploring, comfortably thinking aloud without much censorship. Now she began acting like Jo, but was far angrier than Jo had ever been.

I could at the same time see that the Flock was obviously moving closer together and developing a great deal of healthy self-respect. Why, then, did Renee not only take me and the treatment for granted, but continually point out my mistakes and accuse me of not caring or understanding? I felt baffled, used, hurt, and angry in turn. Nothing I tried seemed to work until the night before we left on vacation, when Josie went through a storm door in a violent statement of Renee's anger.

The shock of dealing with that forced all of us to take a second look. I was able to step back and realize that, just as Renee was acting the adolescent, I was reacting very much like the adolescent's mother. This realization, while not a solution, did make the rest of the summer more bearable, and the explosions became less frequent.

. . .

31

The Flock returned to Harvard with a new closeness among us. We were gaining confidence in our notion that cooperation, not integration, was the realistic goal. We were eager to prove that we could function well in an ongoing group existence.

Jo and I still had amnestic barriers that kept us from communicating internally, but we joined forces in deciding that this multiple need not integrate. Jo was sure that the merging of multiple selves into a single personality constituted some logic problem. I had other reasons.

It was clear to me that, despite occasional bouts with depression, the Flock was more effective than many of the other graduate students. This was even more true now that we had our own apartment and could work undisturbed for fourteen or sixteen hours each day. (I thought we needed the privacy of our own place and had secured a double teaching fellowship that would pay the rent.)

The Flock required only four or five hours of sleep a night. That left a lot of time for work. And the amnesia that in the past had crippled us became an advantage. Our production multiplied because each personality could focus on a separate task. Jo, for example, worked for many hours researching and writing a paper, unaware of what else needed to be done. When I pushed Jo aside to fulfill my graduate-assistant duties, I didn't worry about the progress of the paper. When Jo came back to work, she picked up precisely where she had left off, with no concern about her "lost time." She had near-perfect recall of all that she experienced. This was augmented by her near-perfect amnesia for all the time that elapsed between her points of consciousness.

Being a multiple apparently created more efficient use of my conscious and semiconscious mind. I didn't want to give up my greater productivity to become just like everyone else.

But I knew that the rough times were not yet over. Despite a summer of practice on Lynn, I still overreacted to disagreements among the personalities and was still shaky in most of my interpersonal relationships. I also knew there would be some unavoidable stress connected with the doctoral work, particularly since we had decided to complete two years of study in one and had double teaching responsibilities as well. Multiple personalities couldn't increase the amount of time available in a day.

I decided to seek some ongoing professional help. I hadn't forgotten the horror of Dr. Tate, but I convinced myself that this was different. Now I decided to approach the affiliated psychiatric group, not in crisis but as any other student who wanted to talk with a mental-health professional on a regular basis. Many students were in weekly psychotherapy. My request would not be so unusual.

I discussed my need first with Dr. Matthews, the doctor who had agreed to be the Flock's safety net. I told him my reasons for wanting support in Cambridge instead of initiating regular contacts with him on the North Shore, and cited my financial difficulties as well. "I have to pay Harvard hundreds of dollars each year to cover health care. Why should I pay you sixty dollars an hour on top of that?"

Dr. Matthews agreed that my request for ongoing support with a Harvard affiliate didn't seem unusual, even if the disorder was. He suggested that I make an appointment with Dr. Brandenberg, who served as the director of the group practice that included Dr. Tate. "Dr. Brandenberg may not know anything about multiples," Dr. Matthews counseled, "but she will understand that you have a right to some care."

A few days later, I waited outside Dr. Brandenberg's door and realized that I was tired of excusing the medical community for "not knowing anything about multiples." MPD had been recognized as a disorder for at least a hundred years. It had been brought to the attention of the professional and public communities through *Three Faces of Eve* in the 1950s and again by *Sybil* in the 1970s. Literature related to the disorder had snowballed in the clinical journals.

I could understand that not every mental-health professional had treated a case, but I couldn't accept that mental-health professionals knew so little about it. At the very least, the doctors had access to the journals that had provided Jo with her wealth of information on the topic.

The Flock had seen other mental-health professionals before finding Lynn. They had not recognized the disorder, but the Flock had been working hard to hide it then. Now, however, comfortable with the diagnosis and able to explain the condition articulately, I could not see why it should be so difficult to find a doctor willing to learn.

"I'm not a freak," I told Dr. Brandenberg, "and I'm tired of being treated as though I'm bizarre and unmanageable. I've seen true psychotics in the student population, and they are tolerated here. I'm functional, I'm a good student, and when I came here last year in crisis, I was threatened with involuntary withdrawal from school. That's just not right."

Dr. Brandenberg told me she'd look for someone willing to work with me.

"It bothers me that you should have to look for someone special, as though I'm some sort of freak," I said.

"Some psychiatrists don't believe in multiple personalities," she reminded me.

"They don't believe in multiple personalities," Kendra mimicked as we left Dr. Brandenberg's office. "Since when does one have to have faith in a mental disorder?" Kendra kept a low profile these days, generally expressing herself as part of the Alliance, but when her mitigating influence didn't stop me from doing something she considered dangerous to the Flock, she let me know.

A few weeks later, I called Dr. Brandenberg. No one had yet called to set up an appointment. She said that she hadn't forgotten, and that a Dr. Wu had said she was interested. Another week went by before Dr. Wu called.

I answered the phone, but when the doctor identified herself, Kendra stepped out from the Alliance and pushed the rest of us aside. "My turn," she said internally. "I'm handling this one." She and I were by this time identical in speech and inflection.

"I understand you want to make an appointment," the doctor said.

"That depends," Kendra demurred. "Do you know I'm a multiple?"

"I've read your chart," the doctor said noncommittally.

"Oh, great," Kendra said.

The chart. Well, the doctor would have to get to know the Flock before she understood that the chart reflected more of Dr. Tate's problems than mine. I had read the chart and was appalled by what was written there. After warning me away from further contact and reminding me that he could have me withdrawn from school if I continued my "manipulative" behavior, the psychiatrist wrote that he and Dr. Matthews were going to work closely together on this complicated case.

Dr. Matthews confirmed that he had never heard from Dr. Tate. Nor had I.

Kendra asked Dr. Wu if she had ever worked with a multiple.

"No," she said, "but we can discuss all of this when you come in."

Kendra took a deep breath. By now we all knew the psychiatric routine.

"I understand that you'd rather talk to me in person about all of this," she said, "but I'm afraid I need some answers before I make an appointment. If you've read the chart, then you should understand that my experience with your group practice has not been the best. I don't want to waste your time or mine if we can't communicate. So, do you believe in multiple personality?"

"I believe in you," Dr. Wu replied.

"I'm quite aware that I exist," Kendra said coolly, "and I trust that you are also aware of my existence. That is not the issue. Do you believe in Multiple Personality Disorder as described in the psychiatric literature?"

She said, "Yes."

Kendra said, "Fine."

The appointment was made. Kendra ended the call by giving Dr. Wu Lynn's and Dr. Matthews's phone numbers. "They can tell you a lot more about me than the chart did," she suggested. "If you call either of them, you'll know better who I am before I come in."

She hung up the phone and turned to me. "Renee," she said, "why do you persist in throwing yourself at these psychiatrists? This convinces me that you are the craziest one in the Flock."

The others stayed out of the way when I went to see Dr. Wu. Kendra didn't approve, and she watched carefully so that she could act if needed.

Dr. Wu was young and guarded. When I asked her why she had decided to see me, she explained that she was a resident; she wanted to be exposed to as many different types of patients as possible, and to learn about the disorder. I was delighted: I thought everyone should learn more about MPD. But I was distressed that she had not contacted Lynn or Dr. Matthews. She hadn't had time, she said, and, no, she had never read *Sybil* or any of the clinical literature on MPD.

"What led up to your seeing Dr. Brandenberg?" she asked.

I explained that I wanted some supportive therapy. "I'd like to see someone once a week who can help me with the stress of being a graduate student and a teaching fellow combined with the stress of being multiple. Things are great now—the Flock is calm and cooperative. I'd like to keep it that way.

"You don't have to do any real treatment of pathology, no abreaction of abuse or anything like that," I reassured her. "I just want to keep the Flock from getting into a crisis situation."

I talked for forty minutes, feeling less and less comfortable. Dr. Wu remained cool, guarded, distant. Just about the most unnerving thing to me was lack of response. "Where are you?" I wanted to ask. "Are you listening?" Instead, I continued to explain about the condition, waiting for some sign of understanding, some indication of support or empathy. Even some indication of disbelief would have been preferable to the blank, emotionless mask I faced. "Maybe you'd understand better if you met one of the others," I suggested. She said nothing, and I figured she'd deal with whatever she saw. I slipped inside.

Jo became aware in the doctor's office, the room darkening with dusk. She glanced at her watch. Five forty-six. Where was she? Lynn had neglected to mention that I was going to try again to find a supportive psychiatrist, and Jo had neglected to look at the calendar where the Flock recorded appointments. As usual, her amnesia kept her in the dark.

Jo glanced around the office. She didn't know the woman who sat behind the desk. She squinted to read the titles in the bookcase across the room, thinking that they might help her figure it out. A professor? No, the woman wore a white coat. Probably a medical person. The books were too far away for Jo to make a better guess at identification, but the woman was saying something now.

"So, why is it that you think you could not tolerate hospitalization?" she asked.

"Hospitalization!" Jo thought wildly. "Oh, no, what have they done to me now?" She concentrated on her nerve endings. No pain, no evidence of a suicidal gesture. "Do you want to hospitalize me?" Jo finally asked in her distinctive, halting manner. She glanced out the window and recognized the street as being near campus.

"No, I don't want to hospitalize you," Dr. Wu said, "but you told me earlier that you wanted to avoid hospitalization at all costs . . . or, rather, Renee said that. I wondered why you feel so strongly."

Jo relaxed a little and smiled hesitantly. Obviously this woman knew she was a multiple.

Then she felt annoyed. She was annoyed that Renee would drop her into this situation, and annoyed with this strange woman as well. If this person knew she was a multiple and recognized her as a different personality from the one who had been speaking earlier, why didn't she tell her what was going on? Why didn't she introduce herself? Why did she only ask a question for which Jo lacked referent and context?

Finally, Jo said, "I'm not ignoring your question, but when I find myself in strange places . . . I mean, you know I'm a multiple, and I don't know where I am. . . . I don't know who you . . . Who are you?"

"I'm Dr. Wu," she said.

"A psychiatrist?" Jo asked. When she responded affirmatively, Jo explained, "I'm amnestic and I have trouble answering questions when I don't have the context. So why were you asking me about . . ."

"Your time is up anyway," she interrupted. "Do you want to make another appointment?"

I took over and made an appointment for a week hence, but was far from sure that the others would let me keep it.

"I told you it wouldn't work," Kendra said to me.

Throughout the week, I argued with the others to let me try one more time. "Come on," I said. "She's young and really doesn't know anything about MPD. Maybe she'll relax. Let's give her another chance."

At the start of the next appointment, I asked Dr. Wu if she had had time to call Dr. Matthews or Lynn. No, she hadn't, but she had talked with others on the staff who had seen me last year. "I will not get caught up in your manipulation," she said. "I hear that you're used to setting the rules and getting your own way, but that won't happen this time. I will see you every two weeks rather than weekly. And I will not be available to you in any emergency."

"Let me get this straight," I said slowly. "If I developed a therapeutic relationship with you and then called you to say that things were getting disjointed and crazy, you wouldn't talk to me?"

"I suppose I wouldn't hang up on you," she said, "but I want to make it very clear that I will never see you more often than every other Thursday, those sessions will never go beyond fifty minutes, I will not help you during any crisis, and I will deal with no other personality."

"Great," I thought, "I'm coming here for help in dealing with the disorder, and she says that she'll only help me if I'm able to hide the pathology."

Now that Dr. Wu had defined the limits of our professional relationship, she wanted to know my therapeutic goals. I knew I'd never be back, and decided that I had nothing to lose.

"I'd like to be able to talk with you about the stresses of school and about the additional stress of being a multiple," I said, repeating myself from the last session. "I'd like for you to offer some support," I continued, "and to offer suggestions as to how I might better cope with stress and little problems so that they don't develop into crisis situations. I'm coming to you because I don't think it's right to involve school friends in these needs."

"So your therapeutic goal," she said, "is to be able to tell your friends that you think you're multiple?"

"No," I said, "that is not my therapeutic goal. I have no narcissistic need to tell people about my problem. My fellow students have their own problems. I'm not going to dump my problems on them. That's why I came here—I wanted to find a professional to help me rather than my relying on my friends."

I took a deep breath. "And I don't *think* I'm a multiple," I said, "I *am* a multiple. Thank you for your time."

"Do you want to make another appointment?" she asked.

"No," Kendra said, "we won't be back."

Unable to sleep that night, I tried to figure out what had gone wrong. Maybe I was finally learning from experience. I would never again look for help there. "But why can't somebody outside the Flock do some learning?" I wondered.

With the hope of outside support gone, the Flock compensated by finding support within. One morning at the end of October, I woke to find pages of typed transcripts. These transcripts were the product of brand-new, total inner-Flock communication. Although Jo and other personalities continued to be amnestic and unable to communicate consciously with others in the Flock, on a deeper level the barriers were gone.

The personality who applied this new ability called herself Unity. She hadn't ever presented herself to any external person; she never took the consciousness in a way that interfered with any other personality. She claimed to exist solely to help us communicate better with one another, to help the Flock move closer together.

I didn't know if Unity was new to the Flock or if she had always been a part, unnoticed and unheard. Her background didn't much matter; our new closeness did.

Unity facilitated discussions in a self-induced hypnotic trance. Knowing that conscious awareness of the middle-of-the-night conferences would be important to at least some of the personalities, Unity asked the organizing Karen personality to type transcripts while the conferences were going on. Even I, the least amnestic of all the functioning personalities, had no memory of the meetings. But four times during October and November, I woke to find a transcript from a conference that had reportedly taken place an hour or so after I had gone to bed. I felt no fear about my "lost time," no frustration at finding that the body had operated without my control.

I did feel silly about the whole thing. And I was not alone in that feeling. Based on the transcript, our first intra-Flock session was a test run, filled with expressions of disbelief.

Unity introduced herself and reassured the others that they would not remember what took place at the conference. She suggested that we see how such deep-level communication might work.

The transcript read:

KENDRA (in response to Unity): Come on. After getting us up for this, you might tell us what it's all about.

UNITY: First of all, I did not get you up for this. I told you, you need not know you were up at all.

JO: The reality of the situation is that the body is sitting at the typewriter. Whether any personalities remember it later or not, in some sense, I am *up*.

UNITY: I admit that I'm extending definitions somewhat so that there can be a record of this conference. Would you feel differently if I had let the body stay in bed while we communicated like this?

JO: I can't answer that.

UNITY: We would have been doing the same thing, except that Karen would not have been typing.

RENEE: Jo's right, though. There's a big difference between lying in bed and sitting at the typewriter.

UNITY: Well, I suggest that the two of you come up with a "relevant" difference. You both know that the biggest problem that the "normal" world has with multiplicity is that it insists on the convention of one mind in one body. I suggest that the two of you become more flexible in your thinking if you expect the world to do the same.

JO: There is a relevant difference between flexibility and sloppy thinking.

UNITY: I won't bother to respond to that. Most of what we need to talk about during these conferences has to do with cooperation. Renee has correctly expressed our therapeutic goal as comfort and productivity for all. That's simply not possible without greater connection among us. It need not be conscious right now; it need not lead to integration. We can cooperate quietly, internally, and, as it were, in a dream. But cooperate we must. I will take no position on any given topic. I will facilitate and ensure that all interested personalities have a say in the final external decision on whatever topic we discuss.

After this first dream conference, I felt even more disbelief than I had evidently expressed during the group discussion. I called Lynn. "You're not going to believe this one," I began. "In fact, I feel a little embarrassed even talking to you about it."

Lynn sighed. "Renee, what did you do this time?"

I described the conference to her and read the transcript. "Who would believe this?" I said. "It's just too hokey! I'd like to find a way of denying it myself."

Lynn agreed that the conference seemed strange, but she applauded the Flock's creativity. "Don't you see what's happening, Renee?" she asked. "The others are determined to have a say now.

"I think Unity's a pretty smart lady," Lynn added, "because you are being forced to deal with the reality of the conference through the transcripts. There's no way that you can pretend you're running the show anymore."

"Thanks for making me feel so important," I said.

In truth, I was impressed with the new group cooperation. And, whether I liked it or not, the conference transcripts appeared, at irregular intervals. I decided that it did no good to worry about any conference that took place without transcription.

The first Flock conference happened after our initial visit with Dr. Wu. Following our second appointment, Unity called another caucus.

She asked me to explain why I had gone back to Wu for the second visit, then let the others have their say:

UNITY: Was anyone else at Dr. Wu's office aside from Renee and Kendra?

ISIS: I was. She thinks we're difficult and dangerous, that we've manipulated a lot of people to do our bidding, including Lynn. Dr. Tate let Dr. Wu know that he thinks we used him. Wu is damn sure that that's not going to happen to her. By the way, she has already decided that she would hospitalize us at the least provocation, just to show us who's boss. She thinks you—and, by the way, she does think of you, Renee, in the singular sense— have an ego problem, and that you think you are far more powerful than you actually are.

RENEE: If that's so, then we are all lucky that Dr. Wu didn't meet Isis. At least I don't pretend I can read minds.

UNITY: There isn't any reason to think that Isis's interpretation is less accurate than yours, Renee. Was anyone else there?

RUSTY: I looked at her one time, and she didn't like my new dad.

RENEE: This is ridiculous. Wu doesn't even know Gordon.

ISIS: What Rusty means is that your good doctor thinks that we've manipulated both Lynn and Gordon.

JO: Renee, why do you have to put us through things like that?

RENEE: I just wanted to establish a therapeutic relationship with someone here on campus, just like hundreds of other students. What's wrong with that? I tried to set up something with Wu for the good of the Flock. Don't make me into an ogre.

JOAN FRANCES: Dr. Wu knows I'm just pretending. She knows I'm not a multiple personality. (Groans from the rest of the group.)

KENDRA: Damn it. Renee, do you see what you've started with Joan Frances? Isn't that reason enough to keep away from that fool?

RENEE: OK, we're never going to see Dr. Wu again, but what am I supposed to do for some support? What if things begin to fall apart?

UNITY: How do the rest of you feel about Dr. Matthews?

MISSY: That man's place is scary. And the other girl, who hits her head, might come, and then Renee would be mad.

ISIS: Josie is always a danger, but a lot of us have had fairly pleasant

contact with Dr. Matthews. How about if the rest of us help
Renee out and work together to keep things under control if we
go to see him?

JO: I don't want to see any psychiatrist.

Through full Flock discussion, then, negotiations were made and
compromises were offered until a solution emerged. I would see Dr.
Matthews if I felt overly stressed, and everyone in the Flock agreed to help
out. The greater communication within the Flock made it less likely that
a crisis would occur, but it was good to know that there was somebody
nearby.

DIARY *November 18, 1984*

*When Renee called me, hedging a little on telling me why she sounded
so embarrassed, I imagined all sorts of things. I was completely surprised
by Renee's explanation of the "intra-Flock conference" conducted by a
personality we had not met. I had long since given up looking for a
personality who could always tell what the Flock needed. The literature
suggested that every multiple had a personality who "knew everything about
everyone" and who provided assistance to the therapist. Renee had long ago
stopped worrying about not meeting the criteria of an internal self-helper
personality.*

*Now, suddenly, there is an internal self-helper, who apparently does far
more than offer her therapist polite suggestions: Unity took charge and
provided the climate for Flock cooperation. Not only that, she saw to it that
there were transcripts of the internal conferences. Whether this was intended or not, the transcripts let me keep track of the Flock's continuing
growth. Unity was well worth waiting for, and I am hoping to meet her
when the Flock comes home for Thanksgiving.*

*I wonder if Renee sees how rapidly they are moving toward integration.
Renee and Jo both speak persuasively on why the Flock should not integrate. I don't argue (of course!), but I wonder if deciding not to integrate
is an important step toward that end. This is an amazingly logical disorder,
and I'm beginning to see the Flock's determination that they will not
integrate as entirely consistent with that ultimate plunge.*

Clearly integration is not possible until the personalities like one an-

other enough to subsume into one. In the past, the arguments against integrating have been filled with fear of pathological behavior or fear of denied secrets from the past. Now, when Renee or Jo tells me that she is not going to integrate, what I hear is overwhelming love and respect for all of the personalities.

As Renee affirms all of the personalities, is she beginning to affirm newly recognized parts of self? We're getting closer to that all the time, partly thanks to Unity's group conferences. Now, when Renee makes a decision consciously, she knows, or at least suspects, that Unity has already given everyone a chance to have unconscious input. Renee knows that, more and more, she is acting on the Flock's behalf rather than her own.

I even see Renee's final attempt at securing local psychiatric support as evidence of a new, improved self-concept. There was no reason to believe that Renee would find what she said she was looking for. Maybe she knew this on some level, but needed to have closure on last year's incident with Dr. Tate. The rejection that greeted her served as a catalyst for the new affirmation of self expressed through the intra-Flock conferences. I finally understand that the Flock often requires external stimulation when it's ready for a growth spurt. It's as though everything gets ready internally and then waits to be kicked "on." If the kick doesn't come naturally, they go out looking for it.

Maybe this is one of the essentials for the therapist treating a multiple—the ability to "kick" when needed, and the ability to stand back and watch the multiple manipulate her environment to produce what she needs. I've now been in touch with a number of clinicians who work with multiples. It's clear that my reparenting relationship with the Flock is different from many of the other multiple-therapist relationships, but there are some essentials of good multiple treatment that seem to be present in even the most traditional psychotherapeutic setting.

Any therapist treating a multiple must play a variety of roles for the various personalities. Even if the treatment is confined to the office, the little ones need hugs and attention, just as all children in treatment might. Different personalities have different ways of working through pathology, like any group of patients, and the therapist must adjust to provide an adequate treatment approach for each one.

At the same time, the therapist must give each personality what is needed but must keep in mind that any message is being processed by the entity as a whole. I don't think I'm being arrogant when I say that I'm impressed with what I've been doing intuitively. I've always had great faith in my unconscious, and when I trust myself on that deep level, maybe I'm expressing the same facility that Unity is demonstrating in the Flock.

. . .

32

The Flock went home for Thanksgiving more secure in our internal and external relationships than we had ever been. It was good to be with Lynn and Gordon and great to be with Steve. For the first time in my life, I felt and responded to sexual desire. In the past, I had been sexual because that's what men wanted. But things had changed. *I* loved Steve. *I* desired him.

Thanksgiving morning, Rusty went with Gordon to check out how *The Channel* had been bedded down for the winter. Gordon showed Rusty the engine he had removed and taken apart to repair while the boat was in drydock. He reminded Rusty how the engine worked to propel the boat when there was no wind. "I know that, Dad!" Rusty said huffily.

"It's been a while since we sailed together," Gordon explained. In fact, it had been more than two months. Rusty shrugged. In Rusty's time sense, it didn't seem long at all. He had probably had all of six hours of time in the last two months and was amnestic for the rest. He didn't think he had forgotten anything. But maybe his dad knew something he didn't.

A little uncertainly, Rusty interrupted Gordon's tour of how the boat was maintained in drydock to ask, "Did I forget a whole lot, Dad?" Gordon stopped, thoughtful as always, and finally said, "No, it seems to me that you didn't forget anything at all."

Rusty relaxed then. They turned to leave the cavernous boathouse, passing dozens of vessels snug under tarps. Gordon stopped suddenly and headed back to *The Channel*. "I'll be right back, Rusty," he called. "I forgot something. I'll meet you by the bulletin board that says 'Attention Captains!' " Rusty had never before noticed the sign. He hadn't needed to. He and Gordon had had no reason to stop here on their way in. For the first time, Rusty was struck with the awareness that there were words here in this special place. It was a boat place and a man place. He didn't know that it was also a word place.

Gordon was gone for no more than a few minutes. But in that time, Rusty became transfixed, staring at the letters on the sign. Letters made words. Words could hurt. . . .

"OK," Gordon broke in, steering Rusty away from the sign and out the door, "let's get out of here."

Rusty stumbled after Gordon, tense and disoriented as he walked through the parking lot. A stop sign. Car names. License plates. Words. There were words everywhere.

In Gordon's car, Rusty looked down and studied his sneakers to avoid looking out the window and seeing all the letters, all the words. "The words," Rusty said, his voice quaking, "they're everywhere, Dad. The words, Dad. They're gonna cut me. They're gonna get me. They're gonna kill me."

"No, they won't, Rusty," Gordon said. "The words can't hurt you." Rusty didn't argue, but sat tensely, as though anticipating assault.

Rusty jumped from the car as soon as Gordon drove up in front of Steve's house. I saw Rusty's look of terror as he fled inside the Flock, but I put his concerns aside until later. I needed to get things ready for Thanksgiving dinner at Lynn's, with four generations of Wilsons, Steve, and me. We'd get to Rusty soon; he wasn't going anywhere.

Later, Steve went home alone and the Wilsons' house was quiet. Gordon, Lynn, and I stretched out before the fire. "Time for Rusty?" I asked. I was more inclined to doze in front of the fire than to attend to Rusty's fears. But I decided to leave it up to Lynn and Gordon.

"Time for Rusty," Gordon said.

Rusty smiled quickly at Gordon and Lynn, but then moved to the cause of his anxiety. "Words, Dad," he whimpered.

"Tell me what you see, Rusty," Gordon encouraged in his deep voice, which at times like this soothed, comforted, and took away the sting of old fear.

Rusty saw the sand under his sneakers and the dunes all around him. He saw the ocean grasses waving in sea breeze, heard the crashing of waves and the calling of gulls. Then he saw the stick, moved by some unseen hand, writing words, letters in the sand. "Words. The stick," Rusty said, backing away from memory. "The words, they're gonna cut me up." In Rusty's mind, all of the letters had sharp edges. The hand became the stick became the letters became the pain.

"Words don't hurt," Gordon said, guiding Rusty from his panic back to the memory. "People hurt. Who's holding the stick?" Rusty saw the stick again. He wouldn't look, couldn't look up to see the face, the body behind the stick. Rusty was gone, and Josie was there.

Josie trembled for a minute, ignoring the scene playing itself out in her mind. She fixated on the wall. She would hit the wall before she could be overcome by the memory.

"Josie," Lynn said, noting the change in personality. "It's OK, you're with Gordon and Lynn. Gordon and Lynn are here."

Gordon slid closer to where Josie was cringing. He stroked her back.

"I'm here, Josie," he said soothingly, encircling her so that he could grab her quickly if she lunged for the wall. "Tell me what you see," Gordon urged.

Gordon meant peace. Josie relaxed against him and turned to face her memory.

"Where are you, Josie?"

The wave of memory splashed over Josie, drenching her in the past. She sprawled in the sand. A stick poked viciously at her crotch and thighs. She could feel the scraping pain through her jeans, felt betrayal and violation of her soul.

"You got a prick, huh?" a voice said gutturally. "Is it there? Is it there?" the voice demanded with every jab.

"Stick," Josie whispered to Gordon, reaching back to the present. "Who's holding the stick?" Gordon asked.

Josie looked up and saw her father's face, almost unrecognizable in his torment and rage. Her crotch burned. "Hurts. It hurts. Please, Daddy, no," Josie whimpered, squirming away from the stick and its fire.

"That was before," Gordon said firmly, "not now."

Josie returned gratefully to the present and nestled into Gordon's arms. At peace, she slipped back inside, and Jo found herself in Gordon's gentle, protective embrace. Embarrassed as always at the need for such protection, Jo tensed. "I-I'm OK," she said. Gordon slowly disengaged himself, recognizing that Josie was gone. But he stayed close enough to remind Jo that his touch was nothing to fear.

Jo took in her surroundings at a glance and relaxed, pleased to find herself in Lynn and Gordon's living room. Then a sweet, bitter piece of nostalgia supplanted her comfort. Lynn recognized that Jo's dreamy look focused far beyond the fireplace and plants. "Tell me what you see, Jo," Lynn urged.

She grinned at being caught daydreaming, but answered casually. "Oh, I was just thinking about my father."

At Lynn's encouragement, Jo went on. "I was remembering a day with him at the beach—early fall on the Outer Banks. I sat near some dunes, weaving the sea grass."

Jo could almost feel the rubbery green spikes in her hands. She could almost smell the salt air. "I was about eleven. My father had walked some distance from me and was sitting by his own dune, drawing or writing in the sand with a stick. He looked so dejected and sad. I wanted to walk over and comfort him, but knew he'd never let me. Sometimes he just shut me out, and I didn't understand why." Jo was glad she had many happy memories of time with her father to counterbalance sad ones like this.

She drifted into her nostalgia, and I slipped past her to come out, holding a few more pieces of memory from other personalities.

"Hi there," I said, with the forced casualness I had come to adopt when describing a scene of abuse. "Are you ready for the whole picture?"

"If you are, sweetie," Lynn said.

"As you know, Jo couldn't let herself go over to comfort her father, but Missy could.

"Ray lost it when Missy went over to make Daddy feel better. Although the Flock was eleven then, Missy was perennially five. Maybe he just couldn't deal with what he saw as his daughter's 'little-girl act.' Anyway, his reaction scared Missy. As usual when Missy got scared, Rusty surfaced. I guess Rusty's 'I'm a boy and I've got a penis too' posturing was just too much for Ray to take, and he struck at her crotch with the stick."

Rusty pushed me aside, filled with new understanding and a new sense of well-being. There was no doubt in any of us that Rusty had heard every word I said. "Hey, Dad," he said excitedly to Gordon, "the stick didn't kill me, the words didn't kill me. It's because I'm here," he said, pointing to his head, "and here," he said, pointing to his heart, "not just here," he said, pointing to his crotch. Rusty was gone before anyone could react.

We three sat silently for a minute. Then we all talked at once. "How did he hear me?" I asked. "Holy cow, he's found his real self!" Gordon shouted. "Maybe he doesn't care anymore that his body's a girl's," Lynn trilled. "Rusty!" Gordon and Lynn called together.

I glanced inside. Rusty lounged nearby, enjoying the external bedlam, knowing that I'd be coming to look for him.

He stood up, grinned at me, and then ran a finger down my cheek.

"Check you later," he said and strolled back and back, humming a sea chantey taught to him by one of his dads. "I love you," I whispered as I watched him disappear.

"Where's Rusty?" Lynn asked. "Don't you think he needs to come back and talk about this?"

"No, I think he's doing just fine on his own," I said.

I left soon after, wanting to cherish alone Rusty's gesture, his gift for me. He knew now that he was one of us.

33

I eagerly shared my new understanding with Steve when I returned home that evening, telling him with pride how Josie and Rusty and Jo had worked together to resolve the old damage. Now that Steve really understood that there were many different personalities living in this body, it was important to me that he come to appreciate all of us, as I had. After all, Steve was going to marry the entity, not just me.

The next day, Steve and I spent the afternoon with friends. Jo wanted some time with Steve as well, so I moved aside during the long drive home. Jo glanced around and reflexively checked her watch. She did so without embarrassment, knowing that Steve finally understood all about her.

Jo sat thoughtfully for a while, enjoying Steve's company. He seemed to be aware of her presence, and she was comfortable with that. At least he no longer assumed something was wrong when she came out.

Jo decided that it was time that she and Steve discuss something that had been troubling her. "Steve," she said, "would you rather be involved with me, as a multiple, or with some other, 'single' person?"

He paused and said, "I don't know."

Jo wasn't offended by Steve's response; aside from Lynn and Gordon, Jo still wouldn't let herself feel close enough to anyone to feel rejected. But Steve's answer puzzled her.

"Lynn told me that you and Renee were talking about getting married next August," she said.

"Yes, that's right," Steve agreed. "What do you think of that?"

"Well," she said slowly, "if you're not sure that you would rather be with me than with some other person, I don't understand why you're talking about marriage."

Steve told Jo that he had some real concerns about marrying the

Flock. Last summer, he had assumed that integration was the ultimate goal and that it would be quickly forthcoming. Now it seemed that the Flock had chosen to remain separate personalities.

"You yourself have told me," Steve said to Jo, "that you think integration is philosophically untenable. Whether you're right or not, I don't want to live the rest of my life with a bunch of separate personalities."

He confessed that certain personalities in particular troubled him. He didn't feel he could adjust to male personalities like Rusty, who "might seek sexual expression outside of the home."

Jo was unaware of the dramatic change that had occurred with Rusty the night before, so she considered Steve's arguments. "If Rusty is or would be sexually active in some way, I quite agree with you. But I'm still stuck on your earlier point. Let me respond to your concern about integration."

She searched for an analogy that might fit her understanding of the situation. "I know that I argued against integration not long ago," she said, "but now I don't think that's any more appropriate than arguing *for* integration. Do you remember from your reading of *The Republic* what Plato said about happiness?"

Yes, Steve did remember, but Jo continued, thinking out the analogy as she expressed it. "Plato said that you couldn't strive for happiness. If you lived right, if all of the parts of your soul were in harmonious order, then happiness just naturally followed."

Jo smiled at the ironic aptness of the analogy. "Excuse the pun about separate parts of the soul," she said, "but I do think that the metaphor holds. Integration isn't something that a multiple can strive to achieve. Maybe it's not even something that she can seek to avoid, if she keeps growing healthier. Maybe, once all of the personalities are fulfilled and working harmoniously, integration just naturally follows."

"I hadn't thought of that," Steve concluded, but Jo continued her dispassionate consideration of his reservations.

"However, I do understand your concerns about living with a multiple," she said. "I would think it would be far more trouble than it was worth. I wouldn't marry one either." As far as Jo was concerned, the matter was closed. The Flock would not marry Steve.

The matter was far from closed for me, as I let Steve know a few minutes later. Jo may not have felt rejected, but I did. "I've told you about my being a multiple for almost as long as we've been together," I said angrily. "The other parts aren't anything new. How can you suddenly change your mind about getting married?"

"The other parts may not be new," Steve said calmly, "but my understanding of them certainly is. I can't deal with the idea of marrying someone who contains personalities like Josie throwing herself against walls. Do you know how bad I'd feel if my wife committed suicide? And I can't deal with Rusty thinking he's male. Would you marry a closet homosexual?"

Steve's arguments made no sense to me. "First of all," I said, "I don't like Josie's behavior any more than you do. Her throwing herself at walls is a pathological part of the disorder that is being worked out with Gordon and Lynn. As I, and others in the Flock, learn to handle our own feelings of fear and anger, there is less reason for Josie to appear and release those feelings in her abreactive way.

"The suicidal feelings are like that too. They are reactions to past abuse. We are less suicidal now than we've ever been, and I'm sure that the feelings will soon stop altogether.

"You are also all wrong about Rusty. Yes, Rusty thinks he's a boy, and he is a boy, but not in a sexually active sense. The Flock, as a whole, respect our commitment to you. We don't express ourselves sexually outside this relationship now, and we certainly won't when we're married to you."

"But what happens when Rusty gets a little older?" Steve asked. "Won't he become sexually active then?"

"I told you what happened with Rusty last night," I said angrily. "Why are you making a big thing about Rusty, when I think he's been 'absorbed' by the group? Instead of being proud of my progress, you're ignoring it."

"First you tell me that they're all separate people," Steve said, "and then, when I react to them that way, you get mad. I don't know how I'm supposed to think or act about this."

"Look, you're a single entity with a lot of parts too," I said. "There are some parts of you that I don't like very much, but I love you and want to marry you as an entity. I'm willing to take those less-than-desirable parts in the bargain."

"That's different," Steve said. "I'm one person, not many."

Steve and I had arrived at an impasse. He said he wanted to marry me and he'd probably take Jo and a few of the others thrown in, but he wanted nothing to do with Josie, Rusty, Missy, or many of the rest.

I let Steve know that I loved the entire Flock. He took either all or nothing. I would not deny that they were all permanent parts of the entity. Lynn said that this was the "silver lining in this whole mess."

"How could Steve change like this?" I sobbed to Lynn. "I haven't lied to him. I even stopped trying to hide my being a multiple from him. He was the first person besides you and Gordon that I trusted with the rest of the personalities."

"That's all true," Lynn said, "but remember how Steve has responded to your being a multiple over the years. He denied it for a long time because that was more comfortable for him."

"I know," I said, "but then I really let him see and get to know some of the others. I wanted him to appreciate them the way that you, Gordon, and I have learned to. He went from one extreme to another," I told Lynn. "At first he wouldn't accept me as separate. Now he won't see that we're really all together."

I returned to Harvard after Thanksgiving and wondered how to cope with Steve's refusal to understand. I knew that the Flock was in increasingly better shape. My therapeutic goal of comfort and productivity for all seemed within reach. How could I retain who I knew myself to be and, at the same time, reconcile a relationship with Steve?

I put the question aside for my studies. I talked with Steve every week, but the problem with him was hundreds of miles away. I was always pleased to turn my attention back to papers, reading, and exams.

But Christmas was fast approaching, and the Flock was going to Virginia to spend the holiday this year with Nancy. Steve was meeting us there.

After Christmas, we would have only a few weeks to finish out the school term, and I had no doubt that those weeks would be rough. The Flock was always a mess after a visit with Nancy. In order to be sure that I had a lifeline when I returned, I called Dr. Matthews and scheduled an appointment for January 10.

Steve was attentive, caring, and supportive when we were around other people that Christmas and, when we were alone, firm that he would not marry a multiple.

Nancy sulked through the holiday. When the Flock was around, she criticized our hair, clothes, and "Ph.D. attitude." When we left her to visit other family and friends, she complained that we were ignoring her. I couldn't help comparing this Christmas with the last, which I had spent secure in Lynn and Gordon's family.

Finally, in frustration, Joan Frances turned to her. "Mom, why do you hate me?" she yelled.

Nancy looked sincerely puzzled. "What do you mean?" she asked. "You know I love you. You know how proud I am of you and everything you do."

Joan Frances said no more. Her mother loved her. Of course her mother loved her. How could she have ever doubted that? She must be crazy.

34

I felt depressed and disoriented by the time I returned to Cambridge. I wanted to get away from Nancy, and from Steve, and nestle into my cozy little flat, where I'd feel more centered and in control.

Instead, the disorientation worsened upon my return. Suddenly I began losing large gaps of time. Like Jo, I was amnestic for several hours every day. I could no longer monitor what the various personalities were doing. I would find myself, four or five hours after my last awareness, surveying the work completed by some other personality.

I was relieved that someone was keeping up with the schoolwork, but concerned that I had no direct knowledge of how the time was spent. There were no internal tapes for me to play to catch the gist of what had gone on in my absence. When I called for Kendra, Missy, or any of the others who had talked with me internally in the past, I was greeted only with silence. If it weren't for the handiwork of my unseen companions, I would have sworn that, for the first time in memory, I was alone.

I wasn't alone, but I had lost touch with my Flock. And the pounding in my head and the marks on the walls indicated that Josie had been cycling out as well as the others.

I rejoiced that I had had the foresight before my trip to Virginia to make an appointment with Dr. Matthews. I hadn't envisaged that the Flock would be this bad, but I had certainly been right in my guess that we'd need some support. As my appointment neared, however, I began to worry. Despite the Flock's agreement in November that everybody would cooperate in seeing Dr. Matthews, the Flock seemed seriously disorganized to me. There were no intra-Flock conferences, although I awoke each morning hoping to find a transcript that would shed some light on the current problem.

Dr. Matthews had met Jo, Joan Frances, Missy, and Rusty during previous visits, but I had always stayed close enough to step out in a flash if someone began to panic. Now I no longer had that control.

I finally called Dr. Matthews an hour before my appointment. "I think I might have to cancel," I said. "I'm afraid of what is going to happen if I come to see you." I explained as best I could about the disorganization and amnesia, and Dr. Matthews said that he thought he should talk to Lynn before I came in. By late afternoon, he had not been able to reach her, and called me back.

"What are you afraid of?" the psychiatrist asked.

"I just don't have much control right now," I said. "I don't know what would happen if Josie came out and threw herself at a wall. I know that if I come I've got to figure out what's going on, and I'm afraid that my search might bring Josie to the surface."

Dr. Matthews listened quietly and then said, "I won't permit self-destructive behavior in my office."

"I can understand that," I replied. "I'm not into permitting it myself. But, unfortunately, I don't seem to have that kind of freedom of choice at the moment.

"No one in the Flock is purposely destructive of any person or property. Josie isn't even intentionally destructive of herself. Knocking herself out is the only way she knows how to cope, and actually she's rarely gotten that far. She feels the panic and hits the wall once, and then another personality comes out."

"I won't permit that," Dr. Matthews said again.

I decided that I'd better get down to specifics. "I need to know what you mean by that," I said. "What would you do if it happened?"

"I'd call Security," he said.

"No," I said. This wouldn't work. Security officers would restrain Josie. The physical restraint would send more panic through the system, and no other personality would be able to surface. The scene would end with the Flock strapped down and medicated. "I guess we better not come in," I said to Dr. Matthews. "I'll call you back when I'm in better control."

At first I didn't take Renee's complaints seriously about the lost time and lack of control. By then, with Unity coordinating intra-Flock conferences, I thought more in terms of the entity and "system control" than the fears of a single personality. So, even though Renee was worried, I chalked that up to one personality's overreaction and trusted the Flock as a whole.

Even Renee's description of what seemed to be occurring when Josie came out in the apartment offered evidence that the system was in control in some way. Any real damage by Josie had been avoided. The Flock continued to do what had to be done in terms of writing papers and grading students' exams, and they were making plans for the trip home. I saw my main task as trying to reassure Renee that Gordon and I would deal with all of this when she returned home. I was confident that whatever was surfacing was manageable.

When I got the call after Renee's fiasco with Dr. Matthews, I realized that her fears were extreme and that it was important for her to know that I heard this. I trusted that I could work out some kind of support plan with Dr. Matthews.

I think that Renee must have caught him off guard when she called him prior to her appointment, and he must have responded to what sounded like threats and manipulation. I even speculated briefly that forbidding Josie to come out might have the same effect that Dr. Tate's threats had had—it might keep them going until they got home. When Dr. Matthews finally reached me, I assured him that Renee was genuinely terrified and not being manipulative.

I told him that, once I had watched Gordon respond to Josie, I had relaxed enough to be able to keep Josie from doing any damage. "I don't know how big you are," I added, suddenly wondering whether this doctor was physically capable of controlling Josie, "but I found that I could handle it better when I stopped being afraid of her."

Later, in one of the brief lighter moments of this stressful period, Renee roared with laughter when she told me that Dr. Matthews was built like a football player. He himself had not responded to my implied question about his physical capacity, saying only that he thought he could manage on his own and that he would tell Renee to come in if she called again.

Unfortunately, Renee was by then too untrusting of both herself and the doctor to call.

For the next couple of days, I talked to Renee two or three times a day, something I had not found necessary in all the time she had been away at school. I began to wonder if I had been wrong in believing that we could preserve the Flock's functionality throughout the whole treatment process. I knew that many multiples, including Sybil, had become nonfunctional. I also knew that often a total loss of the ability to function had occurred as the multiple drew close to integration. More and more cooperation and total group decision-making had seemed to be occurring in the Flock. Was this the other side of the coin—the total entity giving in to panic?

.   .   .

Sunday night, only two days before I was to fly to Chicago for semester break, I found myself curled on the sofa, phone clutched in my hand. Lynn was on the other end of the line, talking in soothing tones. She had been talking to Jo. Loathing my amnesia and helplessness, I listened while she filled me in. Then I realized that I felt terrified, but could find no reason for my terror. Quivering, I tried to respond to Lynn's attempts to help me relax and lost time again.

Missy took over then, and Lynn finally found someone in the Flock who could explain the current problems. "It's because of the girl who wants her mommy to love her," Missy said. "She knows now that her mommy won't love her no matter what. She could be the best girl in the whole world and her mommy still won't love her. She says Mommy thinks she's crazy, so now she's just going to be crazy."

Joan Frances, the only personality who still denied the existence of the other personalities, was the cause of the Flock's disorganization. During the recent trip, she had finally given up on ever being able to please her mother. And, typically, Joan Frances had accepted the problem as her own. "It's me," she decided, "I'm all wrong. My mother has always loved and accepted me. I must be crazy." Rather than resorting to suicidal gestures, this time she chose insanity.

Insanity was worse than death, both for Joan Frances and for her mother. A daughter who was a suicide could be forgotten. A daughter who was insane could not be ignored.

Missy didn't have the vocabulary to describe Joan Frances's importance except by analogy. "That girl held Rusty and Renee and Jo and all the other girls in her hand like a puzzle, then she threw them all down. All the pieces fell in different places."

"But, Missy, where's Unity?" Lynn asked.

"Oh, that Unity girl is the glue," Missy said. "There's nothing to stick together now."

"No wonder you all are feeling scattered," Lynn said. "You go back inside now, and let me see if I can help Renee."

I listened while Lynn explained Missy's analogy. "We'll get the pieces back together when you are home," she promised.

Now I understood my feelings of being alone and had a reason for the unexplained terror. Joan Frances had become psychotic. She experienced terrifying hallucinations—blood dripped through cracks in the plaster walls; spiders crawled from people's mouths when they spoke. No other personality experienced her hallucinations directly, but her fear oozed throughout the system. The terror and confusion didn't stop, but I could make some sense of it. Now I could hold on.

The next morning, as I worked to finish grading my students' papers, I felt too shaky to concentrate. I finally set aside the grading to get a handle on the situation. I felt out of sync with reality. Some incipient mental flashing affected me like an internal strobe light. I felt a step ahead of my thoughts, a step behind the world outside my head. Very, very frightened, I called Lynn.

She was with a patient, but it made me feel a little better just to know that she would call back. While I waited, I made a list of what I *had* to do before leaving Harvard for the term. Time seemed to be running out. Functioning was becoming more difficult. I prioritized my tasks in case I couldn't make it through the last day and a half. First priority was to finish grading my students' work. If I missed my own exams, the Flock would suffer, and I was prepared for that. But my students wouldn't suffer because of the Flock's problems.

Lynn called back. I explained the new symptoms and asked her the question that had been forming since the night before. "Am I experiencing a psychotic break?" Lynn agreed that some of my experiences seemed psychotic, but my awareness that I was experiencing them didn't fit in with psychosis. I hung up, comforted by the irony that, since I was aware that my perceptions were crazy, I wasn't as crazy as I thought. I was determined to make it.

*

Lynn met me at the airport and drove me back to her house. I had done it—not only made it through the work for my students, but also finished my own exams. I was safe and felt less distracted by the Flock's disorganization. Rather than simply letting go, I struggled to get from Lynn the reassurance that I seemed to need every trip home. Yes, Lynn and Gordon were willing to see me through the crisis. Yes, they'd help me find a way to patch things up so that I could return to school.

That left only Steve to fret about. I had delayed telling him how bad things were with the Flock because the crazier we seemed, the less he'd want to marry me. Finally, the night before I flew home, I called Steve and told him about the disorganization. As afraid as I was of losing him, I wasn't in any shape to pretend to be what he wanted me to be. Steve offered support and understanding.

Nevertheless, after I had been at Lynn's for a couple of hours, Steve called. "I've been calling you at home all morning," he said, sounding a little wounded.

"Steve, I've been with Lynn since I got here. I told you that things are really bad right now."

"You mean you haven't been home yet?" he asked, the anger and hurt apparent in his voice. "I cleaned the house and even baked a pie. I thought you'd like to offer Lynn something to eat when she brought you home from the airport."

I hung up the phone, feeling depressed and misunderstood. "I'm going through hell," I cried, "and Steve wants me to be thankful that he baked a pie."

Lynn tried to explain that denial had always been Steve's defense, and I got more frustrated. Why didn't anyone hear me? Steve didn't hear me when I told him how bad things were. Lynn didn't hear me when I told her that I wanted support for me, not excuses for him.

I knew I was being irrational, but couldn't contain my frustration. Nobody understood. I had to get out of there.

Lynn was talking on the phone with Steve as I picked up my suitcase and headed for the door. "I'm not going after her," she said.

35

After Missy told me what was happening with the Flock during that late-night call from Cambridge, I knew I had to talk with Joan Frances. If she had truly given up on her pathological notion of what it would mean to be acceptable to her mother, she might finally be able and willing to listen to me. I knew, even if the Flock didn't, that the unresolved guilt produced through incest precluded any real relationship with Nancy. The entity had to accept herself as a survivor of her father's abuse before she could deal with her mother in a nonconflicted way.

I wasn't too worried about the symptoms Renee described. I knew her well enough to know that she would worry about loss of control even if someone else in the Flock was clearly taking care of things. I also knew that, though disorganized, the Flock was not dysfunctional. The student papers did get graded; the Flock's exams were written.

I thought that Renee agreed with me about what needed to be done, and I took the day off from work to meet them at the airport. I was eager for this opportunity to do some intensive work with Joan Frances.

But Renee was terrified. She didn't show that terror openly, but reacted to her fears by complaining about Steve's lack of understanding and a lack of support from me. After a few hours of being what I thought was very supportive, I lost patience and didn't try to stop her when she walked out the door.

Renee had been promised priority for the two weeks she was home. All of the Flock were welcome at my house at any time, and I felt I had amply demonstrated my caring over almost four years of treatment. It was up to them. I treated Renee like the reasonable being she usually was. Steve also had a hard time dealing with Renee's regressed behavior and was as baffled as I was about what she wanted. Predictably, Steve blamed me for not taking over.

. . .

I stood for a minute in front of Lynn's house, trying to decide what to do, where to go. I couldn't face Lynn, couldn't face Steve. I just wanted to get away from everything—from them and from the Flock. I started down the street.

Gordon stopped his car next to me. He was pulling in the driveway when he saw me walking. Rather than go into the house for an update on the Flock's latest crisis, he responded to what he saw. "Come on in the car," Gordon said. "I'll drive you wherever you're heading."

"I don't know where to go," I said, and got into the car. I cried with frustration and confusion. "No one is listening to me, and everything is so crazy inside. I don't know what to do."

"Come on back to the house," Gordon suggested. "Lynn and I have a meeting to go to, so you'll have the place to yourself for a couple of hours. You'll have some time to think, sleep, or do whatever you need to do."

Gordon pulled into the driveway and I blissfully lost time. I didn't want to face Lynn and my humiliation at walking out on her. I didn't want to handle anything. Thank God I could lose time.

Jo found herself sitting in Gordon's car and smiled uncertainly. The quick change from Cambridge to Chicago caught her off guard, but she was glad to be home.

"You just got into town today," Gordon said, carrying her suitcase back to the house. Lynn explained that they were off to a meeting, but that Steve might be calling soon.

A few minutes later, Steve did call. "Hi, Jo," he said. "I'll come up and get you now, OK?"

Jo wasn't sure how to respond. She rarely knew what was supposed to happen. When no other personality shoved her aside to confirm or deny Steve's plan, she said, "I guess so."

Back at Steve's house, Jo and Steve sipped wine in the sunroom. Jo loved this house with its warm wood trim and big windows. She was sad that sometime soon she would have to leave. It had become a safe nest.

Steve gazed past Jo to the small forest of plants that dominated the room's southern exposure. "I'm seeing a psychiatrist now," he said. "I'm trying to learn how to live with a multiple."

Jo was puzzled. She was glad that Steve was in treatment if it was something he was doing for himself, but she didn't understand how she could be the reason Steve was seeing a psychiatrist. "You make it sound as though living with a multiple is like owning an exotic plant," Jo said bitterly. "It sounds as though you wish you could find a *How to Live with a Multiple* book at the local bookstore."

Steve failed to hear the anger in Jo's voice. "That's exactly right," he said. "Since there's no how-to book, I have to see this psychiatrist to learn how to deal with you."

"I am not a plant," Jo said in a controlled voice. "I'm a person. I want you to treat me as a person. I want you to treat me with dignity and respect." With that, she stormed inside herself.

Kendra smiled at Steve impishly. "Well," she said, "you've now struck out with two of them. You blew it with Renee by denying the seriousness of the Flock's current problems. And you blew it with Jo by making her feel that you think she's more bizarre than she thinks she is. That's going some! But don't worry, you won't blow it with me. I'm just going to try to keep things moving along until Lynn is ready to help us put this mess back together."

Kendra smiled reassuringly at Steve to let him know that things really were going to work out. "How about taking me out to dinner?" Kendra asked. "This body hasn't had a decent meal in weeks."

Steve enjoyed being with Kendra, who seemed currently content with herself and with him. They went to dinner and returned home late. Lynn didn't call.

The next day, Kendra, Karen, and some of the others cycled out for brief periods of time. I was too trapped by my anger and hurt to resurface, and no personality had the strength to remain in control for very long. In the past, the Flock had presented a fairly consistent picture to the outside world. Now the personality-switching was like lights flashing on a Christmas tree.

Even Steve couldn't deny the disorganization. Renee and Jo, the two personalities he liked best, weren't around at all. It seemed that he couldn't hold a conversation with anyone in the Flock without having two or three personalities burst in on the talk and then leave as abruptly as they had arrived.

"Kendra," Steve said that evening, "tell me what's going on with the Flock."

"Sorry," Kendra answered politely. "I just don't know what to say about that."

Kendra wanted to do what she thought was best for the Flock, but the other personalities were too scattered for her to get a sense of what any of them might want. The Renee/Isis/Kendra Alliance had dissolved, like everything else, in early January. She thought it was better to say nothing.

Missy pushed Kendra aside. She was happy to share information about the disorganization with Steve. Missy had learned to be an especially good girl around Steve, so that he would love everyone in the Flock. If she helped Steve, she was sure that he'd love her too.

Missy explained her puzzle analogy to Steve and told him that the real problem was "that Joan Frances." She answered all of the questions Steve asked. Then she showed him that she could write identically with both hands, and she drew him a picture.

Steve responded to Missy, chuckled at her jokes, but seemed uneasy. "I wondered what happened to Lynn," he said. "Do you want to talk to your friend Lynn?" "Oh, yes, please," Missy said happily.

But Gordon and Lynn weren't home when Steve called. Steve left a message on their answering machine, and then it was time for bed. They lay side by side in the queen-sized bed, Steve flipping through a newspaper and Missy cuddling her stuffed bear. Missy held on to the consciousness as long as she could, waiting. But by the time Lynn called, hours later, Steve was too sound asleep to hear the phone, and the Flock was too frozen by disorganization to reach for it.

The next morning, Kendra complained to Steve that this was a hell of a time for Lynn to take her "If the Flock wants me badly enough, they can find me" stand. "Jo, Renee, and Joan Frances are all out of commission," Kendra said. "No one else in the Flock is strong enough to keep functioning for long. Why doesn't Lynn realize how bad things are?"

When Steve called Lynn, Kendra refused to speak to her, but Missy wanted to talk to her friend. During the hard last couple of days back in Cambridge, Lynn had reassured Missy that, once the Flock got home, she would make things better. Two days had already gone by and, as far as Missy could tell, Lynn wasn't doing anything at all.

"You're not fixing it!" Missy accused Lynn tearfully. Lynn was calm and distant. "I'm getting ready for work now," she said, "and I don't have time to talk." Kendra took over. "You know where to find me," Lynn said again. "The Flock is welcome at my house at any time, and you know that. I'm going to work now, but I will be home this evening if you want to see me."

That evening, Kendra asked Steve to drive her to Lynn's. "I don't want a car to be there for us," she said. "I don't want it to be easy for anyone to run away."

"I'm not going to apologize for not reaching out to the Flock," Lynn said firmly to Kendra once they were settled. The time was long past, Lynn said, for that to be necessary. "After almost four years," she said, "the Flock should know that I'm here and willing to help."

"If we were capable of really understanding that," Kendra countered, "we probably wouldn't be in the shape that we're in."

Lynn paused, and Kendra said, "Do you know what we're hearing from Steve? He says that you've lost your professional judgment, that you're too caught up in the emotion of all of this to be of help to the Flock."

"And that man Steve said maybe you were mad because you aren't getting any money," Missy chimed in, and smiled, knowing she had the solution, "but I can fix that. Do you want this money?" Missy pulled a twenty-dollar bill from her jeans pocket. Steve had told her to put it there in case someone in the Flock ran away. He wanted Missy to have money to get back home. "You can have this money," she said to Lynn, "and then you can make things better."

"No, Missy, I don't want the money." Lynn sighed and opened her arms. "Come on over here." Missy scrambled to cuddle with her friend.

After a few minutes, Kendra pulled away from Lynn, who, deep in thought, had been patting Missy's arm. Lynn smiled at Kendra. "Part of the problem," Lynn said, "is that you all are hiding what's going on. I hear about Joan Frances's hallucinations, I hear about how disorganized the Flock is, but no one is letting me near enough to deal with the problem. When the Flock got home, Renee spent the whole afternoon both crying 'Help me' and resisting my efforts to do just that."

"Yeah, things are really a mess, aren't they?" Kendra said, and smiled with relief. Now that Lynn understood, Kendra didn't have to worry.

The next day, Lynn called the Flock at Steve's house at midday, just to see how things were going. That evening, the Flock returned to Lynn's. After a few minutes with Kendra and Missy, Lynn found herself face to face with Joan Frances.

For a moment, Joan Frances sat silently, entranced by her hallucinations. The light bulbs in Lynn's lamps glowed like miniature suns; the colors on the walls and curtains dripped as in a Dalí painting. She watched it all with vague interest, not caring to consider what any of it meant.

Then Joan Frances felt a pull, a desperate yearning to pull herself back into reality. She sat up and looked clearly at Lynn. Joan Frances needed, she needed . . . something, and then it would be all right.

"I have to leave now," Joan Frances said.

"No," Lynn answered. "I can't let you go like this."

"I have to leave now," Joan Frances said again. "I have to go to the store."

Lynn was puzzled. "What do you need from the store?"

Joan Frances wrinkled her brow, searching for the answer that was there but still eluded her. "I don't know," she said, "but I'll know it when I see it."

Lynn shook her head. "No, Joan Frances," she said again, "I don't want you to go. I don't want you out alone."

Joan Frances, the personality who had always refused anything Lynn offered, made her first request. "Take me."

Lynn was still uncertain. "What if the hallucinations start when we're in the car?" she asked. "I can't run the risk of Josie's coming out when I'm driving."

"Take her," Missy and Kendra urged. "We'll help."

Lynn acquiesced and drove the Flock to a local shopping mall. Once inside, Joan Frances held back in fear. The bright lights, the sharp sounds, all of the people milling around melted into surrealistic hallucinations. She felt overwhelmed.

Lynn looped her arm through Joan Frances's and the personality who had never before let Lynn touch her now leaned in to her for support. Joan Frances silently led Lynn from store to store, searching toy departments and stationery shops. Suddenly Lynn caught on. Joan Frances was looking for a puzzle.

Together they found it. An egg, a translucent plastic egg, constructed of many intricate pieces, all fitting snugly together.

As they left the store, Missy popped out to say, "That girl needs something else." Joan Frances needed glue, which they found in an office-supply shop. Purchases in hand, Joan Frances relaxed her grip on Lynn's arm and looked around the mall. It was all reality now. No hallucinations. She felt calm and satisfied. Joan Frances had done what she needed to do, and that personality ebbed inside.

I came out for the first time since I had left Lynn's house in fear and anger earlier in the week. "I feel as though I'm waking from a dream," I said and, in saying so, wondered just who *I* was.

"Renee?" Lynn asked.

"Yes," I said, "but there's more." This was a group answer. I was speaking for Renee, but for everyone else too. I felt the entity stir within me.

"I'm not ready to leave yet," I said to Lynn. "Can we just go someplace for a while so that I have a chance to sort this out?"

"Sure," Lynn said. She led me to a restaurant, ordered coffee for both of us, and waited. Lynn looked at me closely. "It is Renee, isn't it?"

"Yes," I said, "it's me." Then, frowning at my inability to explain the inner surges I felt, I said again, "It's me, but somehow it's more."

I cast a curious glance at the packages I was clutching. I had no memory of them, but I felt very possessive. "They're mine, aren't they?" Lynn nodded, and I opened one of the bags to find my egg. I knew it immediately, understood its significance. This was my center, my whole being coming together in a new, coherent way. The Flock still had its separate parts, but those parts were—and this was most important—all parts of a single cohesive being.

I cupped the egg tightly for a moment and then noticed the small tube of glue. The glue was to ensure that we'd never scatter again. We were all parts of a single entity—this time for good.

I ran glue through the cracks of the puzzle egg, sealing it. "Joan Frances had to find the egg," I mused aloud, "and now I have to apply the glue."

36

At last I understood. Renee was right when she first came home, insisting that the issue was reassurances of my love. Poised between truly giving up on her impossible desire to be the daughter who had not betrayed her mother, and fully accepting me, who knew her and loved her with her past acknowledged, the Flock was in limbo, with nothing secure to hold on to. Joan Frances, filled with a burning anger toward Nancy that had, until now, been inwardly directed, was providing the ultimate insult and disappointment to Mother by becoming psychotic. Nancy, of course, had no idea of what was going on, but Joan Frances succeeded in terrifying Renee.

Renee was so afraid that I'd react as Nancy had when Joan Frances had appealed to her for support that she pushed in every way possible to make me reject her. This was the final test of trust.

"Will you love me if I'm helpless, as my mother couldn't?" This was something that had to be asked by Joan Frances, who had nothing to lose and everything to gain. Tonight, no personality would pretend functionality to hide Joan Frances's need. Even Unity had to let go to allow a greater unity to form.

. . .

After Joan Frances's shopping trip with Lynn, I felt strength and inner support that were brand-new and heady. I was Renee, my separate self. A quick roll call affirmed that the others were their own selves as well. But they seemed closer, more responsive. I felt everyone's energy. Somehow, I had tapped into our single power source. I could do anything. Now I was determined to apply my new strength in trying to resolve my relationship with Steve.

Once I returned home, Steve informed me that he didn't want Missy around anymore. He couldn't cope with a five-year-old girl's being in the body of the woman he loved. He had similar complaints about the personalities who had kept things going when I was too confused to manage at all.

I told him I didn't think he'd ever see them again. I felt that our days of uncontrolled switching were over. And the entire Flock had a new feeling of self-protection. We'd never let Steve see anything that would allow him to say such hurtful things.

As I distanced myself from Steve, I sensed his confusion about his own needs and desires. I began to suspect that the fundamental problem in our relationship was something other than the Flock.

Our discussions about our relationship turned into an endless loop. He didn't want to marry me because I was multiple, he said. My being a multiple was less of a problem than he thought, I said, and he wasn't being honest with either of us.

We both knew we needed to talk about this in a new way, and I insisted it had to be done before I went back to school. On the eve of my return to Harvard, Steve and I went to Lynn's house. She had agreed to help with the discussion.

"Steve's not willing to marry me because I am a multiple," I said. "He says that he's not sure what I'm going to be like in a year or in five years. I think that's crap. I keep growing and changing through treatment and through other experiences, but I'm essentially the same person he met and fell in love with years ago."

"It's not the same," Steve said. "Now you've finally convinced me that you are really a lot of separate people."

"But even that's changing," I said.

He agreed that my perception of the various personalities had recently changed, but that was part of the problem. "Just when I learn to accept one thing about the disorder," Steve complained, "it all changes, and I don't know what to think."

"Steve, we all change," said Lynn. "It's true that Renee can't tell you now what the Flock will be like in five years, but she doesn't know what you're going to be like in five years either."

"Look," Steve said to me, "the night of the egg, you were able to say that you, the whole you, were 'in part Missy and in part Rusty' and so on. That's not finished.

"If you could say, 'I am Josie, hitting my head on the wall,' and then stop that behavior because that's not how Renee wants to act, that would be indicative of a new, even more radical integration."

I weighed carefully what Steve was saying. I took a deep breath, not knowing how I would respond. If I met Steve's challenge, then whatever I said would admit even greater change for the Flock than I had already perceived. If I backed away from his challenge, I would deny the unity I felt growing inside me. I knew my Flock as I never had. I trusted them, I trusted me. I knew that my internal others would let me speak only the truth.

Lynn watched me thoughtfully.

As I opened my mouth to speak, "I" stepped out of the Renee personality, turned, and gathered them all protectively in my arms. I then spoke in a single voice that echoed every one.

"I am Josie," I said, "banging my head against the wall. It is an expression of *my* fear, *my* frustration, *my* anger. Up until now, that was the only way those feelings could be expressed."

"You need to experiment with different ways of expressing anger," Steve said.

"I am Kendra, able to stand up for myself. Those freedoms used to be expressed through a separate personality because I was too confused by what other people wanted to have the energy to figure out what I might want. I didn't realize that my needs were important.

"I am Rusty, sailing the boat. It is an enjoyment, a feeling of accomplishment, that I, as an entity, enjoy. That part of me has been male because sometimes it wasn't safe to be a girl. A great deal of strength and confidence grew and stayed safe within the Rusty personality.

"I've spent a great deal of my life keeping my strengths separate because the Flock had been so hurt." I paused. That wasn't quite right. It wasn't them; it was me. "The strengths were held separately," I said, "because I was hurt. I was abused when I was a child."

"That's right, that's right!" Steve said excitedly. "You, *you*, were abused, and you are finally able to acknowledge that!"

Lynn cautioned, "Just listen. There's more she wants to say."

"I am Missy too," I continued. "It took a while for the Missy part of me to work through all her hurt and feel safe. But now, finally, that's a fulfilled, though vulnerable, part of me. I've held a lot of artistic ability there, a lot of fragile creativity. I guess that doesn't have to be shielded any longer.

"And I'm Jo as well, finding joy in my analytic abilities and scholarly work. And I'm Joan Frances, still learning how to deal with Mother." Suddenly I felt too exhausted to keep speaking. There was too much happening inside. They touched and turned and acknowledged until the gestures of support gathered into a single solid hug.

They were me. All of the personalities of the past were now the many aspects of a brand-new me.

I turned back to Steve wearily, but with a faint cockiness. "Are all of your problems solved now?" I knew that *he* needed to hear his response.

"They have been greatly alleviated," Steve answered cautiously.

"So," I asked, "where does that put us in terms of marriage?"

"I think it needs time," Steve said. "Take it easy. Let's see where you go from here."

"How do you feel now?" Lynn asked.

"About that?" I asked, gesturing toward Steve. I just shook my head. I had nothing to say.

Lynn turned to Steve. "What do you think about your response?"

"What I just said makes it look as though there is still one more hurdle to jump. That's not what I'm implying."

I stood up and walked from the room. I needed to be alone for a while, away from Steve, who had prodded me into that final step. I even needed to be away from Lynn, who had lovingly nurtured all of the parts of the Flock so that I'd have the strength to become one. I needed to be alone with me, the single, whole me that existed for the first time since infancy.

Who was I now? I was still aware of internal separations, but the external voice, expression, decision, action, was single, reflective of all of me.

I was the Flock, with all of the personalities, flying in formation in some tightly woven instinct to be one. A group mind with a single thought, moving toward a shared destiny.

I was the thought, the voice of all who were, of all that I could be. Evolving, growing. A person.

I returned to Lynn, my eyes filled with tears, no words sufficient to express my love for her or my love for me. "Hello, Whole Self," Lynn said. "Welcome."

With the same wonderful sense of understatement that Lynn used as she allowed me to be an emotional infant, as she mothered me through my stormy, long-overdue adolescence, and that had allowed all of the different parts of me the expression needed to heal, Lynn added, "What you have done, what you have been through, is all worth it, sweetie. Don't ever think otherwise."

37

Six months have passed since the Flock began to integrate. I'm still getting used to calling her Joan. Although many of the personalities had names that were close—Jo, Josie, Joan Frances—"Joan" is the name that she says she likes the best. The integration is unfolding like a flower. Joan calls what happened those January evenings the start of her "synthesis" and says that she's "not-still-multiple/not-yet-single." She is doing this in her own way. She wrote to me about the experience.

I can't pretend that I suddenly "became one" on January 23. I couldn't deny the separate parts of me. But for the first time I couldn't deny the unity. "I" am all of them and more. That night, for the first time, I spoke for everyone. I was the external voice for the internal multitude. From that moment on, all of the personalities had all of the time, all of the time.

I felt internal nudges who would warn or urge. I'd hear, "Don't get in over your head," as I'd begin to agree to take on another project. Or when I began to feel overwhelmed by work, I'd hear, "Time to get out of here and go for a walk." All of the personalities offered suggestions, made demands, and I felt only a need to accommodate. I felt "well rounded" but not integrated. After a month or so, I decided not to worry about what to call my present existence. Is this integration? I still wasn't sure. What was going on felt good, but I was still afraid that, if I called myself integrated, parts of me would die.

I got busy with school, and then I realized that I heard my internal voices less and less. Living days, weeks, and months in my

*synthesized state wore down the distinctions between the parts. All
of the interests, skills, and resources had been preserved. I certainly
feel the unique traits of each personality, but amplified and polished
by the resources of every other one.*

*Now I guess I'm close to being fully integrated, but I can't say
that without hesitation. I feel as though I can only hold it together
if I don't worry too much about its falling apart.*

I talked with Joan often on the phone during her first "integrated"
semester at Harvard. I noticed during that time that her voice became richer
and truly lovely, reflecting the range of timbre and tone of the separate
personalities. But even with that, I have to admit I was startled by how she
looked after that six-month absence.

When I look at the new postsynthesis Joan, I feel some of the marvel
I felt in seeing my first grandchild, Hilary, as a newborn. I was spellbound
by the many people I saw reflected in Hilary's being. I saw her parents, Neal
and Marianne, but I saw aunts and uncles and great-grandparents as well.
Not knowing Hilary as her own person, I loved her first because of all of
those I saw in her.

I feel as though I hardly know Joan, as her own integrated being, but
I see the Flock in her. I see Rusty's shrug of shoulders, Missy's grin. I watch
Jo's forehead wrinkle in concentration and watch Renee's eyes sparkle as
Joan reaches some conclusion or prepares to tease.

I respect Joan's need to hedge a bit about her state, but I guess I'd be
surprised to see her separate out again. I'm also surprised at how comfortable I am with seeing "only" Joan. I don't miss the separate personalities.
Joan's right. In some miraculous way, they are all there.

January 1986

A year later, Joan finally calls herself integrated. She's solid and whole,
and no less productive. She seems to like my teasing her about her fears
of what she'd lose through integration, and I know she takes pride in her
accomplishments. She's finishing her dissertation, and is quite a sailor.

I like seeing the change in her. She's working as hard as she ever did,
but seems less compulsive. I brought this up last week, during a walk, and
she reflected for a moment on my observation. She told me that she worked

now from a basis of joy rather than fear. Fear, Joan said, is the only thing she has lost through integration.

"I was always afraid before," she said. "I was afraid of not being able to hide the disorder, afraid of something triggering inappropriate behavior. I was afraid that I couldn't control the personalities, but even more afraid that I couldn't handle my own feelings. My life was ruled by the fear that someday I'd get so depressed or so dysfunctional that I wouldn't be able to find my way back. Now I'm not scared. I get sad, depressed, but even in my worst moments I trust that life will get better. I trust myself."

Not much has changed between Joan and Steve. She shares his house, but it seems to me that they are beginning to separate. They continue to be a couple socially, but seem less dependent on each other. Joan is building strength as an individual, and Steve seems willing to let her go.

July 1986

Joan has graduated from Harvard and is teaching and consulting part-time here in Chicago. She gets consistently excellent feedback, but I can tell that she's restless. She wants a full-time, tenure-track position as an assistant professor, and she's told me that she's purposefully looking for a job outside Illinois. Joan has a three-month consulting job lined up in D.C. beginning in January, and she says that she expects to leave Chicago permanently for the start of the 1987–88 school year.

Joan says that she's not willing to stay with Steve unless he'll marry her, and he won't. I think that they both have made the right decision. Joan needs to get away and be her independent whole self for the first time in her life. Marrying Steve would just be a way of putting off her need to leave until she felt stronger. I'm sure that there is no future for a marriage between the two of them.

January 1987

Joan is now in Washington. I can tell from her letters and phone calls that she feels good about her work and integration. She's negotiating for a professorship at a college in the Southwest that will begin in the fall.

I am moving in new directions as well. When I started treating Joan,

I was alone. Now I'm part of a national network of clinicians called the International Society for the Study of Multiple Personality Disorder. The group does far more than "study" MPD, as I discovered when I attended the professional conference last fall. We share ideas for treatment with one another, and that's certainly good for my patients. I've got three multiples on my caseload now, and one more that I suspect is multiple. I take one of them home occasionally, but everyone else is being treated in the office. Gordon continues to work with me as cotherapist. Reparenting is a treatment style that can happen successfully in the office as well as out. The essential factor is that Gordon and I use our relationships with the multiples as models for how the personalities ought to parent and love one another. I will never regret "adopting" Joan as my sixth child, but I am pleased to find that I can give multiples what they need without leaving the office.

. . .

38

No real life has a happily-ever-after. I was integrated, but far from "healthy." Leaving Steve because the relationship had no future was the last good decision I made about partnerships for years.

I left the safety of Steve and found that I was vulnerable to men who were seeking a victim. First Gary, then Sam, then Adam, each more dangerous than the last, sensed the abused child waiting to be hurt again.

Gary was a drug addict—recovered, he claimed. It took me almost a year to realize that he was still using drugs and using my money to support his habit and his mistress.

"A con man," I thought. "Anyone could have been taken in."

But then there was Sam. I let Sam move into my house, and he violated my soul. Nothing was safe from his prying hands and accusations. Once, while I was away on a business trip, he discovered and read the Flock journals and correspondence that I had hidden away in a back closet. He questioned colleagues about my sexual history and recent involvements. He revealed to some of my students that I had been a multiple.

I couldn't tell him to leave. Instead, I became obsessed with convincing him that I wasn't the bitch, the whore, that he claimed me to be.

I was determined to be sexually normal, never wondering if his demands that I feed his sadistic fantasies constituted normality. He told me that I was lucky to have him, and I believed him. He told me that he would destroy every personal and professional relationship of mine if I dared to extricate myself from the relationship. He made good on his threat.

I whirled out of Sam's mayhem into Adam's arms. Adam beat me. A victim of childhood abuse and a survivor of a bad marriage, he said that I was his only hope. We maintained separate homes, but we often had dinner and spent the evening together at his apartment. About once a week, those evenings became nightmares.

Adam liked that I came to his house, made him dinner, and listened to his stories of the day. He praised my deep compassion, my sensitivity to the pain of his past.

Adam didn't like that I left to return to my own house at night. As the time came closer for me to leave, sometimes he'd drink, call me by his ex-wife's name, and taunt me.

"You think you're so smart, don't you?" he'd ask. "I'll slap that Harvard smugness off your face."

My protests that he was smart, that being a stockbroker required a kind of intelligence that I certainly didn't have, failed to calm him. I told him that my going to Harvard was a matter of luck, not brains, and he became infuriated with what he called my false humility.

Again and again, I saw the scene develop but could find no way to escape. No matter what I said, no matter how I tried to withdraw, Adam would grow more angry. "You think you're so clever," he'd say, "you think you're so sly." I silently countered that if that were true I would have found a way to leave before this began.

When I made my first move toward the door, he'd attack. Sometimes a slap, other times a push, or he'd hold me and laugh as I struggled to get away. Finally, defeated, as I huddled hurt and crying, Adam would apologize, begging me to give him another chance: he had interpreted my departure as rejection, but he was getting over it. I felt a certain obligation to tolerate his transference. I was sure that he'd get better. After all, I had.

Then, one night, I returned home after midnight and stared in the mirror at my black eye and bruised cheek, too weary to think of how I would explain it to my students and colleagues. "This is supposed to be better than being a multiple?" I wondered in fury. I called Lynn.

I winced as the phone brushed my cheek and demanded to know why she had taken my defense away from me. "Why did I survive all of that for this?" I asked. I finally told her the details of my tumultuous love affairs. I had hidden much of it from her for the year and a half I had lived away from Chicago, not wanting her disapproval to compound my guilt.

Lynn listened sympathetically. "Oh, sweetie, I wish I had known. I was being so careful not to ask, wanting you to feel that you had a right to an adult life. I was so careful not to invade your privacy."

Anger spent, I felt safe. Lynn would help me figure it out.

"Do you want the silver lining?" Lynn asked tentatively.

My anxiety exploded into laughter. Lynn would point out the "silver lining" in a nuclear explosion. "What?" I asked.

"You're still in one piece."

"That's certainly true," I said. "There were times when Adam was beating me that I wished I could lose time, but I didn't.

"I'm going to work this through," I added, "but I need help."

"Yes, my dear," Lynn replied, "you have my permission to do therapy without me, if that's what you're wondering."

A year more of psychotherapy—traditional treatment this time—and I found security in my sense of self. The doctor helped me see my part in these disastrous relationships. I found abusers and provoked them, baiting them with sarcasm, intuitively finding their weak spots, making myself a deserving victim.

Now I didn't need to provoke abuse, nor did I need to abuse in return. I allowed myself to let go of the past and for a time concentrated on making friends rather than latching on to lovers. This psychiatrist hadn't had much experience with multiples, but he was intrigued with what I had worked through.

He shook his head in amazement as he read old journal entries that I shared with him, and had long telephone conversations with Lynn. "More people should know your story," he said to us both, "and if you write it out, Joan, you might have a better sense of where you are now.

"And give yourself some time, Joan," he counseled. "You have the social guile of a little girl—and a little girl who's had a rough time, at that. You don't need to rush into a relationship. You'll build your own nest once you've had a chance to grow up yourself. You're just beginning to stretch your wings."

Then, in finding myself, I found the strength to face my mother. I had rehearsed my speech to her for months, but had trouble saying the words as we sat together late one night at her dining-room table. "He raped me, Mom," I said. "For years he molested me, and then he raped me."

I held back my tears, steeling myself for her angry denial. And I watched in wonder as a woman accepted a truth that she had carried unseen for years.

"It makes sense," she finally said, and then pulled out of her own flood of memories to offer me the comfort I so desperately sought.

"You have to understand that I didn't know," she said. "I knew that your father had sexual problems, but I never suspected that he hurt you."

No more about my father's incest was ever discussed between the two of us. No more needed to be. My mother put my need for affirmation ahead of the comfort she could have found through denial. I watched the struggle in her face that concluded in her expression of love and acceptance of me. For the first time, she knew me. For the first time, I could see her clearly, without the fog of anger and guilt. Our mutual honesty formed the basis for a relationship.

Lynn read narratives I wrote about my past and about my time in therapy with her and with Gordon. During my frequent trips home, she and I walked the lakeshore and she told me what her experience of our therapeutic relationship had been. I marveled at our special love story; she marveled at how reading the narrative and remembering her own experiences gave her insights into herself and her current work.

"It's not done yet," I said. "I want us to tell our story."

Lynn demurred. "I'm a clinician, not a writer. I can't even find the time to produce a professional paper to express some of what I've learned."

"If you help me tell the story, I'll do the writing."

Lynn agreed and Gordon joined in. We read journal entries, Lynn's clinical notes made on napkins, Gordon's insights recorded on navigational charts. We listened to tapes of the Flock in treatment, to tapes of Gordon and Lynn brainstorming what to do next. And as with the folktales that knit any family together, Gordon, Lynn, and I told one another the stories of my birth and growth.

39

December 3, 1988, a blinking light on the hotel-room phone in Charlottesville, Virginia, led to a message to call Lynn. I was attending a seminar in public policy. Lynn and Gordon, I knew, were visiting a therapist friend in southern California who also treated multiples.

My heart pounded as I dialed the phone. Why had Lynn called? It had been years since she had called me when she and Gordon were out of town. I was no longer in treatment and needing the reassurance that she would be coming home to me, her emotional infant.

I hadn't told her my itinerary. How had she found me in this Charlottesville hotel? What would be so important that she would track me down? And what stroke of luck had made her able to get a message to me an hour before I had planned to check out?

Lynn had found me by calling my sister. Carol and I had finally become friends in the past few years. My sister now knew about my past, and she was the one person I kept informed about my present as well. She always knew where to find me.

My fear dissolved once I reached Gordon and Lynn. They had no special reason for their call. Oh, rehashing the struggles of treating their first multiple as they talked with their friend had made them a little nostalgic, but they really just called to tell me that they loved me. They wanted to say that, though they wouldn't have done anything differently in healing the Flock, they were sure glad I was all grown up now.

We discussed plans for our upcoming visit. A week hence, they would fly from California to visit me in New Mexico. This would be their first trip to the isolated college town I now called home. They looked forward to meeting my colleagues, and the three of us looked forward to a week of relaxed closeness. I envisaged walking miles of mountain trails. Lynn, Gordon, and I would talk about their multiples and treatment techniques, about my research and students, about sailing, about the magic of our family. And we all looked forward to celebrating the book contract we had gotten on *The Flock*.

They called to say they were proud of me, now solidly integrated. They were proud of the Joan Casey the three of us had created together.

As Gordon and Lynn passed the phone between them, we talked for an hour, reaffirming the wonder of our relationship, which had started in such pain and sickness and continued in such joy and health. The three of us had long ago decided that, in some way we didn't understand, the bonds we shared transcended the seven years we had spent together. We renewed our cosmic promise to share our next life as well. (Lynn was adamant that next time around I get to be the mother!)

Two days later Lynn and Gordon died. They had taken their friend's sailboat out and gotten caught in a sudden violent storm. The boat was found pounding itself against a rock outcropping. Their bodies washed ashore two miles apart.

I had made a stop in Richmond to visit my mother and sister before returning west. My sister and I were shopping when Lynn and Gordon died. Even now I think I should have felt something. Even now I think that, if I had been more alert, I would have felt the world tilt slightly at their passing.

Later that night, at my sister's house, I received a message to return an urgent call from Lynn's daughter Marianne. I didn't need to dial the phone to guess that Lynn and Gordon were dead.

I listened calmly as Marianne told me what the Coast Guard reported, and I talked with her about the people I should call. I made as many of those calls as I could handle, and then sat on the porch with Carol.

We talked, drank wine, and were silent. Carol knew what Lynn and Gordon meant to me.

She cried my tears that night. My grief was too deep for tears, my need for understanding too strong to absorb the emotional impact. Steve had wept when I called him. Dr. Caul, a psychiatrist friend of Gordon's and Lynn's and mine, had taken some time to absorb what I said and then called back to offer what comfort he could.

I held Carol that night while she cried for my lost parents. I celebrated then the biological start I had that had led me to Lynn and Gordon. I celebrated the bonds and the cosmic wisdom that had deposited me with my sister at the time of my surrogate parents' death.

Back home in New Mexico, I received a postcard that Lynn and Gordon had mailed to me the morning of their final sail. "We'll see you soon," the postcard read.

Life without Gordon and Lynn has often been hard, and sometimes close to unbearable. I lost the therapists who had given me health, and the parents who had, through their years of reparenting, given me life.

So many times I want to call them, telling them of a new victory; so often I want their soothing voices to help me through some crisis. Recently I realized how frequently I say with regret, "They would have loved this!" and I suddenly thought that it might be no accident that Gordon and Lynn would enjoy so much of my world. I like to think that they have a cosmic hand in my life, leading me toward things and people good and nurturing.

Life has led me to become the parent of a little boy who was himself abused. I have my own family now, complete with a husband as strong and gentle and wise as Gordon. How proud they would be.

My son recently asked me how I had learned to be such a good mom. He reminds me from time to time that I'm newer at being a mother than he is at being a child.

I told him that he and I are alike in that we both took a little more time than most people to find our real families. My true family had taught me how to love and nurture. Because of that, I can love and nurture him.

My life is a testimony to Lynn's and Gordon's love.

Afterword

The story of Joan Frances Casey is remarkable—and not unique. By some estimates, one percent of the population suffers from Multiple Personality Disorder. Although Freud recognized and described this disorder, the American Psychiatric Association only recently—in 1980—included Multiple Personality Disorder in its official diagnostic manual, and the psychiatric community as a whole still does not fully accept it. Indeed, because the disorder is so frequently misidentified, an average of six years may elapse before a multiple receives the correct diagnosis. Clinicians may not know that hearing voices inside the head does not always signify a psychotic process, but rather, as in the case of multiple personality, represents non–thought disordered dialogues among the various alternate personalities. Assessment is often biased in the direction of schizophrenia, depression, borderline disorders, or mania—entities that clinicians have been familiarized with in their training programs. Both psychodynamic and biologically oriented training programs may inadvertently add to this tendency to misdiagnose multiples in the following ways.

Many psychodynamic training programs teach a system of diagnosis and treatment consistent with traditional Freudian beliefs that exclude real trauma and focus rather on the imaginary or fantasied notions that underlie or accompany many of the neuroses. Analytic neutrality is viewed as a valuable aid in unraveling the mysteries of the transference. Few programs are currently staffed with those trained in teaching the treatment of dissociative disease, which is a result of real rather than imagined traumas. It seems unacceptable to many clinicians that Multiple Personality Disorder is a consequence of unconscionable acts by adults in charge. It seems equally awkward for many of these clinicians to abandon their neutral analytic postures long enough to provide the proper warmth, attachment, and flexibility to actually sit through the revivifications of these traumas. Multiple Personality Disorder is still not considered by many to be a legitimate post–traumatic stress response to chronic, over-whelming, life-threatening danger beginning in early childhood.

Thus, although Multiple Personality Disorder is a very real entity, it may be relegated to a conceptual framework that negates this basic truth. In many biologically oriented psychiatric training programs, clinicians become much more comfortable diagnosing conditions that respond to pharmacologic agents—anxiety that improves with anti-anxiety agents, depression that dissipates with antidepressants, mania that is controlled with lithium, and schizophrenia that is improved with antipsychotics. In Multiple Personality Disorder each of the alternate personalities may exhibit simultaneously many of the symptoms that individually these drugs are intended to treat. The drug of choice for multiples seems to be talk—the kind of talk that permits each of the separate traumas to be identified and relived, this time in the company of a safe, healing presence.

Compelling scientific evidence for Multiple Personality Disorder has been derived from studies of brain and nervous system functioning. Topo-graphic EEGs, IQ and other cognitive performance assessments, vision tests, and tests on cardiovascular function have been reported to be significantly different in alternate personalities sharing the same body.

Immunologic and inflammatory responses may also differ between personalities. A patient of mine, Tony, housed an alternate personality whose job was to "never feel pain." Once, Tony appeared in my office shortly after sustaining bee stings to one eye. The eye was very red and swollen. I arranged an emergency opthalmologic consultation but before sending him off to the eye specialist asked if I could speak with the alternate who never experienced pain. That personality appeared, we talked briefly, and it was soon time for Tony to keep his emergency appointment. One hour later I received a call from the opthalmologist who, in an effort to suppress his irritation with me, claimed that he found absolutely no evidence of redness or swelling. The next day Tony returned to my office with his eye swollen shut; I encouraged no alternates to emerge and sent Tony back to the specialist. Soon the doctor called, incredulous, and asked how I could have predicted yesterday that this man would have been stung by bees today. A colleague at the Yale School of Medicine pointed out, in discussing this case, that it takes twenty to thirty minutes to mediate an immune response and that perhaps the alternate who experienced no pain had a different immunological constitution.

Similarly, it is usual for alternates to have different gastrointestinal responses to the same food. One patient whose original had ulcerative colitis and consumed large quantities of Librax to control abdominal pain and diarrhea could not eat spicy food, but had a complete remission of all symptoms within twenty to thirty minutes after the appearance of an alternate who had a perfectly healthy gut and could eat anything. Thus, it is clear that Multiple Personality Disorder is far from being an imaginary condition, and that individuals with this disorder share a number of common features.

All individuals with Multiple Personality Disorder were abused as children; most often this occurred in environments where there was little or no opportunity for protection, retreat, or repair. Commonly sexual assault, by one or both parents or some primary caretaker, occurred repeatedly. While Joan avoids graphic detail in her descriptions of abuse at the hands of her parents, she, like other multiples, did not have a consistently loving adult to rescue her. Ultimately, she created her own protectors from within. Each of these secondary personalities fulfilled a precise psychological function for her such as expression of anger, discharge of sexual or aggressive impulses, keeper of painful memories. The alternates were of different age, sex, and even parentage from the original personality. Only together could all of these alternates provide one another with the necessary tools to live adult life safely.

Thus, Multiple Personality Disorder represents an extreme version of the human propensity for self-preservation. It seems that the psychological equivalent of "fight or flight" in many abused children who are literally too small to do either is to dissociate into other states so that the original is "not there" and is temporarily insulated from fear and pain. This dramatic coping system requires unusual vigilance and extraordinary responsiveness to one's environment. You have to go before it's too late, you have to be cagey because sometimes you have to pretend to be there when you're not. Most of this sequence happens without conscious awareness— you remember being scared and then you remember nothing. The coping system remains in place long after the trauma has ceased and causes profound difficulty for the patient as he or she enters adolescence and adulthood.

Typically, the original personality is unaware of alternate personalities. The alternates, however, may be very much aware of the activities and attitudes of the original. Though they cannot decide when to appear, their presence is elicited often unpredictably in response to environmental triggers encountered in the daily course of events in the life of the original. For the original, this may mean constant confusion as moments, hours, days, or even years are lost to the emergence and "occupation" of alternate personalities. For the alternates, life can hold relentless frustration with the original, who may be perceived as helpless or incompetent. The tension between the original and alternates is reminiscent of an internal civil war. Battles may take the form, for example, of auditory hallucinations (personalities arguing) or the unexplained appearance of injuries (slash wounds, body burns, nail bed maceration, and a host of other self-inflicted mutilations) sustained when an alternate punishes the original.

Each alternate may exhibit symptoms, such as depression or auditory hallucinations, that in isolation may suggest other disorders, such as major depression or schizophrenia, indicating the need for medication. However, drug treatment rarely improves these symptoms in multiples. An intense relationship built on trust with a therapist who guides the patient into new modes of expression through talking and through safe exposure to experiences is optimal. Revivification, or the actual reliving of traumatic experiences, is a necessary part of this therapeutic process.

Lynn Wilson was completely immersed in Joan's case. My training with Dr. Cornelia Wilbur, the psychiatrist who treated the well-known multiple Sybil, and my own experience have taught me that the kind of treatment provided by the Wilsons is ideal. Though therapeutic encounters lasting hours or days are unconventional by the standards of the psychiatric community, where patients are seen in an office for fifty-minute sessions between one and four times per week, I have found that anything less than six hours per week is difficult for both patient and therapist. There must be enough time to allow triggers to surface in the environment. There must be enough time to both elicit and interact with specific alternates. A brief session may be too stressful, provoking the unsafe emergence of alternates outside the session. Suicidal threats and acts of self-injury made by the patient outside sessions are a poignant index of how unsafe this work can be. Thus, I embrace Lynn Wilson's work with Joan as one model for the treatment of multiples. Few therapists, however, can provide this level of treatment intensity, but when adequate resources are available, this kind of work can be highly rewarding.

There is nothing new about twenty-four-hour-a-day therapy and containment for patients with severe disorders. Typically, however, such care is provided in the hospital by a number of staff—psychiatrists, nurses, and other therapists. Lynn Wilson's near-constant availability to Joan essentially reproduced the holding environment of the inpatient setting while making it possible for Wilson to meet the emotional needs of various personalities and to judge when the timing was right for the calling forth of specific alternates.

Some of Joan's personalities were nonverbal, others passive, some hostile. One of Joan's alternates repeatedly smashed her head against a wall to the point of causing bleeding and potential damage to her skull and brain. Lynn Wilson was there to witness the blood and agony, and play midwife to the delivery of the horror that accompanied the revivification of earlier traumas—traumas that Joan was forced to experience again and again if the healing was to take place.

Many experts in Multiple Personality Disorder believe that longer sessions are more effective than conventional, briefer patient-therapist contact. Sybil's treatment with Dr. Wilbur took eight years before integration was achieved. Joan's integration occurred after four years; this is impressive in view of the fact that successful integration of multiples may take between eight and twelve years. Lynn Wilson was able to devote part of her life to and share her family with Joan; the work was effective and quite rapid. When the correct diagnosis is made and the therapist skillful, treatment can be successful in the majority of cases. These experiences can be deeply rewarding for patient and therapist, though it is a treatment that often exhausts both.

On reading an advance manuscript of this book, one of my patients, who had not yet accepted the diagnosis of Multiple Personality Disorder, was astonished to observe the similarity of her experiences and Joan's. My hope is that others struggling with the heroic challenge of the treatment of Multiple Personality Disorder will find Joan Casey and Lynn Wilson's story a great inspiration to their work.

FRANCES HOWLAND, M.D.